# The Wealth of Some Nations

## Malcolm Caldwell

This book is dedicated to the
Sultan of Lewisham in gratitude.

# The Wealth of Some Nations

## Malcolm Caldwell

 Zed Press Ltd., 57 Caledonian Road, London N1 9DN.

The Wealth of Some Nations was first published
by Zed Press, 57 Caledonian Road, London, N.1.
in September 1977.

ISBN Hb 0 905 762 010
     Pb 0 905 762 002

Printed by Wheaton & Co., Exeter.

Typeset by Lyn Caldwell

Designed by An Dekker, Graphic Workshop

# CONTENTS

# INTRODUCTION

'Commerce, like industry, is merely a branch of agriculture. It is agriculture which furnishes the material of industry and commerce and which pays both . . . A nation which has little trade in raw produce, and which is reduced to trade in industrial goods in order to subsist, is in a precarious and uncertain position. For its trade can be taken away from it by other rival nations which devote themselves more successfully to the same trade. Moreover, such a nation is always subject to and dependent upon those which sell it primary necessities . . . In mutual trade, the nations which sell the most necessary or most useful commodities have an advantage over those which sell luxury goods . . . states which devote themselves to the manufacture of luxury goods experience serious vicissitudes. For when times are bad, trade in luxury goods slackens, and the workers find themselves without bread and without work . . . Man in this world has only three original needs: (1) that of his subsistence; (2) that of his preservation; and (3) that of the perpetuation of his species . . . Of these three, the first is the only one which is imperative, indispensable, and individual . . . To give up consumption is to give up life. It is to this original need that we should relate the continuance of humanity, and it is to the means of providing for this need that we should relate the increase of humanity which we call population.'

(Francois Quesnay, 1694-1774, leader of the French Physiocrat school of economists)

It may be asked why I embark with these propositions from another age. Surely the industrial and scientific revolutions have in the interim completely transformed Man's relationship to agriculture? Well, have they? It is one of the purposes of this book to demonstrate the extent to which the basic propositions enunciated by Quesnay still apply, despite all the 'miracles' and 'wonders' of modern scientific research and technological ingenuity, in the governance of our daily lives. Having established as much, we are in a better position to make sense of the economic problems facing both the rich ('overdeveloped') and poor ('underdeveloped') countries of the world today.

Unfortunately, for those whose education has been primarily in the arts and social sciences, we must first tackle complex matters in the elucidation of which some acquaintance with the physical sciences is imperative. I have therefore put as much of these indispensable preliminaries as possible in the first chapter. But it might be helpful before embarking upon this to explain why your trouble in ploughing through it is necessary, and how it will be rewarded later when you have emerged from its thickets into more familiar territory.

During the centuries-long period of Western expansion and establishment of global political and economic dominance, the handful of countries successful as predators were able to break out of the constraints which had, throughout the span of human history, necessarily limited the extent to which labour could be freed from subsistence agriculture to devote its energies and dexterity to providing for needs other than those of the stomach and of the barest subsistence. Labour devoted to manufacturing industry, to commercial enterprise, and to administration, much though it may contribute to enriching society, has to rely upon others to grow the food it consumes. Historically, the surplus of food devoted to supporting the non-agricultural population of industrial countries has come from two sources: first, from improved productivity in domestic agriculture, enabling a shrinking working population engaged in the fields to reap a growing harvest; and, second, from purchases of food made abroad from the proceeds of sales of manufactured goods (and of certain services, such as shipping, insurance and the like).

We may analyse the economic history of the last few centuries, centuries which have seen the emergence of drastic disparities in wealth between one group of countries (the overdeveloped) and another (the underdeveloped), in two ways: one way is to apply the tools developed by Marx and his successors to account for the development of capitalism (and its concomitant and reciprocal colonialism/neo-colonialism/imperialism); the other is to shift our focus to the physical exchanges involved and to account for the outcome in 'real' terms (in terms, that is, of the flows of raw material resources and of the increasing utilisation, geographically uneven in impact, of finite, non-renewable, mineral reserves, amongst which the fossil fuels are of particular importance and significance). In the chapters which follow I introduce the reader to both these approaches, and show how *both* are indispensable to understanding, and how the particular phenomena and processes upon which they respectively help to throw light are, in fact, so intimately related as to be in effect inextricable.

I do this in four chapters. The first endeavours to do two things: to equip the reader with the minimum of technical information necessary to make what follows comprehensible; and briefly to survey aspects of modern economic history in the light of what is being discussed. The success of the chapter is to be measured by the extent to which it enables the reader to think in and manipulate the categories and ideas it introduces. I am aware that I have tried to do in a few pages something that could only satisfactorily be done in several textbooks of considerable bulk. But I hope that I have been true to the underlying principles and that I have so organised their presentation that my grasp of them is satisfactorily conveyed to others. My reason for undertaking this task first is quite simply that I would like by doing so to have ensured that those who go on to complete the text will see the remainder in the light of what has been initially presented. The importance of this will become apparent, but it is worth saying here that, in my view, the phenomena of underdevelopment and over-development, which constitute the subject matter of chapters two and three, cannot be understood without an insight into the role of the fossil fuels in determining their very different, though causally related, fates. Nor can the significance of the possibilities for what I have called 'transcending' under- and overdevelopment which I investigate in the final chapter be fully appreciated until the objective natural limits to Man's manipulation of his environment, viewed in the context of the crisis of world capitalism and imperialism, have themselves been adequately grasped.

Chapter two introduces a necessarily synoptic discussion of the Marxist perspective on the phenomena of poverty and inequality in an age of apparent — or at least promised — plenty and abundance. There is much that will be familiar to at least some readers in this, but I had to present the arguments as they do form a key component of the whole picture and of the whole argument. Chapter three, on the other hand, contains some less familiar matter, or rather a somewhat unfamiliar interpretation of matters much in the news. It rests heavily for its cogency upon the two chapters which precede it, and cannot, I believe, be followed fully unless it is read after — and in the light of — their contents.

In the final chapter, I restrict myself in the main, though not entirely, to two case studies of relevance for the future, if what has gone before is at all accurate in its diagnosis. On the evidence available to us, it seems that the leaders and the masses of China since taking power in the revolution which triumphed in 1949 have come to their own conclusions about the prospects and possibilities open to Third World countries of liberation in a world shaped by the past, by the present configuration of world forces, and by natural circumstances the implications of which can only be understood by subjecting them to rigourous scrutiny informed by Marxism-Leninism-Mao Tsetung Thought. There is much of interest and relevance in the resultant policies which, in general, point away from the direction pioneered by those countries we have here described as overdeveloped. China, therefore, constitutes our first case study; we shall, however, also look at the experiences of the other socialist countries of Asia (North Korea, the Socialist Republic of Vietnam, the Lao People's Democratic Republic, and the Democratic Republic of Kampuchea), all of which have, in their various ways, departed from the model established by the first socialist state, the USSR, a model which I argue is more a variation of that of the overdeveloped capitalist countries than one pertinent to a future where the first essential of a tolerable long-term strategy must be its abandonment of the old road discredited by its looming dead-end destination.

I have taken as my second case study the example of Britain. This may at first glance seem inexcusably parochial, but a moment's consideration will show this not to be so. It is true that, if we look only to such obvious indices as per capita GNP, incidence of ownership of cars, dish-washers, and so on, and other such evidences of material prosperity, Britain may not now appear as the most suitable candidate to be nominated for the label 'overdeveloped'. But I hope chapter three will have by then afforded the clue to the reasoning that has led me thus to nominate it. Britain was the first country in the world to head down the road of overdevelopment with its inescapable blind alleys. It has been accordingly the first to encounter the problems and frustrations associated with such an outcome. It is worth looking at the possibilities of reversing a seemingly inexorable destiny in post-imperial Britain. I shall, however, refer to several other overdeveloped countries in my discussion, just as I have done when analysing the condition itself in the chapter which immediately precedes the last. By singling out the British case I do not in the least intend to imply that it is a singular one: on the contrary, I am arguing that there is a great deal to be learned from its dilemma of pressing relevance to all those other countries committed to the overdeveloped trajectory.

My intentions in embarking upon this short introductory text will have been fulfilled if some part of the readership it attracts is led to carry out further work designed to reveal more conclusively, and with a greater wealth of corroborative detail than I have been able to deploy here, the total poverty of conventional political-economic thought among leaders of all major movements of the rich countries today, whether these leaders be of the traditional right, of the traditional left or of traditional liberal persuasion. If the necessarily much greater proportion of my readers who are in no position themselves to carry out such work nevertheless come to question their former allegiances and their former views, and to seek out allies and social forces pressing in the directions I suggest are indicated, I shall be more than satisfied. I take it as self-evident that the peoples of the Third World are fast coming to command of their own destiny, and that they are — for a variety of reasons — bound to head, after liberation, along that way trod as pioneers by the Asian socialist countries, a path holding out vistas of far greater hopefulness for the human future than those to which we in the rich countries, as we grapple with the end of empire, have become accustomed and to which we desperately cling despite their increasingly obvious treachery.

Perhaps the hopes expressed in discussing the problems and prospects of the rich capitalist and imperialist countries are illusory; perhaps we are headed for a catastrophic breakdown of the West which nothing can halt or even delay, and which signals, in effect, the end of the humanist vision of 'progress'. There are certainly those of the 'doom and gloom' school who affect to believe this. I do not share their perspective. But even supposing there were to be, over the next couple of centuries or so, a breakdown of Western society, encompassing, say, the splintering of Europe into a host of minor political entities each united by regional, religious and cultural links, and a North America isolationist and absorbed by intractable domestic problems — with perhaps anarchy reigning in some parts — it would represent no irretrievable historical tragedy for two reasons. The first is that such periods of apparent retreat into disorder and away from civilisation (as understood, that is, in periods of apparent ascent towards higher and higher levels of organisation and prosperity, as vulgarly represented by the vision of an affluent United Europe risen above the barbarity of war) in fact play an essential role in the broader historical pattern. The so-called Dark Ages in Europe can now be seen to have been the fertile breeding ground of the Renaissance and all that it represents in terms of human achievement. Only through such seeming relapses can men and societies be purged of intellectual and cultural sclerosis, and — tempered by exposure to a diversity of unfamiliar hazards and dramatic changes — find renewal of vigour and daring to launch another assault on the perpetual sisyphean challenge of constructing a durable 'better world'.

The second is that historical continuity is ensured by the passing of the baton to other civilizations at the other extremity of the cycle of growth and decay. In our time, the most significant phenomenon by far is the Asian Revolution, now releasing untold riches of human dynamism, purpose and creativity, long dammed up by the crushing weight of imperialism and domestic reaction (a palsied and senile reaction, intellectually bankrupt and vacuous). Already the achievements of China, North Korea and Vietnam have, each in their different way, suggested the abundant contributions to the human tradition and heritage which are to come.

I am, therefore, an optimist. But I would go further and argue that, starting from acceptance of the inevitability of the decline of the West and of a steady retreat from 1960's-style affluence, we can tailor our political and economic aims to these realities and plan for accommodation. Such realism is obviously preferable to blundering desperately ahead along conventional lines, encountering graver and graver frustrations and setbacks, eventually to succumb to some combination of social chaos, totalitarianism, extremist violence, corroding cynicism, and Hobbesian anarchy. In the end, I am buoyed up by the hope and expectation of our achieving much smaller, homeostatic, and more self-sufficient societies in the West amid the ruins of the dreams become nightmares. It is in that spirit that I write.

## BIBLIOGRAPHY

1. Arnold Toynbee, *Mankind and Mother Earth*, (London, 1976).
(Toynbee's last book, published posthumously, is a highly successful
attempt to present a properly proportioned — i.e. non-Eurocentric — world
history; not least of its merits is that it keeps constantly in mind the
ecological aspects of historical change.)
2. L.S. Stavrianos, *The Promise of the Coming Dark Ages*, W.H. Freeman
& Co., (San Francisco, 1976). (Argues that the medieval dark ages were, in
fact, a time of tremendous preparation for the great burst of Western
creativity and achievement which followed, and that the Western world is
again entering a 'dark age' which will again afford the opportunity for
experiment and renewal.)
3. Perry Anderson, *Passages from Antiquity to Feudalism*, NLB, (London,
1974).
4. Perry Anderson, *Lineages of the Absolutist State*, NLB, (London, 1974).
(These two books trace, within a Marxist framework of analysis, the trans-
itions from classical antiquity to feudalism *via* the Dark Ages and to the
threshold of Western capitalism *via* feudalism; read in conjunction with
works cited hereafter — notably Wallerstein, referred to in the bibliography
to chapter two — they provide a survey and summation of modern scholar-
ship on the rise of the West and the origin of capitalism; at the same time
both Anderson and Wallerstein notably advance our knowledge and understanding of these historical events which so shaped five or six centuries of
human history.)
5. Alexander Gray, *The Development of Economic Doctrine*, (Allen and
Unwin, 1972). (Originally published in 1931, Professor Gray's short
history of economic thought went through innumerable impressions; it was
re-printed in 1960. It remains one of the best introductions to this
important — and often neglected — field in economics and makes clear the
place of the physiocrats in the tradition.)
6. M. Barratt Brown, T. Emerson & C. Stoneman (eds.), *Resources and the
Environment*, Spokesman Books, (Nottingham, 1976). (This collection of
essays offers a socialist perspective on resource problems, and constitutes a
useful introduction to the subject.)

# FOSSIL FUELS AND ENTROPY

'For one thing, most of the substances employed in plant growth, metabolism, and reproduction contain elements other than the carbon, hydrogen, and oxygen that were captured in photosynthesis. Hence — and most importantly for a discussion of the relation of green plants to food and population — all but three of the elements needed by any green plant for its internal affairs, like the rest of the elements in compounds (e.g. proteins) for which we look to green plants when we rely on them for food — must, and do, come from the soil . . . It is not possible to bring about the dream of increasing the uptake of only carbon dioxide and water by plants, and to produce food that way. The dream has often been promulgated by people who should know better. Whether the proposition is looked at from the standpoints of carbon/nitrogen ratio, of thermodynamics, or microbiology, or any other way, the conclusion is the same . . . that same single endpoint of impossibility is reached *necessarily*. Increase of uptake of nothing more than carbon dioxide from the air without expenditure of fossil fuel is impossible. It could be done . . . only by waving a magic wand.'

(Hugh Nicol, *The Limits of Man*, Constable, London, 1967, pp. 208, 225)

I intend in this chapter to explain in outline the role and importance of the fossil fuels in the economic history of the last couple of centuries. Put in the barest and sparest terms possible, it may be said that the present level of human population, and the present level of comparative comfort shading into affluence enjoyed by a substantial part of it, have been attained by transforming the energy latent in the fossil fuels into energy for human beings (food) and energy for the powering of labour-saving machinery (fuel). The fossil fuels are, however, in finite supply, and while we may substitute energy derived from other sources to power machines — sources such as solar energy, nuclear power, and subterranean heat — there is no known or even theoretically conceivable substitute for the fossil fuels in enabling the production of food to remain at its present volume, a volume much in excess of the optimum 'natural' one which would be possible in a world unable to call upon the carbonaceous reserves (fossil fuels) we are currently squandering. It follows that we either conserve — as far as possible — the remaining fossil fuels for agricultural purposes in order to postpone and make more ordered re-adjustment to a world economy independent of them (and at a level of population and comfort not too different from that prevailing prior to the 'fossil fuel revolution' of recent centuries), or we face cataclysmic events for which we will be ill-prepared and which will inflict untold suffering. On balance, however, it seems likely that, as the reality becomes more and more inescapable, piecemeal adjustments will be made here and there, but with more success in some kinds of societies than in others — and the presently underdeveloped countries seem in a much better position, in this respect at least, than the overdeveloped who are burdened with an 'energy-addiction' which threatens agonising withdrawal symptoms.


## THE ORIGINS AND DISTRIBUTION OF FOSSIL FUELS

What *are* the fossil fuels? The two main groups are the coals and the bitumens (or petroleum group). Before discussing their composition and distinctive properties, a word is in order about their origin and incidence. There seems little doubt now that both petroleum and coal are products of prolonged geological processes by which organic matter, accumulated in sedimentary deposits, was transformed by low-temperature anaerobic decay. The evidence suggests a mainly marine origin for petroleum and a terrestrial one for coal. In the first case, billions of microscopic marine organisms sinking at death with the silt and mud to the bottom of the sea were there sealed in before decomposition. Wide-ranging differences in types of petroleum indicate that the constituent matter varied, but was primarily organic. The processes may have begun as long as 400 million years ago — and continue today. But the time-scales involved in the complete transformation are such that the existing stock of petroleum may be said to be finite. The actual occurrence of accessible petroleum deposits is the outcome of geological convulsions and upheavals and subsequent protracted adjustments. For a variety of reasons deposits are unevenly distributed over the globe, an aspect upon which I shall have much subsequent comment to make.

The assertion that petroleum stocks are, in effect, finite can only be challenged along a number of limited lines, of which we need note but two here. The first, working from the hypothesis of an *inorganic* origin of the fluid, postulates that oil is the product of a continuous process by which methane is sweated out from the earth's core and polymerized into hydrocarbons of a higher molecular weight. While it is true that scientists have been able to show in a laboratory situation that oil *can* be made from inorganic chemical components, the weight of evidence both from geology and from chemistry is heavily against the inorganic hypothesis in general. The second rests upon the contention that what it takes Nature millions of years to achieve can be simulated in the laboratory and telescoped into something like twenty minutes to half-an-hour. It was estimated in 1971 that if all America's agricultural wastes — vegetable waste as well as manure — were collected and subjected to the proven process, about 2.5 billion barrels of oil could be produced each year — about half the 1971 requirements. But no debit was made for the energy required to heat the initial material to 720° F. and to put it under a pressure of 1,200 pounds per square inch, nor was account taken of the fact that most agricultural 'waste' plays an important part in the exchanges governing food production. Businessmen cannot afford to be as naive as journalists and academics, and it is the surest sign of all that we may take it that petroleum is in finite supply — and that peak production is in sight — that the big oil companies are now diversifying into coal, uranium, and mass transit systems, and have been doing so for some considerable time.

The origins of coal are easier to establish and less controversial, since embedded fossils, stratification, and interbedding with sedimentary rocks provide incontrovertible evidence. Coal is thus revealed as the product of partial decomposition, under anaerobic conditions, of buried vegetation, largely terrestial vegetation from a swampy environment. There are many varieties of coal; the differences are often of great economic significance. Global incidence is, as in the case of petroleum, uneven. Coal stocks are unquestionably finite.

But in both cases we must ask: how finite? There are any number of estimates — often wildly divergent. The problem is that there are so many variables, with a number of unknowns (and unknowables); the best I can do is to present careful estimates for each of the two major fossil fuels, and then to draw attention to the theoretical approach, whose cogency derives from mathematical logic rather than from statistical measurement.

In the oil industry, reserves are what it is believed can be recovered under a given set of technical and economic circumstances; resources are what is actually there. For the oil industry resource or resource base would be represented by oil-in-place; reserves will be determined by the fraction of the oil-in-place that can be extracted economically. Coal figures tend to be presented on a somewhat different basis from oil figures in some contexts. However, it is important to note that the use of the various terms is not consistent, with resulting doubts and confusions. Over the years, many attempts have been made to estimate fossil fuel reserves. The growing sophistication of techniques in recent times has certainly reduced some of the earlier purely speculative estimates and the uncertainty. At the same time, a rapidly expanding world population and the process of decolonization have imparted a greater urgency and geographical extension to exploration for fresh sources of petroleum. One of the two main fossil fuels, coal, had until recently received relatively little public attention for some time, it being thought somehow obsolete. Now, however, intense prospecting for coal is again afoot. To the best of our knowledge, coal — or at least coal of the better qualities — is unevenly distributed, and some seams are so awkwardly sited as to be, in effect, uneconomical to work at present or realistically prospective prices. Others are of low grade or otherwise unsuited to general use. Table I shows just how poorly distributed the fuel is; an alternative estimate is given for reference and comparison in Table II.

### TABLE I

Estimates of Total Original Coal Resources of the World by Continents* (in billions of short tons)

|  | Resources determined by mapping and exploration | Probable additional resources in unmapped unexplored areas | Est. Total Resources | % of world total | % of world pop. |
|---|---|---|---|---|---|
| USSR | 6,500 | 3,000 | 9,500 | 56.4 | 7 |
| N. America | 1,720 | 2,880 | 4,600 | 27.3 | 6 |
| Asia | 500 | 1,000 | 1,500 | 8.9 | 56 |
| Europe | 620 | 210 | 830 | 4.9 | 13 |
| Africa | 80 | 160 | 240 | 1.4 | 10 |
| Oceania | 60 | 70 | 130 | 0.8 | 0.5 |
| South and Central America | 20 | 10 | 30 | 0.2 | 8 |

*Original resources in the ground in beds 12 inches thick or more and generally less than 4,000 feet below the surface, but including small amounts between 4,000 and 6,000 feet.

Sources: adapted from National Academy of Sciences — National Research Council, *Resources and Man*, W.H. Freeman & Co., (San Francisco, 1969) p.202. P. Averitt, *Coal Resources of the United States*, U.S. Geological Survey Bull. 1257, and J.A. Hodgkins, *Soviet Power: Energy resources, production and potential*, Prentice-Hall, (Englewood Cliffs, N.J., 1961); population figs. from the U.N. *Demographic Yearbook*. Because of rounding, the last two columns do not add up exactly to 100.

TABLE II

*World Coal Production and Reserves*

| | Coal production, 1972 million metric tons | % | Total reserves (proved + indicated and inferred) — billion metric tons | % |
|---|---|---|---|---|
| USSR | 500 | 22.6 | (4,122) | 61.4 |
| USA | 541 | 24.5 | 1,100 | 16.4 |
| Canada | 15 | 0.7 | 61 | 0.9 |
| Total N. America | 560 | 25.4 | 1,164 | 17.3 |
| China | 400 | 18.1 | 1,011 | 15.1 |
| India | 74 | 3.4 | 106 | 1.6 |
| Japan | 28 | 1.3 | 19 | 0.3 |
| Total Asia | 554 | 25.1 | 1,143 | 17.0 |
| Poland | 151 | 6.8 | 46 | 0.7 |
| Total Europe (East) | 194 | 8.8 | 61 | 0.9 |
| UK | 117 | 5.5 | 16 | 0.2 |
| W. Germany | 102 | 4.6 | 70 | 1.1 |
| France | 30 | 1.4 | 3 | 0.04 |
| Total Europe (West) | 274 | 12.4 | 92 | 1.4 |
| Total Europe (E & W) | 468 | 21.2 | 153 | 2.3 |
| Australia | 54 | 2.4 | 16 | 0.2 |
| All others | 73 | 3.3 | 114 | 1.7 |
| WORLD | 2,208 | 100.0 | 6,712 | 100.0 |

(Source: J. Beamish-Crooke, Central Planning Unit, National Coal Board)

What the tables illustrate, among other things, is how vitally important it is that the countries of Asia, Africa and Latin America — with nearly three-quarters of the world's population — conserve for their own use every single drop of oil to be found within their legitimate territories and seas, since their coal resources in relation to population do not appear to be considerable. (It is, however, true that recent coal prospecting in countries as diverse as Indonesia, Tanzania and China has revealed unexpected riches; this does not in the slightest weaken the conservation argument.)

## SUPPLY, DEMAND, AND THE THREAT OF EXHAUSTION

How long will coal supplies last? Here we come up against many imponderables, but first let us look at a theoretical estimate based upon the best available data and the latest projection techniques for the full cycle of production of an exhaustible resource. The appropriate figures and explanation are given in Appendix A to this chapter. Using this method, the conclusion is that if coal is used principally for its energy content (rather than for other uses such as serving as a raw material for the petro-chemical industry), 'the time required to exhaust the middle 80% of the world's coal resources would be about 300 to 400 years (but only 100 to 200 years if coal is used as the main energy source)'. (1) The shorter of the two estimates assumes a return to coal for direct energy production, thus releasing remaining reserves of oil and natural gas for other purposes for which the fossil fuels are needed as a raw material.

The importance of the above figures should be stressed. Since the time-span for oil exhaustion is even shorter than that for coal, and keeping in mind the doubts attached to the substitution value of the energy alterna-tives hitherto suggested in public discussion (nuclear power in particular), we would be wise to take the shorter of the two estimates as the basis for our thinking. It is of great importance to note that with a consumption period of 100 to 200 years for the middle 80% (we may eliminate the long periods of time at relatively low rates of extraction required to produce the first and last 10%'s of ultimate total production), *peak* production could come somewhere within the next 50 to 100 years. Furthermore, as peak production approaches there must be fierce competition for control over remaining reserves unless, by that time, energy demand itself has already levelled off.

What about the alternative uses of coal? Synthetic materials (such as plastics and nylon) are made largely from fossil fuels. Plastics and synthe-tic fibres make up a sector of the industrialized economies which is growing at a particularly rapid rate. In the last two decades their usage increased by over 50% as a component of final demand as reflected in the American GNP. Synthetic rubber is also a by-product of the petro-chemical industry. As oil sources become exhausted, more and more coal will have to be diverted to feed this fast-expanding sector, thus accelerating the projec-tions previously established. Indeed, questions are already being raised as to whether oil or gas should now be used at all for fuels, since both are so valuable chemically. Many organic chemists consider that the burning of fossil fuels for energy production to be one of the least desirable uses for these large organic molecules. Professor Neilands of the University of California has recently pointed out that the hydrocarbons in the fossil fuels represent the patient work of the sun and that it is totally irrespon-sible to burn them up in internal combustion engines: on the contrary, they ought to be carefully preserved for the manufacture of synthetic medicines and other such essential purposes. Moreover, there is the whole question of protein synthesis, which may yet have a crucial part to play in a hungry world: here again coal and oil are essential inputs.

Such global considerations are, however, an artificial approach to the real problems, for the world is still divided up into more or less indepen-dent, self-centred, and contending sovereign states, some (such as the

Soviet Union) possessed of ample coal reserves for the foreseeable future, and others apparently more or less bereft of supplies (for instance some of the countries of Latin America, Africa and South East Asia). So, to the problem of total supply must be added that of distribution, a problem compounded by the relative wealth, power and command over real resources of a minority of nations, and by poverty, neo-colonial dependence, and surrender of resources on the part of the vast majority of existing states.

Studies of oil resources have been, if anything, even more numerous and thorough than those conducted on coal. There are a number of reasons for this. First, the industrial countries were initially launched on coal, and have over the years used up the more accessible (and therefore economic) of their own seams. Faced with alternative import strategies, they saw the economic logic in importing oil rather than coal, even for requirements traditionally satisfied with coal. Second, in any case the changing needs of the industrialised countries dictated growing dependence on oil. Most of the countries concerned — but not all — were comparatively poorly endowed with oil. A good deal was known, and had been from time immemorial, about the whereabouts of domestic coal, even if it was no longer an economic proposition to work it, but there was some urgency to establishing where oil was to be found in a highly competitive situation. Most commonly, accessible oil deposits were to be found in countries not possessed of effective sovereignty, and therefore wide open to exploitation. The search for oil on the part of the rich nations is still accelerating in intensity, symbolised by such extravagances as the notorious Mohole Project,*and by active U.S. armed forces participation in petroleum exploration (it being the case that the immense U.S. military machine is totally dependent upon combustion of the fossil fuels and therefore has its own interest in oil apart from that engendered by its role of defending U.S. industry abroad, it is estimated that the B-1 bomber fleet would, if the project goes ahead, in its lifetime use more fuel than that required to keep *all* U.S. mass transit systems going for ten years).

* The object of the Mohole Project was to drill a hole of far greater depth than ever before attempted into the ocean floor for the purpose of studying the composition of the earth's interior. The term is derived from the so-called Mohorovicic discontinuity in the earth's crust, a feature recognised from seismic data many years ago. It may be 5-10 km. deep under the ocean floor, and some 30 km. beneath the continents. The major oil companies were interested in the project because they were themselves going to be involved in deeper and deeper ocean drilling. Cost estimates rose from US $5 million to US $125 million, and the whole operation was eventually terminated by an Act of Congress. (2) Scandal resulted from the awarding of the contracts for the project; there was alleged to have been political influence.

There are both empirical and theoretical estimates of total oil availability. Both converge on the essentials of the situation. Below (Table III) I reproduce two relatively recent empirical tabulations of estimated ultimate recovery (EUR) of world crude oil by geographical area.

TABLE III

Comparative tabulations of EUR* of World Crude Oil:

| *"Free World" outside USA:* | Weeks, 1962 | Ryman, 1967 |
|---|---|---|
| | (billions of US barrels) | |
| Europe | 19 | 20 |
| Africa | 100 | 250 |
| Middle East | 780 | 600 |
| Far East | 85 | 200** |
| Latin America | 221 | 225** |
| Canada | 85 | 95 |
| Total | 1,290 | 1,390 |
| United States | 270 | 200 |
| Total "free world" | 1,560 | 1,590 |
| USSR, China & "satellites" | 440 | 500 |
| World Total | 2,000 | 2,090 |

Source: Adapted from National Academy of Sciences — National Research Council, *Resources and Man*, W.H. Freeman & Co., (San Francisco, 1969) p.194. W.P. Ryman, Deputy Exploration Manager, Standard Oil Company of New Jersey.

*EUR = Produced + Proved + Probable + Future Discoveries

**Includes off-shore areas; the Far East estimate is certainly an underestimate, since China alone would now appear to have reserves exceeding these attributed to the whole Far East in this table. See Appendix B.

The theoretical approach is based upon an observed mathematical relationship between the rate of discovery at one date and the rate of extraction at a later date. On this basis, it would appear that the American domestic petroleum industry, exclusive of Alaska, reached its all-time maximum rate of production somewhere about 1969 or the early 'seventies, but it will not be possible to assign an accurate date until some time has elapsed — certainly five years. Nevertheless, the production figures over the last few years are intriguing:

TABLE IV

Annual United States domestic crude production
(thousands of barrels)*

| 1965 | 2,848,514 |
|------|-----------|
| 1966 | 3,027,763 |
| 1967 | 3,215,742 |
| 1968 | 3,329,042 |
| 1969 | 3,371,751 |
| 1970 | 3,517,450 |
| 1971 | 3,453,914 |
| 1972 | 3,459,052 |
| 1973 | 3,288,580 |
| 1974 | 3,056,936 |
| 1975 | 2,918,924 |
| 1976 (est.) | 2,843,592 |

* 1 metric ton of oil = 7.3 barrels (approx.); 1 million barrels a day
= 50 million metric tons per annum (or roughly 77 million metric
tons of coal equivalent — mtce.)

We need hardly stress the significance of the above for an understanding
of the urgent world-wide activities of the United States oil giants. The
middle 80% of ultimate total (realised) U.S. production, by the same kind
of computation as that referred to above, would take a mere 65 years
(less than one human lifetime at U.S. life-expectancy rates), namely the
years from 1934 to 1999. It should be noted that despite intensified
domestic prospecting since the OPEC-induced oil price rises of the early
1970's, American dependence upon oil imports continues to grow; whereas
in 1973, 35% of requirements was imported (7% from the Arab world), in
1976, more than 40% was imported (17% from the Arab world). By 1985,
it was thought in 1976, the overall dependence could be 50% or more*

For the world as a whole, the same source (3) gives two estimates of
prospective world production. The first, based upon a smaller ultimate
total, suggests that peak production will occur about 1990, with the
middle 80% requiring only the 58-year period from 1961 to 2019. The
second — and more optimistic — gives the peak about the year 2000, with
the middle 80% of production occurring somewhere between 1968 and,
say, 2032. Whichever estimate we accept, the conclusion is inescapable

*In fact, the dire winter of 1976-77 catapulted the United States into
accelerated dependence: in January, 1977, the U.S. imported half of its
oil consumption — and more than half of this came from the Arab
countries. While the wintry weather persisted, no relief or reversal was in
sight. (4)

that the present oil regimen will be a brief one in retrospect, and that bitter international conflict over control and costs can only go on intensifying in the years immediately ahead. If we are to go on relying upon the fossil fuels for energy, it will not be oil that will meet the major part of our needs after the next few years.

Our own opinion, based upon considerations parallel to those detailed for coal above, is that these careful projections may veer on the side of optimism. Moreover, it ought to be pointed out that since the curve of the complete cycle of production of an exhaustible resource is of the classical bell-shape, if the growth of demand for the product in question is exponential, the two curves projected diverge long before the point of peak production, far less that of exhaustion. It is general realisation of the implications of this that has created the sense of crisis that is already palpably with us.

There are, of course, other fossil fuels, and the science journalists and technological optimists frequently refer to them. Natural gas is commonly cited. For the U.S., peak production is expected about 1980. Already it is obvious that the gas shortage for powering industry and for heating homes in America is acute. The exceptionally severe winter of 1976-77 in North America exposed with cruel sharpness just how serious the natural gas situation had become. In the older industrial states of the US Middle West and North East industry was partially paralysed by failure of supplies, while houses, schools and hospitals faced shortages and periods of gas-starvation. The pricing system and over-confidence in reserves are both factors in the history of the crisis. By February 1977, 19 states in the USA were in a critical condition, with factory after factory closing down. Economists predicted that the crisis was no isolated disaster: similar conditions would recur — with increasing frequency — for the foreseeable future, unless some totally unexpected development were to occur. Neighbouring Canada has natural gas to export, but, aware of the developing shortages, the Canadian government moved some years ago to restrict sales to the United States, an action much resented in Washington. The Canadians rightly felt that their first priority must be their own long-term interests, particularly on entering a period when exceptionally bitter winter weather has been forecast as a long-term trend. In the early months of 1977, however, in view of the urgency of the problem in the United States, Canada somewhat relaxed its export restrictions to ease the malaise of its southern neighbour.

Gas, in 1969, still accounted for more than twice the amount of energy generated in power stations in the United States by oil and nuclear power combined. In the rest of the world the picture is less clear; in any event, there is no serious expectation that natural gas can play more than a marginal role — important for a time in certain areas — in the overall energy equation. Natural gas liquids present a rather similar picture. As far as oil shales are concerned, the informed view is that their organic contents hold out more promise as raw material for the chemical industry than as a major source of industrial energy, for which use their impurities would constitute a grave handicap. Putting all these fossil fuels together with oil, the final judgement of the American National Academy of Sciences is as follows:

> 'If these substances continue to supply the bulk of the world's energy requirements, the time required to exhaust the middle 80% of the ultimate resources of the petroleum family — crude oil, natural gas, natural gas liquids, tar-sand oil, and shale oil — will probably be only about a century.'

To recapitulate, however, it is certain that the petroleum family, in addition to supplying us with energy, will increasingly be in demand for other uses such as providing raw material for the plastics and synthetic fibre industries, two of the fastest growing sectors in the world economy today, as we saw. In addition, petroleum will also increasingly figure as an input in the research into, and eventual production of, synthetic proteins. The huge detergent industry is also based upon organic raw materials extracted from petroleum. There are many other competing uses, including the very important one of providing the vital raw material and power input for the key fertiliser industry. These uses, taken together, are sure greatly to accelerate depletion.

We should stress again that the use-curve is bell-shaped (Appendix A). Long before the peak is actually reached in about 40 or 50 years' time (possibly sooner as demand continues to swell), the countries most dependent upon oil, and especially those countries most dependent upon imports, will have to take decisive action to guarantee their access to the world's remaining reserves and, in turn, to prevent their rivals from pre-empting them. Obviously, the fight will favour the strong. It seems extremely improbable from all the accumulated evidence of human history that the battle will be a peaceful one. Oil and imperialism have always been inextricably bound together.

In contemplating the coming struggle, we should bear constantly in mind that the rich industrialised countries are quite incapable of fighting — or indeed of functioning — without huge and continuous flows of oil. In contrast, guerrillas have little — if any — need for it, at least in the earlier stages of their struggle. As for the respective civilian populations, Gabriel Kolko has surely made a sound point when he argues that:

> 'The nations of the Third World may be poor, but in the last analysis the industrial world needs their resources more than these nations need the West, for their poverty is nothing new to peasantry cut off from export sectors, and trading with industrial states has not changed their subsistence living standards. In case of total rupture between the industrial and supplier nations, it is the population of the industrial world that proportionately will suffer the most.' (5)

The real lessons of the Vietnam war will be slow to percolate general consciousness in the West, but they are, once properly understood, truly alarming for those in the rich countries (and the rich in the poor countries) who fancy that their wealth and power are themselves adequate safeguards for their own perpetuation. Nothing could be further from the truth, as the rest of the 20th century will amply testify.

Table V gives global figures of world energy reserves. It should be noted that column 4 is wildly optimistic in superficial appearance, as it relates *likely* total reserves to *present* consumption — that is, discounting both population increase and rising standards of living (and energy consumption) in the poorer countries as well as the rich. Consumption growth rates may have declined since the 1973 Middle East war, but they are still firmly upwards, per capita as well as globally.

TABLE V

*World Energy Reserves*

| | Proved Reserves | | Total Reserves | |
| --- | --- | --- | --- | --- |
| | billion tons coal equiv. | Ratio to present consumption (yrs.) | (Proved + likely additions) billion tons coal equiv. | Ratio to present consumption (yrs.) |
| Coal | 460 | 120(a) | 6,700 | 1,800(a) |
| Lignite | 135 | 130(a) | 1,050 | 1,100(a) |
| Total solid fuel | 595 | 125(a) | 7,750 | 1,600(a) |
| Oil | 129 | 31 | 405 | 98 |
| Natural gas | 74 | 41 | 300 | 167 |
| Shale oil/tar sands | | | 150-750 | |
| Uranium (1) | 19 | | 50 | |
| Uranium (2) | 1,300 | | 3,400 | |

(a)  Solid fuel at 50% recovery
(1)  If used in conventional reactor
(2)  If used in breeder reactor.

NOTES: Solid fuel reserves are *ten times greater* than the ultimate reserves of oil and natural gas taken together.
A downturn in world oil production (from conventional sources) is expected before the end of this century, and probably before 1990. Oil shale and tar sands could yield up to twice the quantity of oil contained in conventional oil field, but much of this is in very low-grade deposits. Development lead-times will be very long, and costs high. No significant contribution to world energy requirements from shales and sands can be expected until after the mid-1980's. Uranium reserves are limited, but their life would be very considerably expanded if a successful breeder reactor is developed.

(Source: J. Beamish-Crooke, Central Planning Unit, National Coal Board.)

One popular misunderstanding concerns the significance of new finds. Recently, great prominence has been given to the magnitude of new coal, gas and oil finds in various parts of the world ranging from China to the North Sea. It is tempting to assume that successive discoveries will delay exhaustion indefinitely. But note should be taken of three points. First, despite all the new finds, there does appear to be a strong secular tendency for the ratio of world proven oil reserves to annual production to decline (though the picture for coal is at the moment different because of the much slower growth rate of production and the much larger reserves), and this is the really significant figure. Second, while no one disputes the local and temporary importance of such finds as those now being tapped in the North Sea, they ought to be kept in some kind of proper perspective. To keep the world's reserves-to-production ratio constant at its present level would necessitate the establishment of reserves the expected ultimate size of the North Sea oil province every couple of years or so, since they are equivalent to only about twice current world annual oil output. At levels of demand anticipated before the end of the century, this figure could have shrunk to six months or so. Third, it can be shown that — with exponential growth in demand/production — the actual magnitude of total reserves makes surprisingly little difference to the time-span for depletion. Let us apply this to coal and oil. With known reserves, and consumption continuing to rise at existing rates, coal would last (according to one calculation) for 111 years, and petroleum for 20. *If* reserves in fact turn out to be *five times as large* as at present thought, these figures would shift only to 150 and 50 years respectively, if, that is, consumption continues to grow exponentially at the average annual rate of growth.(6)

## OTHER LIMITING FACTORS

It is as well to point out here, as a kind of parenthesis, that even supposing all our informed expectations are somehow totally confounded, in the sense that oil and coal resources prove to be, in effect, infinite, there would *still* be at least a couple of limiting factors which would come into operation anyway. The first is pollution. By the early 1970's, at least eight million tons of oil a year were finding their way into the world's oceans. The two Thor Heyerdahl expeditions in 1969 and 1970 discovered to their surprise and dismay that no part of the Atlantic, however remote from shipping lanes, was free from contamination. A Japanese student who undertook a marathon four-year walk round the coasts of the archipelago in the early 1970's found oil-ball pollution everywhere without exception. Professor Jacques Piccard has forecast that the world's oceans will all have been killed by oil pollution before the end of the century. Discharged oil works in a number of ways to destroy marine life, including the plankton which forms the vegetable first stage in the complex chains feeding all marine life. Bacterial breakdown by oil spillages actually deplete of oxygen 400,000 times their own volume of water. Tankers of half a million tons will soon be plying the world's waterways — none immune from accident. Should a storm wreck one of the giant rigs now being planned for work in the North Sea, oil spill could amount to over 50,000 barrels a day (a rate equivalent to 2.5 million tons a year); it is freely acknowledged that oil rig security is an impossible assignment. There is obviously something fundamentally illogical and wrong in destroying potential food in the oceans as an unavoidable by-product of extracting and transporting oil, much of it intended — one way or another — to raise food production on dry land, as we shall see.

The principal pollution problem with coal is smoke emission, though one should not underestimate the havoc that can be caused to the rural environment by unregulated open-cast mining. Industrial smog is expensive to combat, but is in itself expensive in a host of other ways, such as corrosion of structures and injury to the health of humans exposed to it. If, as now seems inevitable, world coal production and consumption (combustion) increase rapidly in the decades ahead, in order to make good short-falls in petroleum availability or to circumvent rising oil prices, the problem of smoke pollution could become a very serious one in the industrial countries, and at some point a limiting factor — either in the sense of the real costs of putting up with the consequences of extensive coal combustion, or in the economic sense of the sheer cost of curtailing and minimising the resulting smoke emission.

The second ultimate limiting factor is the effect on the atmosphere of prolonged and intensive combustion of the fossil fuels. We just do not know what the long-term consequences will be of all the artificial heating that now goes on in a variety of ways — intentional and unintentional. We do know that the atmospheric temperature has risen perceptibly since the onset of the industrial revolution, and that this has, and must have, manifold ramifications for climate and environmental conditions generally. How resilient the environment is remains to be seen, but already there are those who feel and have expressed alarm about the atmospheric changes going on about us. As a result, the whole field of climatological research is receiving an urgent impetus.

## THE ORGANIC CHEMISTRY OF FOOD PRODUCTION

Let us now, however, turn to consideration of the peculiar characteristics of the fossil fuels which impart to them a unique status and role in post-industrial revolution economic life. Petroleum is a complex and variable mixture of hydrocarbons. It seems likely that it was the fats and proteins in the starting materials which were the precursors of these hydro-carbons. Petroleums from different sites diverge markedly in a number of properties: the proportion of light to heavy hydrocarbons; of aliphatic, aromatic and cycloparaffin compounds; and the content of porphyrins, sulphur, and metal trace elements. Coal is largely made up of carbon, hydrogen and oxygen. Its qualities vary with the degree of vicissitudes to which it has been subjected in processing. In general, the less altered varieties such as lignite have more of the gases hydrogen, oxygen and nitrogen and less carbon than the 'higher' ranking bituminous coals and anthracite. The original materials (land vegetation) consist largely of lignin and cellulose. Some coals contain sulphur, phosphorus, and traces of other elements. Hydrocarbons and other simple organic compounds obtainable from coal are probably not present as such, but form at high temperatures by thermal breakdown of the complex original substances.

It is now necessary, if we are to appreciate the distinctive characteristics and economic contribution of the fossil fuels, to make a considerable digression into the scientific laws governing food production.

Much nonsense has been talked about improving world food production, most of it in ignorance of scientific principles which were established in their essence a century or so ago. No systematic presentation of the complexities of the subject can be attempted here — the curious reader is referred to the bibliography at the end of the chapter — but a number of areas demand some exposition.

Most commentaries on the present energy crisis fail to make clear the important distinction between energy for machines and energy for human beings. Yet food is to Man what fuel is to power stations, cars, and other mechanical contrivances. Nor are human requirements neglible. Rendering statistics into terms that make comparisons possible, it has been shown that the daily human power requirement in the U.K. in 1961 was $8.2 \times 10^6$ kW, as compared with an average daily output from electrical generating plant in the U.K. of $17.5 \times 10^6$ kW. Now, this human power must derive from substance — there being no known or conceivable mode by which we might be galvanised by periodical charging with electricity or some other power source. (It should be noted and borne in mind that *ultimately* all power must have a 'meal' or 'meals' of substance, too: obviously oil- and coal-fired thermal power stations are as dependent upon combustible 'diet' as we are; while in the case of hydro-electricity, nuclear power, solar energy, and other such sources, there is a large initial investment and some running costs in substance).

The substance from which human beings — in common with all other animals — derive their energy is food. Food can only be produced by the action of the sun on the substances of air, soil, and water. The chloroplasts in plants operate in the process known as photosynthesis to transform solar electro-magnetic energy into chemical energy, some of which becomes available to us as food. In the 'natural' state, prior to any deliberate and conscious human intervention aimed at raising the productive capacity of a given area of land, there is a necessary equilibrium the parameters of which are defined by the efficiency of the photosynthetic transformations allied to the particular qualities of the soil, upon the substances of which the indigenous plantlife must call for the substance of its own growth. *Agriculture* is the series of processes whereby a given area of land is artificially induced to yield food for more animals and people than it would naturally support.

We can deduce from the very slow and erratic growth of world population prior to the industrial revolution that agricultural innovation up to then was slow and insecure. Rather limited piecemeal improvements spread slowly, and there were periodic sharp setbacks in certain areas as a result of injudicious land use practices (as in North Africa) or historical vicissitudes of one kind or another. What was it, then, about the industrial revolution period that transformed human prospects in population terms?

Obviously industrialisation *as such* cannot produce the wherewithal to feed expanding human numbers. Most industrial endproducts are inedible, and even those that are edible can only be so on the basis of original agricultural or fishery inputs: tinned pineapples and fish fingers are obvious examples, but even in the case of synthetic proteins the raw materials involved are the fossil fuels — themselves the product of accumulations of animal and vegetable matter in the remote past. It is to changes in agriculture itself that we must look for the key.

But first we must make an important distinction: that between food and food*stuffs*. The first category consists, broadly speaking, of those protein-rich nutriments available for human consumption such as many meats and some plants, notably the leguminous group including peas, beans and lentils, and also — though mainly indirectly via grazing livestock — the clovers and alfalfa (lucerne). The second includes the cereals, root crops, sugar, oils and fat. The latter by themselves cannot sustain life, and it is the leguminous crops that are at the core of all self-sufficient agricultural systems (i.e. agricultural systems independent of imports and capable of growing all the food required by the resident population).

Modern temperate climate agriculture had its beginnings in what has become known as the Agricultural Revolution in Britain in the eighteenth century. Conventional economic history texts discuss this in terms of concentration of holdings, elimination of fallow, higher crop yields in improved rotations, better drainage, selective breeding of livestock, and the more widespread use of such root crops as turnips which enable more cattle to be kept alive through the winter. It is seldom explained how extra protein was introduced into the system. Without extra protein, none of the other innovations or improvements would have had the consequences that demonstrably followed. Turnips and cereals are low in protein, and could not, by themselves, have sustained the doubling in average weight of the chief breeds of sheep and cattle which the eighteenth century witnessed, alongside other gains in yields (milk, grain and hay, for instance). The answer lay in the greater use of the broad-leaved, arable, annual, 'Dutch' clover (so-called because it had been introduced into England from the Low Countries in mid-seventeenth century; in fact, however, the first cultivators of clover were the Baltic Letts in the 6th century A.D. and all 250 present day species of clover are descended from the original strain).

To understand the importance of this, we must elaborate upon the distinction between legumes and non-legumes. On the roots of leguminous plants are little nodules, which specific bacteria from the soil, will in appropriate circumstances, colonise. When this has been accomplished, the bacteria are capable of converting air-nitrogen directly into protein-rich plant tissue, within limits set by the supplies of calcium, phosphate, sulphate, potassium, and trace elements in the soil. (The proposition that energy per se cannot produce substance is an elementary one, but one which, as we shall see, is frequently ignored or overlooked in popular discussion of food/population problems; I shall return to it several times as it is central to the argument of this chapter, and therefore of the book as a whole.) Nitrogen thus fixed by leguminous plants, as well as directly contributing to protein production, enriches the soil with nitrogen for other crops, whether growing contemporaneously with them or succeeding them in a rotation.

Incorporation of 'Dutch' clover into British agricultural practices, along with subsequent and related improvements, constitute what should be called the First Agricultural Revolution. The enhanced capability for nitrogen-fixation improved the quality and quantity of cereals and grazing, and therefore the production of bone, flesh and milk in human and domestic animal alike. At this point, the part played by fuel and fuel-related and fuel-dependent fertiliser was of little consequence. It was the systematic application of fuel to food production from the end of the nineteenth century onwards which constitutes the Second Agricultural Revolution.


## AGRICULTURE AND FUELS

If the First Agricultural Revolution can be identified, at least at the outset, as a British or European phenomenon, the Second affected most of the temperate world outside of colonised Asia and Africa (though we should note in passing, and anticipating somewhat, that its specific manifestation in Britain was the discovery of how to sow perennial 'wild white' clover deliberately *and with added doses of lime, phosphate, and potash*). The Third is currently in progress in East and South East Asia — notably China, North Korea, Vietnam, Laos and Cambodia — as we shall see in Chapter Four.

Before looking at the Second Agricultural Revolution, it may be as well to sketch in the antecedents of the vital conjunction of fuel/fertilser and agriculture. No doubt the connection has been there from the beginning in its simplest form: for instance, the burning of tree and bush cover in shifting 'slash and burn' cultivation provides ash fertilser for the crops that are then sown. The value of returning faeces to the soil was also early recognised where intensive agriculture became necessary, as in parts of China from the later part of the first millenium B.C. onwards. But the connection was local, sporadic, and pragmatic in most places throughout most of the pre-nineteenth century history of agriculture. Even in the first half of the nineteenth century the changes that were to be observed were of minor significance compared with those that were shortly to follow. We should note developments under two heads: direct and indirect.

By direct is meant the application of fuel products, or products in the manufacture of which fuel plays an essential part, actually on to or into the soil itself as an aid to fertility. Before the accession of Queen Victoria, little that was new had made an appearance. A beginning had, however, been made in applying soot from coal-burning domestic chimneys as a fertilser, and small amounts of ammonium chloride and sulphate of ammonia had become available for agricultural purposes as a by-product of the new municipal gasworks springing up across the country. Thus some nitrogen from coal was put to use that might otherwise have been simply dissipated. The 'burning' of limestone in order to make quicklime should also be noted as another early agricultural use of coal.

By indirect applications we mean those which improved the efficiency of agriculture by a roundabout route. Examples abound, from the evaporation of sea-water by coal-burning fires in order to yield salt, to the smelting of iron by coke-fired furnaces for the manufacture of better farm tools. Salt, in turn, contributed to the preservation of food, and — insofar as salted food made longer sea voyages possible — to an expansion in the range of food imports.

With the flowering of the Industrial Revolution — first in Britain and then elsewhere in the Northern Hemisphere, Japan, and Australasia — it was the indirect applications of fuel to food production and thence to population which proliferated first. Construction of railway networks eliminated the recurrence of localised food shortages, made fresh food more readily available to the growing urban populations, and accelerated international division of labour whereby distant and hitherto unused or underused cultivable land could be made to supplement and complement the immediate hinterlands of the metropoles. Countless other developments hinging on the power of coal and with implications for the feeding of a now rapidly growing world population might be cited: steamships, wire fencing, the Suez Canal, the electric telegraph, agricultural machinery, and so on; to some of these we return below.

The orthodox economic history texts make a great deal of the logistic aspects, stressing the opening-up of North America, the Argentine, and

Australasia by improvements in communications. It is certainly true that the colonisation and cultivation of these hitherto sparsely populated land masses played a most important part in the total picture of the industrialisation of the West (both in providing food for the urban worker and in absorbing surplus population from the Old World). But once again the conventional analysis does not explain where the extra protein came from to make these developments possible. The explanation is not called for, of course, if it is merely assumed that the Red Indian and the Aborigine were incapable of making the best use of the environments they inhabited: had their 'primitive' incompetence indeed been the true explanation, then all that would need to be posited is that the White Man, with his superior economic-technological genius, quickly evoked the dormant potential of these vast thinly-peopled plains and pastures.

However, the fact is that the Americas were poorly endowed with indigenous legumes, while Australasia was originally devoid of a native forage legume. It was not until the second half of the nineteenth century that this was put right, with the introduction — in part deliberate, in part fortuitous — of such plants as alfalfa in America and subterranean clover in Australia. And it was not until the last couple of decades of the century that these countries began to undergo the fateful transformation into producers of protein (meat, milk, eggs) on a grand scale as introduced grasses and clovers rapidly extended their range. But of course something else was necessary as well: the supplementary sustaining fertilisers to make good the deficiencies of the native soils. Where the raw materials, such as phosphate rocks, gypsum, lime or chalk, were not present and to hand, they had to be imported. In any case, they had to be processed. In either case a high cost in fuel had to be met.

But what had gone on in the way of fossil fuel application to food production prior to the last quarter of the 19th century was but a prelude to what was therein and subsequently to come. The developments were multiple, and we can but suggest the variety here. The first group of relevant developments consisted of improvements in transport world-wide. Railway mileage increased very steeply, all but doubling from 1890 to 1913 (when the world total exceeded 1.1 million kilometres). Of particular importance for the older industrial countries was the opening up of vast food-providing acreages in North America and elsewhere:

Railway mileage open to traffic: (in '000s)

|               | 1870  | 1910  |
|---------------|-------|-------|
| United States | 53.4  | 242.1 |
| Canada        | 2.5   | 26.6  |
| Argentine     | 0.6   | 17.3  |
| Australia     | 1.2   | 16.9  |
| Russia        | 7.1   | 45.1  |

Over the same time span, the population of Europe, excluding Russia, rose from 206 million to 339 million; another 32 million non-Russian

Europeans emigrated during this period, notably to the first four of the 'lands of recent settlement' in the table above (and we should bear in mind that, simultaneously, there was a significant shift of Russian population into Asiatic Russian 'lands of recent settlement'). Between 1881 and 1915, the USA took 22 million European immigrants, Canada 2.6 million, the Argentine 4.3 million, and Australia and New Zealand 3 million.

The steamship, of course, greatly facilitated this decisive population shift, so important for the feeding of the older industrialised countries. In 1850, less than ten per cent of the world's shipping was steam-driven (and two-thirds of this was plying the inland waters of North America). But between then and the first world war there was a complete reversal of the balance: by 1914 only 8% of the world's shipping was propelled by sail. Over the same sixty-odd years, the average size of steamships in service increased tenfold — the largest latterly exceeding 50,000 tons. Such expansion in capacity was made possible by the use first of iron and subsequently of steel in construction. There were also improvements in engine design, and (after 1904) a rapid turn over to oil as a fuel in place of coal (apart from the obvious advantages oil had in ease of handling, it generated more power per unit of fuel weight consumed — an edge in performance which was sharply increased after general adoption of the Deisel engine from the 1920's onwards). In short, innovations in shipping made possible the unprecedented movements of people and goods which sustained the impetus of industrialisation and economic growth in the late nineteenth and early twentieth centuries. More and more passengers could be carried on one voyage, and fares tumbled accordingly,

Another innovation played an extremely important part: refrigeration. (It should be noted that producing low temperatures is costly in fuel.) In 1880 a cargo of frozen Australian meat reached London, and a few years later the food situation of the world was transformed. From the lush pastures of the 'lands of recent settlement' (themselves transformed by imported legumes and the application of imported fertilisers) meat and dairy produce at extremely low prices began reaching the markets of industrial Europe. British real wages all but doubled from 1870 to 1914, in a period that now seems a remote Golden Age of steady and even falling prices.

The second major cluster of changes revolve round use of the fossil fuels more directly to increase food production. We have mentioned earlier some elementary forms of fertiliser utilised prior to the development of agricultural chemistry in its modern garb. But a more self-conscious, less pragmatic, approach had to wait until the latter part of the nineteenth century. Sulphur played an important role (largely empirical at first) from the first half of the century. Even before 1840, sulphuric acid had been used to dissolve bones and rock phosphate in order to make available their phosphate for application as fertiliser. After the patents of 1842, it became possible to manufacture 'superphosphate' (incorporating phosphate, sulphate, and calcium) from fossil phosphate (the supply of fresh bones being, of necessity, limited).

A true understanding of the role of fertilisers, however, had to await a succession of trials, experiments, speculations, observations, and advances in theory which bore fruit only after about 1865, when an appreciation of the indispensability and function of nitrogen, potassium, phosphorus, calcium and sulphur in increasing agricultural production was steadily gained. It was some twenty-five years later before commercial fertilisers regularly incorporated potassium. The key point for present purposes is to understand that the manufacture of these new fertilisers that were becoming available by the end of the nineteenth century was in one way or another — directly or indirectly — indebted to the fossil fuels. Direct indebtedness was accounted for by fossil fuel by-products such as the sulphate of ammonia accruing from gas works (before 1939, over ninety per cent of synthetic ammonia capacity was based on coke or coal). Indirect indebtedness included utilisation of the basic slag by-product of steel production (rich in phosphate, lime, and magnesium). After 1904, the Frasch process, later to be supplemented by others, greatly facilitated the production of elemental sulphur, so integral to the fabrication of superphosphate. Some estimates suggest that Frasch process sulphur alone (like all parallel processes dependent upon the fossil fuels) may support up to one sixth of the population of the countries employing superphosphate in agriculture (through its contribution to protein generation). Statistics such as these, though they so rarely figure in economic or indeed demographic discussions, are of the essence of a balanced and scientific approach to world resource/population problems.

As the twentieth century progressed, so too did the fertiliser industry, with petroleum and natural gas playing a steadily increasing role. By the early 1970's, the estimated production proportions of world ammonia capacity were roughly 9% from coal, 27% from naptha and other petroleum liquids, 56% from natural gas, and 8% from other sources. There is no discernible slowing down in the rate of growth of synthetic ammonia production round the world — nor, indeed, can there be if the world's agriculture is to sustain the rapidly swelling world population. Technical innovations in the petrochemical industry are also constantly necessary to keep up production of the fertilisers so desperately needed by the modern world's agriculture, a highly vulnerable creation resting on extremely shaky foundations, and — despite all the marvels of agricultural science — constantly at risk of catastrophe. Some appreciation of the precariousness of an economy built upon dependence on imported fossil fuels may be had by studying the experience of Japan towards the end of the Second World War, when the allied blockade was almost total. If the retort is made that Japan is a special case of import dependence, we may safely grant that without relinquishing the basic point, for it is impossible to conceive of the present international economy functioning if there were not continuous movements of increasing quantities of fossil fuels across national boundaries. What happened in October 1973, as a consequence of the Arab countries' restriction of petroleum supplies, and the multiple subsequent repercussions (the diversity and number of which continue to proliferate), can only give a hint of what the fossil fuels now mean for the support of human population on this planet.

Associated with the production of petroleum chemical ammonia there is the increasing production of ammonium nitrate and urea. Production of urea has the advantage of using the carbon dioxide separated from the synthetic gas used in ammonia plants and otherwise emitted into the atmosphere. Urea use has expanded rapidly in agriculture this century. The USA alone used about 3.5 million tons in 1970 — 37% as liquid fertiliser, 35% as solid fertiliser, and 15% as cattle food supplement. Much of the urea used in American agriculture is imported. The growth rate in world petroleum-based ammonia production, to give some indication of the acceleration, averaged 15% per annum from 1964 to 1971 (but part of this increase was due to oil replacing coal as the feedstock); over the same period, sulphur recovery from natural gas and oil grew by 11% per annum, this form of sulphur production accounting for over 30% of the world total in the end year. It is as well to recall that sulphur is the most important single commodity in the chemical industry, and one whose consumption per capita has been taken as a measure of a nation's industrial progress. Not least of its uses, of course, is in the supply of fertiliser.

Much more could be said concerning the direct use of the fossil fuels in the manufacture of fertilisers. The important point to grasp — and there is no possible danger of over-emphasising the point — is that without an adequate continuously rising supply of the fossil fuels there can be no rapidly expanding fertiliser industry, and without a rapidly expanding fertiliser industry there can be no sustained rise in world food production (as at present organised) and without that rise — in turn — world population cannot continue to expand in numbers at the rates characteristic of the last few decades. It is as simple as that.*

In the third group of applications of the fossil fuels to agriculture I embrace a miscellaneous bag, in no way trying to be exhaustive. A brief walk round a modern agri-business concern (the world 'farm' seems

---

*It should be borne in mind, though, that there is strong evidence that fertiliser absorption in modern agri-business is reaching saturation point, where further increments of fertiliser application yield lower and lower increments of output. The rate of yield increase of crop and livestock products is decreasing steadily in the overdeveloped countries, and '. . . much of the evidence regarding the trend in output per unit area supports the argument of an approach to the biological limits. Potential increases in output per unit area will probably be more dependent on human effort

somehow out of place) should alert the observant visitor to a great variety of applications. Some are self-evident, such as the use of fuel to run the farm tractors and other mechanical contraptions. Others are less so; we might cite, for instance, the use of electricity in battery farming (electricity overwhelmingly drawn from coal or oil burning thermal electric power-stations). Yet others are obscure, such as the use of fencing (the metal component of which of course was manufactured by smelting from raw ore and subsequently worked up in a factory using fossil-fuel powered machinery; to be comprehensive we should mention its distribution from the factory and installation by fossil-fuel using vehicles — but this last point would apply to most things on a modern farm too). Everyone is familiar with the crucial role of fencing in making possible the protein-producing agriculture of the American West and Mid-West, and probably also its role in Australian meat and wool farming, but an obscure calculation of 1913 suggests that the capital sunk in fencing in England and Wales then was of the magnitude of that sunk in the railways, a statistic which some may find incredible and which I certainly repeat only with the warning that I have found no way of checking its accuracy or even the plausibility of the comparability suggested. I leave to the ingenuity and industry of the visitor the continuation of this list — but probably the task of drawing up an exhaustive listing would prove impossible. Again, the important point to grasp is the utter dependence of modern agriculture on the fossil fuels. This discussion omits the fossil fuel dependence of the supply, delivery, and distribution networks, which is dealt with in chapter three.

Another matter to which attention should be given is the part the fossil fuels play — through their role in modern transport — in moving fertilisers not based on the fossil fuels as raw material around the world. An early example was guano, which was mined out at rates incomparably in excess of deposition, and therefore may also be regarded as finite. Chilean nitrates of soda afford another well-known example, but what may be less well-known is that the commercial product has valuable properties which other nitrogenous fertilisers lack and which make unnecessary the complementary movements of lime and chalk needed in conjunction with the latter. Tropical rain forest, about which wild hopes were in the past entertained by economists, is deficient in chalk and limestone (added to which we may note in passing that, once tree cover is removed for continuous

* cont. and attention than previously' (7). The second sentence quoted is germane to chapter four, below. This being said, it must be added that fertiliser application is still far below optimum throughout the underdeveloped countries, and massive increases in fossil fuel-based fertilisers can be absorbed in agriculture there for the foreseeable future — if available, and if available at acceptable prices. (8)

cultivation, the soil quickly loses its fertility). But here again, the list is almost endless, as valuable fertilisers and supplements are shuttled from country to country, and inside countries, in ever-increasing quantities. Of the 1970/71 world consumption of fertilisers (68.2 million metric tons), 28% entered international trade (and, even before October 1973, world consumption was rising faster than world production, a situation in which shortages would in any case have inevitably made themselves felt). In short, there is invariably a high fossil fuel energy cost associated with delivering non-fossil fuel based fertilisers from where they are to be found to where they are required.

At this point it may be as well to deal with the air-fixation of nitrogen, which has probably generated more nonsense from economists than anything else in this (or possibly any other) field. It has, in its time, been hailed as the panacea postponing indefinitely the spectre of world famines. The reasons why this is not so are extremely complex, but I will attempt, as a non-scientist, to explain at least some of the more important.

In the first place, air-fixation of nitrogen requires large quantities of cheap electricity — to fix one ton costs roughly five tons of coal equivalent. It is true that the electricity could in theory ultimately come from nuclear plants (though there would still be a fossil fuel cost in construction and maintenance). But there are serious doubts — which increase with time rather than diminish — about the extent to which we ever could, or should, so expand the production of nuclear energy that it would carry the burden of ever-increasing demand. The doubts arise in a number of areas: disposal of nuclear waste; safety of the power stations themselves; radioactive pollution; availability of uranium; the feasibility of fusion energy production; and the military implications of proliferation. There is another argument against plunging into large-scale nuclear energy programmes, and that is that, however successful, they could only be stop-gaps, merely postponing the ultimate reckoning when the Man-energy-food equation must return to equilibrium without calling upon fossil fuel 'capital', and that, in the interim, all the problems which press more and more insistently upon the world today would have been greatly exacerbated.

Secondly, air-fixed nitrogenous fertilisers can only be used in conjunction with earthy supplements embodying sulphur and calcium, for a variety of reasons connected with soil and plant science; the more old fashioned nitrogenous fertilisers (as we have noted in the case of Chilean nitrate) are superior in performance, not that there is anything surprising in this, for, as Professor Nicol points out, microbes and plants are old-fashioned, too. Thirdly, only the leguminous plants, as we observed above, have the ability to convert air-nitrogen directly into protein-rich plant tissue, the basis of our diet, and the leguminous plants do not need nitrogenous fertilisers (with minor exception); on the other hand, non-leguminous plants, providing our starchy foodstuffs, utilise the nitrogenous fertilisers precisely to manufacture more starch, sugar and fat. Professor

Nicol summarises the argument by stating that the underlying exchange involved in the fixing of nitrogen and its application to plants to raise yields (with the necessary additional inputs, as pointed out above) is of fossil carbon for carbon in crops here and now, and that this results in an increase in protein-poor foodstuffs at the cost of a reduction in irreplaceable fossil fuel deposits.

All this arises from the implications of maintenance of the carbon/nitrogen (C/N) ratio in soil and plants. The C/N ratio expresses the ratio of organic carbon (excluding carbonates in the soil) to the organically combined nitrogen (or the total combined nitrogen, since the normal proportions of ammonia and nitrate are small); the C/N ratio of most topsoils is roughly 10 (plus or minus 4), and that of protein about 4. Since C/N ratios in mature crops range from 18 for clover hay to 40 in cereal grains, there are problems for all land animals (including Man) in raising the proportion of protein in their diet to about a sixth of the dry matter. Man can solve the problem by consuming pulses, young vegetables, and/or meat, the latter from animals which have succeeded in solving their part of the problem. The significance of carbon as a plant nutrient, of organic manures in facilitating effective plant consumption of nitrogen, and of the role of the carbonaceous fossil fuels in the exchanges governing increases in crop yields is dealt with in detail by Professor Nicol, to whose work I refer those anxious to pursue the matter further (9).

## PROBLEMATIC SOLUTIONS

This demonstration of the integral and vital role of the fossil fuels in maintaining modern agricultural production is not, as I have admitted, in any way exhaustive. The catalogue of connections could be much extended. However, I would now like to move on to a discussion of some of the developments which have, over the years, been propelled into temporary prominence in public debate on 'solving the world's food problems'. Let me first back track and pick up at the point where I embarked upon a consideration of fertiliser production from fossil fuel raw materials, for it is important to understand the character of the changes which have, since the beginning of the century, enabled world population to climb from well below 2,000 million (2 billion) to over 4,000 million at the time of writing (1977).

There are aspects of economic history, as we already have had occasion to note, that are seldom referred to in the standard texts, even though some of them are of such importance in the whole process of development that their exclusion seriously distorts the picture and detracts from our understanding of its dynamics. One such was the perfection of means whereby 'wild white' clover could be successfully sown in order to increase the crop of grasslands, thus enabling greater ultimate off-takes of meat, milk and wool. Until it had been demonstrated that 'wild white' could be deliberately sown in places where it did not naturally occur — or occurred sparsely — the potential of British grasslands remained low. But the development of seeds that could be made commercially available and 'took' when sown would have been, on its own, ineffective; it happened that at about the same time (that is about 1905) it was shown that to enrich grassland with 'wild white' required that lime, phosphate, and potash be applied to prevent the depletion of soil nutrients consequent upon increasing the crop. 'Wild white', in alliance with lime, phosphate and potash, subsequently went round the world to wherever natural conditions favoured meat, milk and wool producing grasslands. When new grasslands were established where there had been none before (as in Australia and New Zealand), fertilisers had to be imported in huge quantities to make good the natural deficiencies of their respective soils. Bear in mind that the enormously increased output of protein thus made possible had — and has — an enormous cost in fossil fuels, and that future sustenance of the world's population (not to speak of the desirability of improving the diet of the world's hungry majority) will require that demands on the fossil fuels at least keep pace with numbers (or expand faster than numbers, in the second case). To give some idea of what would be involved in fulfilling the aspirations of adequately feeding a possible* world population of 6,400 million at the end of this century, we need merely note that while Europe consumes 170 kg. of fertiliser per hectare of arable land under permanent crops, Asia's figure is 21 kg., while those of Latin America and Africa are 18 and 8 respectively (and many parts of the so-called Third World have intrinsically poorer soil than northern hemisphere lands and correspondingly higher fertiliser requirements if comparable yields are ever to be attained). Much of this fertiliser helps produce not food as such but foodstuffs; here of interest is the disparity in protein intake between Western and Third World diets and what would be required to even out

---

* Estimates of the likely century-end population have fluctuated a great deal in recent years. The highest and wildest estimates have already been overtaken by events. Of course this is not a safe field for prophecy, however well-embedded in informed speculation. But I would suggest that there are now grounds for discounting extravagant and sensational projections. In the first place, as we shall see in chapter three, population is already stabilising, if not falling, in the overdeveloped countries. In the second, the countries of the Russian bloc seem, despite frantic official efforts, quite incapable of creating circumstances wherein parents will voluntarily have more than the bare minimum of children. In the third, China has undertaken an enormously successful campaign to stabilise population. And, finally, in the really poor underdeveloped countries of the 'free' world two things are already happening to decelerate growth: one is a resurgence of

the difference. Even the most cursory and approximate calculation affords an idea of the magnitudes of fertilisers called for in the next thirty years — and correspondingly the magnitudes of fossil fuels demanded.

It may seem that I am unnecessarily hammering away at this point, but the reason is to set up the general background to our look at some of the 'solutions' that have been hailed in uninformed discussion from time to time. Because it was, for some time, almost front-runner in the food stakes (though somewhat broken-winded now), I start with the so-called 'Green Revolution', about which countless words have been written in recent years (with, incidentally, a high fossil fuel and timber cost).

Basically, what we shall refer to as the green revolution involves substituting special high-yielding laboratory seed strains for those traditionally used in grain production. While seemingly spectacular results, in terms of yield, have been attained as a result of introducing 'miracle' rice, wheat and maize, a host of problems has from the beginning accompanied their use (I give a number of bibliographic references below). An important non-technical one arises from the class structure of the societies in the 'free' part of the Third World where the special seeds have been made available, but we shall delay consideration of this to the next chapter. What I mean by the technical problems — problems related to the plant physiology, soil requirements, treatment of unanticipated nutritional or health side-effects, and so on — have been numerous and serious, but may best be summed up by referring to the simple observation that in food production as in all natural exchanges you get nothing for nothing. Hybridisation results in seeds with higher potential productivity, but this manifests itself as a greater weight per acre of plant matter, which has to come from somewhere (in accordance with the general principles I have outlined above). It comes by heavy application of fertilisers (and by application of pesticides — many of which, like dieldrin, endrin and isodrin, are petrochemical products, and the first two of which have been banned since August 1974 in the USA as posing an 'imminent hazard' to human health), without

*cont. Malthusian 'positive checks', in the form of all those influences which increase the death-rate, or (in Malthus' own words 'the whole train of epidemics, wars, plagues and famines'; and the other is adoption of draconian and fascistic anti-natal programmes in countries such as India and Singapore, programmes involving compulsory or coerced sterilisation of the lower orders and other such violent measures. As a result, even the moderate Bucarest Conference (1974) estimate of 6,407 million as the end-of-century world population may be too high. The world growth rate was 1.9% per annum in 1970; by 1975 it had fallen to 1.6%. A 1976 report concluded that the world's population now may *not* double from its present 4,000 million for there 'is every indication that growth will continue to slow through the last quarter of this century.'(10)

which crop failures are inevitable.

Scientific arrogance has too frequently in the past brushed aside the traditional wisdom painfully acquired and matured by peasant and farmer through generations of practical experience in applying and fitting their agricultural techniques to local requirements. A mechanistic application of 'scientifically established' innovations can have catastrophic consequences (for which the peasant/subject has to pay, not the scientist). An illustration of this from introduction of the 'green revolution' in wet rice-growing Asia may be given here, though we might equally have looked at some of the 'silent spring' disasters precipitated by adoption of modern 'agri-business' in the West. Blanket adoption of a single HYV (High Yielding Variety) of rice adds to the danger of a specific crop disease or infestation wiping out the harvest, whereas local variability in strains sown limits the spread of any particular threat. HYV's characteristically require heavy dosages of pesticides, but these may have — as they do with wet rice cultivation — serious side-effects. For example, pesticides applied to guard the rice plants may kill the fish which share the flooded fields. These fish supply when harvested, invaluable protein to supplement the basic rice grain diet, but in addition also keep down pests while they are alive and actively seeking food for their own sustenance. Again, HYV strains, which maximise grain weight as opposed to stalk weight, may make it impossible for farmers to maintain draught animals. These — aside from their intrinsic usefulness in the fields — also served to provide human food (milk and meat) of high protein from a foodstuff (straw) otherwise discarded as inedible by humans because of its high cellulose content. One should not forget, moreover, the very valuable manure draught animals produce; particularly in tropical conditions, chemical fertilisers have to be supplemented by organic manure if good sustainable results are to be obtained. (This comes back to the logic of the C/N ratio.)

Now, an aspect of the green revolution which requires notice is that many of the so-called 'developing' countries which have taken up cereal production with HYV's are — partly for geographical, partly for historical reasons — exceptionally dependent upon imported fuels and the related petro-chemicals, including fertilisers and pesticides. In the Philippines, for example, 90% of domestic energy requirement (including of course those related to agriculture) is derived from imported oil — a handful of the giant Western oil majors having controlled the market for many years, without making (until after the 1972 coup) any major effort to survey and develop possible local sources of crude. Thailand is in much the same situation of import dependence, but it is further along the path of having its own reserves opened up. One could cite numerous other examples, but the interested should repair to the bibliography for further guidance.

Ignoring for the moment the fact that soaring oil prices impose crippling balance of payments burdens on these poor non-oil producing countries, what has happened to them affords a revealing insight into the unsound foundations of modern world agriculture. Imports — as we have already mentioned — played a role in increasing the productivity of European and other 'Western' agriculture from quite early on, Chilean nitrate providing an example. But with a number of exceptions (including those with the luck to have neighbours with disposable surpluses) the countries concerned were able to carry through their agricultural revolutions on the bases of their own fossil fuel stocks. Furthermore, until the post-war period, the rich countries controlled most of the disposable cheap fuel of the poorer (colonial and neo-colonial) countries to make good any deficiencies at home. Fuel was cheap, and the fight for markets less intense than it has since become as more countries have developed industrial sectors (the special circumstances of the great inter-war depression would require separate consideration): the main point is that agricultural production was pushed up on a much more secure basis than is the case with the later-comers to agricultural revolutions today. Lacking adequately developed domestic and home-controlled fossil fuel extraction and processing industries, the non-oil producers among the 'developing' countries are at the mercy of circumstances beyond their own control. Were the major oil exporting countries — for good financial and economic reasons from their point of view — seriously to restrict supplies entering world markets, the plight of the agricultural sectors (employing most of the population and feeding most of the rest) of poor oil-importing countries would be desperate. They cannot do in months what it took a country like Britain decades to do: find, mine, and achieve the capacity to process their own domestic reserves of fossil fuels, possibly coal (and coal industries do not develop overnight — nor can they quickly be rejuvenated, as countries now requiring, because of the oil crisis, to switch back to coal are finding to their cost). In this situation, however, as in many others as we will see during out survey of the international economic situation, the case of China is of outstanding importance and relevance.

I think it is safe to conclude that the green revolution is based on false premises and expectations, and that in important respects it has intensified rather than helped alleviate the problems associated with feeding the world's rising numbers. Briefly, here are some further candidates sometimes seriously advanced as contenders for 'solving' the hunger problem, and first among these the illusion of 'improving photosynthesis'. Here we come back again to basic principles. Photosynthesis cannot create substance. It can, by harnessing solar electro-magnetic energy, transform some substances into others by the agency of pigments called chlorophylls. Carbon dioxide and water are transformed into organic compounds consisting of carbon, hydrogen and oxygen, while free oxygen gas is released from the water. Plant growth, *per se*, is conceptually distinct from photosynthesis, and since many other substances other than carbon, hydrogen and oxygen enter into plant growth, including those for which we look to green plants for our food, notably protein, it follows that the majority come from the soil. If the soil be enriched with nitrogenous fertilisers and the necessary earthy matter, the local C/N ratio will be lowered. It can only be righted by the plant's increasing photosynthesis by increasing the area (i.e. bulk) of chlorophyll-containing leaf and stem — up to the limits set by the availability of the earthy matter (e.g. phosphate, potassium, magnesium, etc.) necessary for the additional green matter above the ground and corresponding root increment below. The end result is to increase the bulk of sugar, starches, fibres and oil (i.e. foodstuffs). The prospects of keeping land animals alive will have been enhanced little if at all unless there has been a simultaneous increase in protein-rich sources such as beans.

Second, we may take the old favourite of improved irrigation. No one doubts that much could be done to improve water control in many parts of the world in such a way as to provide the conditions for more secure and effective agriculture. But what many idealists have in mind here is turning the vast deserts of the world into lush fields and vegetable gardens. A few calculations using the fossil fuels as coinage soon dispel these illusions. There are a number of energy-consuming stages. One is the distilling of sea-water: Nicol estimates 50 tons of oil a year to feed one adult on one acre. Next, there is the problem of piping the distilled water to where it is needed: the quantities of oil equivalent would of course depend on the miles of piping required, the height of the site above sea level, and many other factors; in any case it may be conceded that the fuel cost would be astronomical. Again, because many deserts have serious qualitative deficiencies as plant hosts requiring correction by application of very large quantities of bulky amendments such as gypsum, we have to allow for a further colossal energy cost in effecting the needed applications; it might be possible by applying a nine-digit tonnage of gypsum to newly irrigated land of a suitable kind ultimately to feed from an area of 150,000 sq. km. (roughly the size of England, Nepal or Tunisia) a population of 20 million, according to Professor Nicol's calculations, (in a world where world population increases at an annual rate currently over three times that*) — and at an extravagant cost in energy. Excluding the energy costs in such essential adjuncts as piping, pumping, and the processing and transport of

---

*It is of course true that each country must adapt its own strategy in accordance with its own specific resource endowment: we do *not* constitute one world for any purpose except perhaps that of the collection of statistics. A desert country richly endowed with oil which could be extracted at low cost, and possessed of a reasonably stable population, might well decide, under an autarchically-inclined revolutionary regime (along the Cambodian pattern), to cease exporting the oil and to devote it instead to irrigation — thus making possible food self-sufficiency as an alternative to importing food.

fertilisers (and in transporting the human colonists with all their possessions, tools, and other requirements), we can easily calculate the oil cost in water supply for irrigation alone at one billion tons a year. For comparison, US oil production in 1970 was just over one half of that — and the US was in that year far and away the world's largest producer, with 23% of the world's total. Total world oil production in 1975 was only 2.7 billion tons. We may add that the area of desert land in the world is steadily increasing. Hungry people in Asia, Africa and Latin America, in foraging desperately for food, have laid waste vast areas in the three continents. The southward spread of the Sahara has attracted much attention in recent years, but the desert is also eating into formerly cultivable land northwards, at a rate of a quarter of a million acres a year. Another half a million acres of irrigated land throughout the world are lost each year by waterlogging and salinity. A process of 'desertification' is accelerating under pressure of immediate human food needs, commercial timber extraction, and — in general — uncontrolled and unsound land practices.

Reference has sometimes been made to rain making as a panacea. It is, of course, subject to the general argument that water by itself cannot sustain growth. More seriously, we are growing more aware of our profound ignorance of the consequences — proximate and ultimate — of what we do when we interfere with the world's water cycles. The Americans used rain-making over North Vietnam during their aggression: how much of the abnormally rainy or dry weather in neighbouring countries thereafter was the indirect result? Have the recent floods in Bangladesh anything to do with human interference in the catchment areas upstream (begun during the colonial period)? To what extent have the droughts and famines in Ethiopia and other parts of Africa in recent years been the result of pushing out cultivation into barren areas during periods of water availability which turned out to be totally abnormal? We have a lot to learn in terms of existing techniques before embarking upon aerial rain-making (which, in any case, is costly in fossil fuels — it is hard at present to imagine atomic-powered aircraft!). To correct existing mistakes and deficiencies and to allow for the evidence that the years 1957 to 1972 were the best for world agriculture for 150 years in terms of weather and the prediction that a favourable cycle of such duration is unlikely to return for some time — perhaps for centuries — such fossil fuel as is available for all purposes connected with water supply ought to be conserved for conventional purposes of which we have some experience. There are many more 'solutions' to the world's food problem current in popular discussion, but we need proceed no further in their refutation. Once the general principles governing food production have been grasped — however hazily — the reader is in a position himself to construct the case against any suggested new 'miracle' or panacea. For instance, one could look at the new 'miracle' technique of food production recently much talked about: nutrient film technique (nft — the up-dated label for hydroponics, or growing food on water). It is claimed that this process of producing food crops in a film of water less than one millimetre in depth constitutes a system 'totally independent of soil or any other solid growing medium'(11) and thus applicable to arid or otherwise inhospitable regions where soil quality is low. Amazing yeild claims have been advanced for this technique, experimentally applied: ten crops of lettuce a year in Queensland, Australia; 400 tons an acre of cucumbers in California; and 130 tons an acre of tomatoes in England. Aubergines, peppers, and beans are also the subject of current experiments, the last of the three being of particular significance in that here we have a high protein crop.

## ENTROPY, INEQUALITY AND POPULATION

Let me try, before concluding the chapter with a look at the significance of entropy, to sum up what we have been saying about the basic chemical considerations governing food production. First, energy unaided cannot produce food substance (hence the total irrelevance of fission and fusion energy to world population/food problems — except to the extent that by replacing use of the fossil fuels as motive power for machines they thereby increase the stock available for food production purposes). Second, having regard to the C/N ratio, and to the nature of the whole process of food production, we must combine more carbon and nitrogen if we are to have more food; it follows that we must call upon the world's stored reserves of carbonaceous fossil fuels (which themselves represent the cumulative result of hundreds of millions of years of small long-term imbalances in the carbon cycle). Highly simplified though this presentation is, it ought to be sufficient to guide the reader to more systematic and detailed analyses and discussions.

World population has been enabled to grow to its present numbers by oxidizing fossil fuels thus winning food in excess of the limit set by solar energy, green plants, and so on in the natural (i.e. pre-fossil fuel utilising age) cycles. Oxidization of the fossil fuels entails reducing the stock of available energy, which leads us to a consideration of the concept of entropy.

The Concise Oxford English Dictionary defines entropy as the 'measure of the unavailability of a system's thermal energy for conversion into mechanical work'. I do not promise in what follows to give an unexceptionable gloss on this bare definition, I would be satisfied if non-scientific readers were made sufficiently curious to pursue the matter in the pages of other writers infinitely better qualified than I. Nonetheless, since the concept is of the utmost importance for the subject matter of this volume, I have no option but to attempt some elucidation.

There are two qualitative energy states — free (available) and bound (unavailable). Free energy may be conceived of as that potential energy (for instance, a coal seam or oil well) available for our purposes. The First Law of Thermodynamics states that energy can neither be created nor destroyed in any observable process. When coal is extracted and burned, or oil extracted and used to fuel a car, all that happens is a transformation from potential to kinetic energy — not an increase in the quantum of energy. Moreover, and here we come to the Second Law of Thermodynamics (the Entropy Law), the transformation in the case of heat energy is one-way and irreversible — what has happened is that the original free (available) energy has been dissipated so diffusely in the form of heat, smoke, and ashes, that it has become irrecoverable for human purposes. Jumping in a foolhardy fashion to the generalisation, we may say that in any closed system the amount of bound (unavailable) energy continuously increases — or, to put it in other words, that entropy continuously increases. This may appear puzzling when we make statements such as that the entropy of a finished product — a sheet of metal say — may be lower (its *disorder* less) than that of the original ore from which it has been produced, but this can only be at the cost of increasing entropy elsewhere in the system (e.g. burning coal in the smelting process, etc.).

For our purposes, the essential aspect of the Entropy Law is in its irrefutable logic: the free energy of our system can only be run down, never increased. All our vaunted marvels of modern technology have been achieved by frantically tapping low entropy availability — and turning out relatively meretricious products at a net cost of degrading free into bound energy. In the words of an economist with some knowledge of what is involved:

> 'what goes into the economic process represents *valuable natural resources* and what is thrown out of it is *valueless waste*. Economists are fond of saying that we cannot get something for nothing. The Entropy Law teaches us that the rule of biological life and, in man's case, of its economic continuation is far harsher. In entropy terms, the cost of any biological or economic enterprise is always greater than the product. In entropy terms, any such activity necessarily results in a deficit.' (12)

The free energy at out disposal is of two kinds: solar and terrestrial. The former must realistically be seen as beyond our control. We must, therefore, make do with manipulating our earthly stock of low entropy as our needs and demands rise. But that stock is finite while the former is, to all intents and purposes, infinite. Yet the process of so-called economic 'development' has been a process of switching our dependence from solar to terrestrial sources (evident in such changes as those from draught animals to tractors and from manures to artificial fertilisers). A moment's thought should enable the reader to see for himself that, as the pace of economic 'development' quickens — and the food needs of the world's population grow — there will be more and more calls for such changes, in order to achieve in the here and now certain limited goals (for some, ownership of two cars; for others, the feeding of ten mouths from an area formerly supporting five) *at the expense of human beings yet unborn.* Let us look at this briefly. Admittedly we have to make provision for feeding ourselves here and now — and can only do so at present population levels by tapping terrestrial low entropy (the fossil fuels). But at the moment perhaps some 95% or more of annual drawings (growing annually at 4%-5% per annum) on the capital stock of fossil fuels are being frittered away on the generation of energy for purposes — mechanical and industrial — other than food production. This 95% squandering means quite simply that — in order that we may have all kinds of meretricious and unnecessary things — the stock available untouched for feeding future generations is being rapidly and irreversibly run down. For those who scorn such analyses, pointing out that new reserves are continually being established and in any case that (admittedly higher cost) marginal reserves (such as tar-sand oils and shale oil) will soon become profitable to work with rising energy prices and improvements in technology, let me just pose this question: if we have to go to the lengths to which we are now being driven in this generation — for example, drilling for oil way out in the wilds of the inhospitable frozen wastes of Alaska — to what desperate straits will the next generation and the next (not to look further) be driven to stave off starvation for the world's poor and to maintain the momentum of rising affluence for the rich minority? The situation as adumbrated in the pages above is not a fanciful and speculative flight of political imagination, but is an irrefragable inference from established scientific principles. The logical structure of the argument is unassailable, even if we cannot put precise quantities and measurements to the parameters (such as how many tons of coal and oil remain recoverable, how long these will last, how demand will develop, etc.).

Faced with these realities, or rather acting in ignorance of them, the world plunges ahead with its pillage of the dwindling fossil fuel reserves. And for what? Detergents (US consumption of synthetic detergents rose from 4% of total soap + detergent market in 1945 to over 80% in 1964; the other developed countries have followed a similar trajectory); synthetic rubbers (from 52% to 66% of 'free world' plus Polish and Czech total rubber consumption between 1960 and 1970); synthetic fibres (from 4.5% of estimated world consumption of fibres in 1960 to over 31% — estimated — in 1975); plastics (one of the fastest expanding growth sectors in the world: West German consumption of plastics per capita rose from 1.8 kgs. in 1950 to 55.0 kgs. in 1970; world consumption rose thirteen-fold over the same period); and so we might go on. It is to be noted that in each case there is a clear switch away from a renewable resource — soap, natural rubber, wool and paper (the biggest single use of plastics is in packaging), for example — to a non-renewable petro-chemical in-put. But this is of course only a part of the story, for we have to add to this the colossal burning of fossil fuels more directly in cars, central heating, and hundreds of other modern consumer uses. And then again in industry where the catalogue really is endless. The most important — literally vital — use of all, in supporting human population by way of fertilisers and in other ways to sustain food production, accounts for but a modest (though steadily rising) percentage of the whole. For overdeveloped countries, the generally accepted figure is that food systems today absorb about 16% of the nation's energy budget. Only about a quarter of this is, however, in agriculture as such, the rest going in processing, distribution, domestic preparation, cooking, and the like. † (Much of the latter could be cut out with a different organisation of production and social structure — something we discuss in chapter four.) From 1940 to 1970, the total energy inputs to the US food system trebled, while the 'energy subsidy' (reflecting the units of energy input required to produce one unit of food) doubled — from 4.5 to 8.8.*

† Even the more inclusive figure 'is not complete, since it does not include the energy expended in other countries in producing commodities such as fish-meal and phosphate fertilisers which are important inputs to UK [and other overdeveloped countries' — M.C.] agriculture. On this basis, if every field in the world were cultivated to the UK average, something like 50% of the present total world fuel consumption would have to be devoted to food production. *This is one of many cogent reasons why the whole world cannot go over to a fuel-intensive agricultural system as practised in industrialized countries.* ' (13)

* It is worth alerting the reader to the ambiguities inherent in any discussion of food production and 'efficiency'. Professor John Hawthorn, in his invaluable paper cited in the bibliography, writes thus in illustration: 'A fairly recent study of the Kung bushmen shows that they secure a good high-protein diet based on nuts, animals and about 20 different types of vegetables by food gathering two-and-a-half days out of seven. Over this exercise a man at work achieved an output-input ratio of 7.8. A similar study of the Dodo tribe in Uganda gave a ratio of 5. The Tsembaga people of New Guinea are said to do even better with a ratio of 25. In contrast, the average UK farmer works on a ratio of 0.4. For a given input of energy the Kalahari bushman achieves nearly twenty times as much output as his British counterpart. However, to succeed in this very efficient process he requires just over 1,040 hectares of land per person, and one man's work for one day provides for himself and three others. His British counterpart provides for himself and forty-seven others and requires only 0.78 hectares per person. His productivity per hectare is therefore more than 1,300 times that of the bushman, but the effective figure is higher because this calculation is based on the total area of the UK with out allowing for buildings, roads and inland waterways.'

I would like to conclude this chapter with a summary of the situation by Professor Nicol, who was one of the first writers to draw attention to the 'limits of man':

'The unique energy-entropy ecological relation shown by human populations stems from recent acquisitions of energy through oxidizing subsurface deposits inaccessible to feral consociations and to Man using only primitive techniques. Extra food thereby won has permitted an increase of human (and some animal) populations beyond the limit set by equilibria between current solar energy, green plants, surface stocks of ionizable matter, the microbial population, and — through the microbes — the C/N weight ratio (of non-carbonate carbon to combined nitrogen).

The present-day stock of oxidizable matter may be regarded as a shrinking source of energy, or in entropic terms of its random dispersal, in energy-less compounds, throughout the atmosphere and the seas. A decline in human populations is thus foreseeable: to set in, at latest, when maximum output of oxidizable materials has been attained.

There must be a return to equilibrium with surface resources energized by contemporary solar income alone. Human populations are in theory perpetually renewable at some quite low level of subsistence, numbers, and culture. That level is arguably akin to those of about 1600 A.D., on the assumption that the situation differs from those of pre-Columbian times in that surviving "know-how" about living in approximate balance with the surface environment is equally available all over the world.' (14).

# REFERENCES

1.   National Academy of Sciences, *Resources and Man*, (San Francisco, 1969) p205.

2.   D.S. Greenberg, *The Politics of American Science*, Penguin, (London, 1969) pp219-260.

3.   National Academy of Sciences, ibid.

4.   Cf. T. O'Toole, 'U.S. Oil Imports Soar to Record in January', *International Herald Tribune*, 9/2/1977.

5.   G. Kolko, *The Roots of American Foreign Policy*, (Boston, 1969) p50.

6.   Cf. D.L. Meadows et al., *The Limits to Growth*, Earth Island Ltd., (London, 1972) pp55 et seq.

7.   Centre for Agriculture, *Land for Agriculture*, (Reading, 1976).

8.   S.P. Dhua, 'Need for Organo-mineral Fertilizer in Tropical Agriculture', *The Ecologist*, 5.5. (1975).

9.   H. Nicol, *The Limits of Man*, Constable, (London, 1976).

10.   Worldwatch Institute, *World Population Trends — Signs of Hope, Signs of Change*, (Washington, 1976).

11.   *Daily Telegraph*, (London, 24/1/1977).

12.   N. Georgescu-Roegen, *The Entropy Law and the Economic Process*, Harvard University Press, (Cambridge, Mass., 1971).
13.   P. Chapman, *Fuel's Paradise*, Penguin, (London, 1975) p36.
14.   H. Nicol, ibid, pp161-162.


## BIBLIOGRAPHY

1.   Hugh Nicol, *Microbes by the Million*, Penguin Books, (London, various eds).
2.   Hugh Nicol, *Microbes and Us*, Penguin Books, (London, 1955).
3.   Hugh Nicol, *The Limits of Man*, Constable, (London, 1967).
(Three of the late Professor Nicol's expository works for the layman. As an undergraduate in the early 1950's, I heard Professor Nicol expound his views on the energy limitation to economic growth in a talk on the BBC Third Programme. Much later he became a personal friend and patient mentor, always ready to make good the deficiencies of an education in economic 'science' that had left me (like countless others in the same predicament) completely ignorant of some of the most important relevant physical laws. My debt to him in this volume is obvious.)
4.   Konrad Krauskopf, *Introduction to Geochemistry*, McGraw-Hill Inc., (New York, 1967).
5.   A.M. Smith, *Manures and Fertilisers*, Nelson, (Edinburgh & London, various eds.).
6.   E.J. Russell, *Soils and Manures*, CUP, (Cambridge, various editions).
7.   A.L. Waddam, *Chemicals from Petroleum*, John Murray, (3rd. ed., London, 1973).
8.   Shell International Chemical Company Ltd., *Chemicals Information Handbook*, (London, 1972-73).
9.   A.V. Slack, *Chemistry and Technology of Fertilizers*, Interscience Publishers, (New York, 1967).
(A selection of references covering the most important technical aspects.)
10.   Ingrid Palmer, *Food and the New Agricultural Technology*, United Nations, (Geneva, 1972).
11.   Ingrid Palmer, *Science and Agricultural Production*, United Nations, (Geneva, 1972).
12.   *The Green Revolution*, Proceedings before the Subcommittee on National Security of the Committee on Foreign Affairs, House of Representatives, 91st Congress, 1st Session, 5/12/69, U.S. Government Printing Office, Washington, 1970.
13.   Marvin Harris: 'How Green the Revolution?', *Journal of Contemporary Asia*, 2.4. (1972).
14.   H.M. Cleaver, 'The Contradictions of the Green Revolution', *Monthly Review*, (June, 1972).
(A few sources relevant to consideration of the 'green revolution'.)

15.    N. Georgescu-Roegen, *The Entropy Law and the Economic Process,* Harvard University Press, (Cambridge, Mass., 1971).
(Absolutely essential reading for all seriously interested in the questions tackled in this chapter and in the volume as a whole; Professor Georgescu-Roegen is an economist who has thoroughly explored the implications and ramifications of the Second Law of Thermodynamics for the discipline and methodology of economics.)

16.    Walter C. Patterson, *Nuclear Power,* Penguin Books, (London, 1976).
(A useful introduction to the continuing debate on the advisability and feasibility of banking on nuclear power for the future. Readers are also advised to keep their eyes on the periodicals *Sanity,* London, and the *Bulletin of the Atomic Scientists,* Chicago, and to consult the bibliography in Walter Patterson's book.)

17.    Rachel Carson, *Silent Spring,* Penguin, (London, various eds.).

18.    Frank Graham, *Since Silent Spring,* Hamish Hamilton, (London, 1970).
(Two best-selling contributions in the pesticide controversy.)

19.    Gerald Leach, *Energy and Food Production,* Science & Technology Press, (Guildford, 1976).

20.    John Hawthorn, *'Energy — Brake or Break; The Energetics of Food Systems'.*
(Two recent succinct and cogent contributions to the debate.)

21.    Leon Howell & Michael Morrow, *Asia, Oil Politics and the Energy Crisis,* IDOC, (New York, 1974).

22.    Jean-Marie Chevalier, *The New Oil Stakes,* Penguin, (London, 1975).
(Two useful looks at the structure of the world oil industry and its impact on the various sectors of the world economy.)

# THE DEVELOPMENT OF UNDERDEVELOPMENT

Systematic concern with, and study of, the phenomenon of 'under-development', at least in non-Marxist and non-socialist circles in the West, really dates from the second world war. Prior to that time, while the back-wardness of the colonial and semi-colonial countries of Asia, Africa and Latin America was recognised and accepted as a fact, it was generally assumed that the condition of backwardness was being, albeit slowly, over-come with the help and guidance of the more advanced powers who ad-ministered them. Even some Marxists in the West were inclined to accept the need for the advanced countries to exercise trusteeship over the back-ward until such time as the latter might in due course catch up sufficiently to be entrusted with all the responsibilities of self-government. Some went so far as to proclaim that even when imperialist countries had undergone proletarian revolution they would need to retain their colonies for the economic advantages they yielded: these advantages, it was said, helped sustain Western civilisation, which was seen as the sole ultimate guarantor of progress for the peoples of advanced and backward countries alike.

Of course there were other socialists, both in the West but more partic-ularly in the oppressed nations themselves, who even then saw things in a quite different light, tracing the backwardness of the backward precisely to imperialism itself, and seeing the cure for it, therefore, in the revolution-ary or evolutionary assertion and achievement of independence. The debate, in left-wing and other circles alike, remained, however, largely hypothetical and theoretical until the second world war.

The second world war totally transformed the picture, for at least two reasons. In the first place, the Pacific war matured the nationalist move-ments of Asia and advanced their prospects more in three and a half years than had been the case in the preceding three and a half decades. Indepen-dence, from having been a largely utopian vision and rhetorical battle-cry, suddenly became an imminent possibility. All the problems that it would inevitably bring in its train were, therefore, thrust on the agenda of public discussion very much more forcibly and insistently than hitherto. In the second place, the United States ruling class — seizing the opportunity offered by America's achievement of world primacy in both economic and military terms — accepted responsibility for planning the post-war world. It is worth looking for a moment at what was involved here, and how it tied in with the need to develop development economics.

The prolonged inter-war economic crisis and recession had been an alarming experience for the Western business community and those responsible politically and professionally for safeguarding its interests. Influential Americans attributed the catastrophic decline in business activity not just to some God-sent commercial malaise, about which little could be done, but also quite specifically to some malfunctionings which could be traced to human acts and decisions. In particular, it was natural to see in the general resort to mercantilism, protectionism and autarky a major contributory factor: the 'Open Door' and free enterprise were articles of almost religious faith (even though the USA reserved the right to protect its own domestic market and its own colonial interests). Prominent among the culprits, according to this view, were the old colonial powers such as Great Britain, Holland and France. Their resort to restrictions in production and export of key raw materials from their colonies — in order to shore up prices — was bitterly resented in America, the main customer for such commodities. Moreover, Britain's system of imperial preference, and the sharp protectionist measures taken by France and Holland to preserve their own stakes in their colonial empires, badly hit American overseas trade. On the one hand, Washington felt that US business was being 'held up to ransom' (in being asked to pay 'unnatural' raw material prices), and on the other that it was being 'shut out of world markets'. And, indeed, the US share of world trade did drop during the 1930's.

With the onset of the war in Europe, American leaders set afoot a process of investigation into the world economy, in order to elaborate a sound programme for reconstructing it along the lines Washington desired (and US business required) in the post-war period. The scale and thoroughness of these investigations, a major part under the auspices of the Council on Foreign Relations (an unofficial body but one integrated with the administration via the numerous governmental and bureaucratic figures who took part in its activities), were exemplary. By 1943, the blueprint for the post-war economic disposition was virtually complete.

It started from the assumption that without a much greater degree of US government intervention in the international economy and assistance to American business interests than hitherto there would be a grave danger of slipping back into depression when hostilities ceased and the huge war machine (which had brought full employment to the States for the first time since the hectic boom years of the 1920's) was dismantled. Capitalism was to be restored and revitalised world-wide, but now under US hegemony, and with its *modus operandi* dictated from Washington. To stimulate activity, dollars were to be pumped freely into the system through American aid, overseas military spending, greatly stepped-up US foreign investment, and new bodies such as the International Monetary Fund, the International Bank for Reconstruction and Development and the various United Nations agencies (all US-dominated). A number of key objectives could thus be pursued. American industry would benefit by orders for its products from all over the 'free world' (the American empire). Adequate supplies of raw materials at acceptable prices could be guaranteed by making aid to such war-weakened countries as Britain, France and Holland conditional upon compliance with American terms. The dollar would replace sterling (which had never recovered from the first world war) as the international currency, management of which could guarantee a flow of international purchasing power sufficient to maintain a high level of economic activity and of economic growth in the capitalist countries.

In the management of such a system, a great deal of economic expertise was obviously called for. As far as the discipline of development economics is concerned, the problem with which it had to cope, stripped of all altruistic platitudes about 'closing the gap' and the like, was the integration of the former colonies and semi-colonies into the international capitalist economy under US hegemony. They had to supply a smooth flow of raw materials to the rich industrialised countries of the West and to Japan. They had to be made hospitable to foreign investment. And they had to be fashioned to provide an expanded market for the goods produced in the advanced countries. None of these objectives were compatible with the aims of revolutionary nationalist movements, such as that which had swept China out of the American empire by 1949. Development economics, therefore, was bound from the start to be ideologically skewed, with all due respect to those practioners, and there were some, who genuinely, if naively, felt a calling to assist the poor of the world. It should be noted that the fledgling discipline was lavishly funded by the big foundations (themselves financed by business), especially those of the United States, and to some extent directly by business (in the form of endowed fellowships, chairs, etc.).

This digression should clear the ground for the attempt, which follows, at a highly compressed account of the development of underdevelopment, from a basically Marxist perspective. Little effort shall be made, except in passing, to rebut conventional developmental wisdom, having noted its parentage and bias. Much of it is irrelevant symbol-manipulation where it is not directly servicing imperialism. I say that I shall approach the topic of underdevelopment from a 'basically' Marxist perspective, for there is healthy disagreement among Marxists on certain aspects (some of them important) of the process. What I write will not meet with the agreement of some — perhaps any. Its Marxist credentials may be questioned. But it embodies at least my own understanding of the matter. Thereafter, I pick up some important themes related to the development of underdevelopment and discuss them.

## HOW IMPERIALISM GREW

### The Growth of Industrial Capitalism

By the 18th century, some West European countries, notably Britain, had capitalised upon certain historical, geographical and technological opportunities and advantages sufficiently to be able to make the transition to a quite new stage of economic development: industrial capitalism. Which precisely of these opportunities and advantages were ultimately the most important or ought to be credited with the greatest causal significance is a matter of continuing controversy (see references 1-7 in the bibliography to this chapter). But we should at least mention a number of the key factors, the order of listing in no way reflecting any prejudice on the author's part about their comparative weighting.

The Romans were the first to succeed in embodying in their legal code adequate safeguards for the property owner and the merchant. While the Roman empire could not itself effect the transition to capitalism, Roman commercial law, surviving through the dark ages, became in time the perfect legal instrument facilitating the transition from western European feudalism to capitalism. Islamic law, Chinese law, and Japanese law were all defective, judged from the commercial point of view, and their defects undoubtedly hindered sustained vigorous evolution of business activities.

Western European feudalism in itself had peculiar features which made it specially hospitable to the seeds of capitalism. Dispersion of power among the monarch, the feudal nobility, the burghers of the cities, and the dignitaries of the church, enabled the second to work towards establishment of capitalist relations of production in agriculture (as and when price and wage relations favoured it) and the third to create for themselves in the growing independence of the cities the conditions conducive to unfettered expansion of manufactures and of both domestic and international trade, and therefore to accumulation of money capital and bullion.

Geography played a part in at least two ways: first, the climate and soil of western Europe were (and are) ideally suited to pretty reliable high yield mixed agriculture; and, second, the Atlantic seaboard countries of Europe have a uniquely advantageous site for commanding international trade. The former blessing, especially once complemented by introduction of clover into agricultural practices, speeded accomplishment of the essential switch of labour from land to factory. The second gave the western European powers (whose modern boundaries had gradually been forming and stabilising from the middle of the 11th century to the start of the 14th) not only an interest in an unprecedented variety of produce, ranging from the cold climate products of Scandinavia through all intermediate variations to exotic tropical produce entering into Mediterranean commerce via the Arab world. It is true that vigourous trading cities and principalities around the Mediterranean to some extent shared these advantages (and played a prominent role in the evolution of the European economy at various periods accordingly). But the Atlantic seaboard powers had an additional advantage which was to prove crucial: access to the oceans which were to become the highways of the world market to come. Open sea sailing techniques and experience made the exploratory pushes down the west coast of Africa and finally round the Cape and across the Atlantic to the Caribbean and the Americas possible when the need and opportunity for such expansion arose.

Finally, arising from the seaward expansions of the 15th and 16th centuries onwards, the countries of western Europe were able to seize and concentrate in their own coffers a wealth of plunder of a magnitude far beyond any ever before imagined, far less seen, in world history hitherto. To the gold and silver looted from Latin America, to the Dutch fortunes built on the bones of the Indonesian people, and to British booty from India, has to be added the huge rewards of the trade in human flesh, supplying slaves to pioneering white planters and mine-owners in sparsely populated lands of recent settlement, such as the Americas. Ernest Mandel has estimated the total haul from such brigandage at over one *billion* pounds sterling — a staggering sum for the times: as late as 1770, the entire British national income was a mere £125 million. He concludes:

> 'It was this systematic plundering of four continents, during the commercial expansion of the sixteenth to eighteenth centuries, that created the conditions for the decisive lead acquired by Europe from the industrial revolution onward . . . the enrichment of which was paid for, in the literal sense of the word, by the impoverishment of the plundered areas.' (1)

The capital thus accumulated by the most primitive of means enabled western Europe to make the transition to industrial capitalism; its loss to the rest of the world aborted whatever progress had been made along the same lines and speeded them down the road to underdevelopment.

## The Development of Underdevelopment

Since the 18th century, there have been distinct phases in the development of underdevelopment. From the beginnings of the industrial revolution proper, in the second half of the 18th century, until the last third of the 19th century, there is a first stage. During this period, industrial production proper is restricted to the pioneering countries of western Europe (and to their off-spring in North America). In this sphere, surplus value is extracted from wage labour employed in increasingly large-scale manufacturing industry. The peripheral countries of eastern Europe, Asia, Africa and South America continue to contribute to the coffers of the industrialising countries; 'primitive accumulation' goes on in innumerable forms, the proceeds largely accruing to nationals of the imperialist powers and, to a much lesser extent, to their 'native' agents. Manufactured exports pouring out of the industrialised countries of the northern hemisphere flood the more accessible parts of the Third World and hasten the disappearance of local pre-industrial manufactures and handicrafts. But capital is still — measured against the magnitude of the task of transforming the countries of western Europe and North America into recognisably modern industrial powers — comparatively scarce, and therefore is devoted almost exclusively to metropolitan purposes. Moreover, the relatively underdeveloped modes of long-distance transport and communications effectively restrict the opening up of vast areas of hinterland to exposure to the cascade of cheap new manufactured goods. For both reasons, *some* semi-peripheral countries succeed in taking the first hesitant steps towards autonomous industrialisation (for instance, Russia, Japan, Spain and Italy). In others, attempts to do the same are thwarted because the accumulation of capital is already controlled by local agencies of the imperialist powers.

By the last third of the 19th century the picture is being fundamentally changed in a host of ways. Technical innovations in transport and communications (the steamship, the electric telegraph, the opening of the Suez Canal) combine with the growing release of capital, expertise and productive capacity from the tasks of completing the domestic transport networks of the industrial countries to make possible a real revolution in international communications. A genuine world market, co-extensive with all populated parts of the globe (minus a few isolated pockets), now exists. The products of Western industry can reach everywhere — and everywhere assault the remaining bastions of handicraft and pre-industrial manufacturing production.

The enormously expanded capacity of the industrial countries to generate capital permits of its export on an unprecedented scale. This, too, dooms such efforts as have been made elsewhere in the world autonomously to follow the example of the pioneering capitalist countries (except where — as in Japan — it proves possible to take effective steps to prevent foreign investment pushing in from the leading industrial countries). The export of Western capital all over the world aborts, thwarts and distorts Third World development in many ways.

In the first place, the fact that industrially experienced Westerners, possessed of (or with access to and disposal of) immeasurably greater resources than any available locally, now dominate the non-agricultural sector means petrification of local elites in the pre-capitalist rural economy, or — to the extent that they have already developed outside it, or are felt useful outside it — their co-optation to the economic and political needs and requirements of the imperialists. The actual forms of such arrangements and accommodations varied widely in detail from one Afro-Asian-Latin American country to another, but the outcome in every case is quite clear and unequivocal: every economic activity in the colonial or semi-colonial

country is now subordinated to the over-riding interests of the metropolitan powers. Only activities compatible with or complementary to these
interests are permitted to survive or to develop. These include the distribution of Western imported goods into the interior in petty trading and
peddling; the purchasing and delivery to Western warehouses and to exit
ports of smallholder cash crop produce; clerical work in Western offices,
banks, insurance houses and the like; all kinds of comprador functions for
Western trading and agency houses; all kinds of services, ranging from
domestic service to hotel-keeping, and the running of bars, casinos and
brothels, etc.; interpreting and catering to the tourist trade; some constuc-
tion work; dealing in land; repairing machinery in small workshops; and so
on.

Another aspect of the matter is that production of raw materials is now
rapidly modernised. The enormous growth of industry has, of course
increased demand for raw materials many times over. But the growing
*efficiency* of production exacerbates the problem, for — as each unit of
capital and labour turns out a greater number of units of output — the
significance of the raw material cost in each unit of output must rise.
Capital, therefore, impatiently reaches out worldwide to replace older
organisations of production of raw materials by new ones; slavery in the
southern states of the USA gives way to capitalist planting, farming and processing; the Culture System in Indonesia gives way to the organisation of
production by big capitalist corporations ('the Corporation System');
Britain moves directly into Southern Africa, the Malay states; and so on.
The price of raw materials embarks upon that century-long secular slide
downwards (1873-1973). (Many oscillations make the actual course of
prices exhibit a wave pattern, though.)

But the 'modernisation' of raw material production is relative, for such
'modernisation' in no way urges the economies of the Third World forward
towards independent and balanced economic development. On the contrary, it freezes them into an unbalanced and dependent pattern, characterised by primary sector predominance, and by secondary and tertiary
sectors specifically fashioned to facilitate imperialist exploitation of their
resources and labour. Moreover, the failure of Third World economies to
move ahead, in conjunction with the surge of their populations, ensures
that the labour remains cheap. This is attractive in itself to the Western
investor, but it also means that there is little incentive to replace labour by
machinery, further defining the nature and trajectory of the now rapidly
underdeveloping countries. In turn, the existence of attractive labour-
intensive investment opportunities in the Third World eases the problems
of over-accumulation of capital in the metropolitan countries — a
phenomenon already apparent by the end of the 19th century.* (seeover)
But perpetuation of a low-wage economy (and of a pre-capitalist subsistence agriculture sector) makes the domestic Third World market unattrac-
tive to the domestic Third World would-be manufacturer and investor,

whose entrepreneurial and investment choices therefore harden, on the one hand, into those avenues left open by the imperialists and on the other into traditional outlets (land, jewellery, usury) or into Western-owned and managed enterprises.

A third stage emerges out of the prolonged inter-war depression and the interlude between Britain's relinquishing the reins of overall responsibility for maintaining the rules and momentum of the international capitalist economy and America's picking them up. As suggested earlier, there has to be accommodation to the phased termination of the older forms of colonialism and neo-colonialism associated with the middle era of 'classical' imperialism. Besides, the pace of technological change and innovation is accelerating, producing complex international economic repercussions. There is also a much more conscious attempt at international economic management and at international economic integration for the benefit of the bourgeoisie of the imperialist countries and of their compradors, political gauleiters, mercenaries, and the like in the now post-colonial (or neo-colonial) Third World.

But even the comparatively brief post-war period cannot adequately be characterised as if it is a single stage of development evincing uniform features throughout. In particular, the 1970's have witnessed a sea change in international economic circumstances the long-term significance of which cannot be exaggerated; I discuss it specifically in the next chapter. However, we can risk a number of generalisations about the quarter of a century following the end of the second world war.

The first thing to notice is that capital investment to the countries of the Third World, though of continuing importance, is of relatively less weight compared with inter-investment by the imperialist powers among themselves. There are many reasons for this, among them greater political instability in the now independent countries and consequently enhanced risk attaching to investment; the threat of nationalisation and expropriation by incoming radical regimes; the transfer of *some* raw material production to the imperialist metropoles themselves (a leading example of which is the substitution of a host of petro-chemical products for formerly imported natural inputs — e.g. synthetic rubber for natural rubber); and the increasingly common practice on the part of imperialist enterprises of financing their Third World activities out of profits made on the spot.

A second aspect is that the post-war years have seen a rapid spread of industrialisation in at least some of the countries of Asia, Africa and Latin

* An increasing organic composition of capital in the industrial countries (i.e. an increase in the proportion of machinery per worker) depresses (or threatens to depress) the rate of profit; exporting surplus capital to the underdeveloped countries counteracts this tendency, for there the organic composition of capital is low (and the rate of surplus value high).

America. It is, needless to say, industrialisation of a particular type. Much of it is undertaken by Western and Japanese and multinational corporations in order to derive the benefits of a cheap and plentiful labour force, savagely repressive labour legislation that is inconceivable today in the richer countries (except the Soviet bloc ones), generous investment incentives offered by right-wing Third World governments, official and unofficial corruption, and other such advantages. Another major section consits of joint ventures in which, by the nature of things, the economically stronger rich country partners tend to dominate. Yet another category consists of entirely local enterprises which spring up to provide services for the others — picking up any opportunity left open by them. Then there are the Third World state-run industries covering an enormous span of processes and products.

Two things must be stressed, though. In the first place, such industrialisation as has taken place has been to the gain of the imperialist powers, directly or indirectly: directly, by supplying a market for machinery (the manufacture and export of which have grown steadily in relative importance in the overdeveloped countries); indirectly, by enabling imperialist interests to reduce and partly evade the consequences of the squeeze on their profits consequent upon post-war policies of full employment, provision of social welfare, and greater co-optation of social democratic parties and the trade unions into the management of metropolitan capitalism. In the second place, in none of the Third World countries which have experienced a considerable industrialisation is the resulting pattern of enterprises remotely similar to, or even comparable with, the pattern typical of the countries which much earlier achieved fully autonomous national economic development. On the contrary, what we have is a highly specific pattern of *dependent* development.

This basic dependency has a number of features. Not all of them occur in all cases, but at least some of them occur in all. Nor are all of them peculiar to underdeveloped countries of the Third World, for some occur in poorer developed countries. But the bunching of them in all underdeveloped countries produces a quite distinctive, qualitatively different, economic pattern from that evinced by developed countries. Let us review some of these features.

One is the dependence upon foreign aid, a dependence that tends to grow with the passage of time and that inevitably puts a great deal of power in the hands of those providing the aid. And those able to provide aid are, naturally, the rich and the powerful heavy-weights of the international economy, notably the United States, Japan, the EEC countries, and, to a lesser extent, Russia and some of her stronger East European satellites (such as East Germany). Conditions attached to aid are seldom, if ever, beneficial to the recipient country's short- and long-term economic prospects. But that is not the point: they are beneficial to the favoured local elites and most certainly to the aid-giving countries. Some aid simply buys political support in the international community and perhaps also military advantage in the way of bases and the like. But most has a hard economic purpose: construction of infra-structure vital for modern sophisticated investment projects; restriction of local credit to reduce local competition and to preclude local state activity in areas deemed profitable terrain for 'market forces' (namely, foreign investors) to operate in; dictation and imposition of legislation granting favourable conditions to foreign investors; and the like.

Another is the scale of that segment of the economy effectively in foreign hands. This inevitably cramps the scope of local initiative (except to the extent favoured by the ruling elites and their foreign advisers for their joint and several reasons). In some cases, as in Kenya or Malaysia, foreign-owned plantations take a lion's share of the cultivable land, exacerbating the problems and poverty of land-hungry poor peasants. Whatever example we take there is the threat of sudden withdrawal of the foreign operators if they feel that a switch of their investments elsewhere would be more profitable. This in itself can create very serious problems for the deserted host economy, but it is also an extremely powerful instrument to be held in reserve to deal with undesirable 'radical' tendencies appearing locally in the neo-colony. It is true that even the poorest of countries can, with correct political leadership, embark on the road of autarky, as the Cambodian experience shows, but where radical leadership is hesitant, is partly dependent upon liberal middle class support, and is pledged to 'peaceful transition to socialism', foreign investor non-cooperation and sabotage can be fatal (as in the Chilean case).

Yet another factor is the almost invariable presence, prominence and influence of foreign advisers, whose mandate and horizons are inevitably poles apart from the horizons of the local poor and from a mandate tailored to redress local poverty and to iron out local inequality and privilege as the *top* priority (rather than as some vague commitment, for political cosmetic purposes, in some unattainably distant future). Here we return to our earlier comments on the post-war evolution of development economics, for the imperialist powers require a considerable number of trained people to oversee implementation of aid programmes, allocation of budgetary resources in a 'rational' fashion, drafting of legislation relevant to foreign investment, and a great variety of other such matters. Other expert Western development economists are deployed training local personnel to assist in, and some day ultimately to take over, these operations. Local candidates for such training readily offer themselves, for the rewards of success are made highly attractive; during training at postgraduate level typically in the USA, or Australia, or western Europe, Third World students being groomed for the role of watchdogs of imperialist interests in their own countries are carefully indoctrinated for the task. This indoctrination does not necessarily take the form of outright scholarly propaganda for 'freedom' and free enterprise: orthodox economic courses, and as part of them orthodox economic development courses, embody quite enough built-in biases to guarantee in the majority of graduates at least a fairly endurable internalisation of received economic science 'wisdom'. In any case, the successful graduate himself is soon in a position sufficiently privileged, and sufficiently beholden to continuation of the neo-colonial dependence of his own country on the imperialist powers, readily, perhaps even unconsciously, to rationalise his own role. Most such graduates, however, are I suspect, simply out to make as much money as possible, and therefore their case needs no complicated psychological explanation; if it is money that fascinates and motivates you in a poor Third World country obviously the best and most direct way to go about accumulating it is to serve as an agent of the ultra-rich imperialist countries.

Finally, we should note that the way domestic capital behaves in dependent neo-colonial industrialisation is very different from its behaviour in past industrialising processes. The reasons for this are complex, but the outcome in neo-colonial countries is clear: local capital, although participating in the industrial sector, also tends to wash back into its traditional — and less productive or non-productive — uses (land speculation, usury, services, etc.). There is not, in other words, a steady progression from less to more advanced uses, such as accompanied industrialisation in the now developed world. One explanation is to be found in the share of local investment opportunity pre-empted by foreign concerns. Another is the restricted local market, its demand held down at a very low level by the poverty of local wage labour and peasantry, and by the extensive un-and under-employment.

After a couple of decades of capitalist 'development' in the poor countries, under rich country tutelage, what is the outcome? From 1970 to 1975 real production per capita in the 30 poorest countries of the world (including such giants as India and Indonesia, which together account for nearly three-quarters of a billion people) did not rise at all; if anything there was a slight decline. In 1975, the average per capita output in the rich industrial countries (with a combined population roughly of a size with that of India plus Indonesia) was US $5,080 a year. In the 30 poorest countries it was still about US $130. Over the 1965-1975 decade the gap had steadily widened. In the rich countries productivity had risen rapidly (in Japan by 100%, in West Germany by 73%, in Canada by 43%). In the poor it had stagnated or edged ahead at a barely perceptible rate.

## WHY IMPERIALISM SUCCEEDED

### Early Equivalence in Development

I should like to backtrack again now and have a second look at international economic history over the last few centuries. Until two or three hundred years ago, international trade in non-renewable real resources, including energy resources, was negligible. When the Western powers first reached Africa, the Americas, and Asia each part of the world still retained almost intact its original real resource endowment. The main items entering into trade were small exotic articles with great value in small bulk — the precious metals, spices, and a whole variety of other natural products and artifacts in virtually global demand among the rich but of restricted origin. It was the demand for spices in the 16th century which brought the Western powers to Asia almost simultaneously by both available routes (i.e. the westward and the eastward sailing). It should be noted that the spices had a number of medicinal, germicidal and cosmetic uses in addition to their best known use in rendering meat edible. In effect, the spices performed the functions later to be taken over by canning and refrigeration — both of which had to await the effective exploitation of the fossil fuels. They became obsolete with the adoption of 'Dutch' clover cultivation from the early 18th century on (see above, Chapter One).

As far as possession of the most valued items of trade was concerned, it could not be said that Europe was better off than the rest of the world. On the contrary, the reason why Europe went to Asia, and not Asia to Europe, is that Asia was more self-sufficient, and had little need, and but scant desire, for the products of Europe. That it was not a question of inferior technology is amply borne out by the fact that Indonesian or Arab merchants were perfectly well able to trade with the Far East, South and West Asia, and both East *and* West Africa — and as far north as the Ivory Coast at least. These feats of navigation and seafaring had been first accomplished some centuries prior to the European voyages of exploration which so pre-occupy many Western accounts of the past.

Broadly speaking, at the time of establishment of more or less continuous contact between further Asia and the West (there had been sporadic contacts for many centuries), both culture-spheres were still in the stage before systematic use of inanimate energy sources as capital. That is, use of the fossil fuels was negligible and certainly of little or no economic account. Leaving aside for a moment the question of those peculiar social and geographical factors characteristic of each and ultimately relevant to economic development, what can we say about the progress which each had made on the basis of harnessing the 'income' sources of inanimate energy? We can do no more than suggest the broad lines of a comparison here. Income sources of inanimate energy include wind and water — and, if we allow for cases of total and irrevocable depletion (now alas, all too common), wood. I noted above the sea-faring prowess of the Indonesians. More generally, the ocean-going vessels of several parts of Asia and Arabia were at least the equal, and in some respects superior, in design and workmanship to those of Europe as late as the start of the 15th century. Sailing ships marked one of the most important forms of harnessing wind power. Another was the construction of windmills to facilitate such operations as grinding grain. The windmill appears to have been an Asian innovation, entering Europe through the Middle East. The Chinese seem to have pioneered in the important techniques associated with interconversion of rotary and longitudinal motion, later to be so important for the steam engine, and to cause so much trouble to European engineers in the early stages of the industrial revolution. Water-power was also used to generate energy, notably by the water wheel and mill, in both East and West. Water control, in a more general sense, was much more highly developed in Asia than in Europe. This arose from the requirements of wet rice cultivation, in part, and in part from the water needs of cities, the largest of which in Asia at this time were very much larger than the largest to be found contemporaneously in Europe. Wood was used for metallurgical purposes in both regions — the technology of cast iron and steel were first mastered in China, and the Javanese were casting their own cannon before the arrival of the Europeans. As an addendum, we should note that both culture-spheres were already using gunpowder on first encounter: the significance of gunpowder is that this particular use of sulphur marks the first significant employment of a combustible fossil fuel mineral to generate power (and to obtain food, to the extent that the firearms were turned against edible animals and birds). In short, there was little — if any — distance between West and East, at least in strictly technological terms, as of, say, the 14th-15th centuries, and the differences between Africa and the West were only marginal. There were, however, other factors, including, as suggested above, the sociological and geographical.

## The Enabling of Imperialism

A gap subsequently did open up. Once opened, it widened through time, and continues to widen to this day. By 'gap' I mean a disparity in all kinds of indices generally associated with development in the conventional sense. Naturally, it is not the indices that are important *per se*; what concerns us are the realities which the indices imperfectly seek to reflect. Among the more familiar of these indices are: per capita GNP (Gross National Product); expectation of life; infant mortality rate; literacy rate; degree of urbanisation; percentage of the labour force in the non-agricultural sectors of the economy; per capita per diem calorie and protein intakes; housing space per family member; and ownership of cars and consumer durables per 100 of the population. To begin with, few of these diverged much, if at all, (and some were obviously irrelevant until fairly recently in historical terms). The foundations of their future divergence were nevertheless being laid from the moment that Western metallurgy, and in particular the technology of armament manufacture, and Western navigational skills, including techniques of naval warfare, became clearly superior. Africa, India and South East Asia thereby lay exposed to military conquest and economic exploitation. Simultaneously China and Japan chose to shut themselves off from the outside world to the maximum extent attainable in their respective circumstances.

Accepting as given that a gap had clearly begun to open up in some important respects by the second part of the fifteenth century at the latest — and therefore begging on this occasion the intriguing questions of the whys and wherefores — the next step of the argument involves us in some consideration of what processes, with what results and long-term implications, were actually going on during the colonial period. It is convenient to restate the orthodox model first, and then to discuss its infirmities and misrepresentations.

Conventional approaches start from the assumption (implicit or explicit) that there are a sufficient number of characteristics shared by all societies before the transformation associated with industrialisation is firmly launched to justify us in using some such general concept as W.W. Rostow's 'traditional society'. Rostow's best known work, *The Stages of Economic Growth*, has come under considerable scholarly attack since its first appearance. Nevertheless, there is no doubt that the basic idea behind it is so deeply entrenched in the orthodox view of the development process that it is worth subjecting it to systematic criticism. I paraphrase his position below.

Prior to the onset of marked economic growth in Western Europe, Rostow claims, the world consisted entirely of 'traditional societies' differing markedly in detail from one region to another and from one political unit to another but all exhibiting a core of common characteristics conducive to stability and socio-political and technological conservatism. For a variety of reasons, Britain, and subsequently her nearest neighbours and some overseas territories with close links, broke out of the chrysalis and embarked upon an historically unique process of self-sustaining economic growth, the essential facet of which was that certain economic magnitudes started to grow at compound interest — or in other words that economic growth became an intrinisic or normal feature of society. Rostow argues that the available economic-historical evidence suggests that *all* societies that have hitherto followed the pioneers in the process of industrialisation or 'modernisation' have gone through a similar series of 'stages', and that one may conclude that those societies still trapped in traditional low-level stability will have themselves to go through these 'stages'. He identifies these as: traditional society; pre-conditions for take-off; take-off into sustained economic growth; maturity; and high mass consumption. We may represent this diagramatically: see figure 1 overleaf.

It is no accident that Rostow sub-titles his work 'A Non-Communist Manifesto', nor that he acted as President Lyndon B. Johnson's special advisor on the Vietnam war at the height of American involvement. In fact, memoirs of the period show very clearly that even his administration

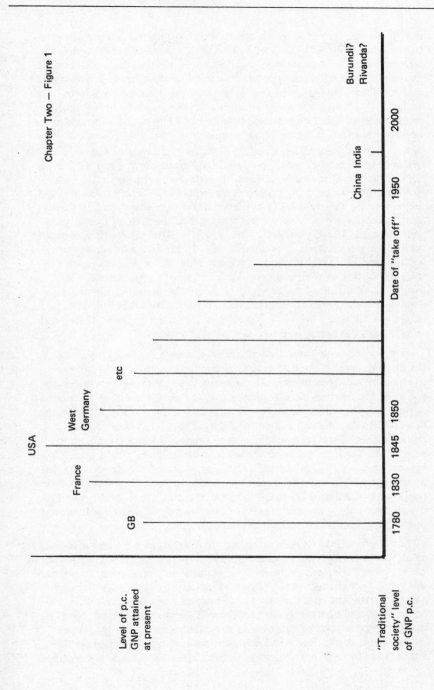

Chapter Two — Figure 1

colleagues were appalled by his out-spoken bloodthirstiness and enthusiasm for bombing. The thinking behind the stages model is saturated with Europo-centrism. It is not only that there is implicit in the whole concept the idea that growth arose spontaneously in the West, while it was triggered off elsewhere by the impact of modernising Western influences. More importantly, Rostow plays down the whole phenomenon of imperialism colonialism, and therefore abstracts from historical reality. To undermine Rostow's position, a digression is necessary.

We may measure a high standard of living in a number of ways. Probably the most frequently used and familiar measuring rod is GNP per capita. The fact that this is expressed in monetary terms is in itself — quite apart from the many problems associated with trying to impart to it some meaning and plausibility as a measurement — misleading, in that it draws attention away from the really significant features of the development process. A high standard of living or high GNP per capita means that the average person has a considerable bulk of durable possessions embodying non-renewable real resources such as the metals and petroleum (in the form of plastics, synthetic rubber, etc.) and enjoys a high protein diet won by combustion of the fossil fuels. How this came about historically, and what it entails for the consumers of the countries that remained poor, constitute the really interesting questions. Again, let us try to sketch out in a diagram the barest outlines: see figure 2 overleaf.

It will at once be noted that in this case, unlike the first (Rostow's), the development of the first industrial countries is not seen in isolation from the fate of the countries that remained, or more accurately became, poor. On the contrary, it is suggested that the development of the presently rich countries was achieved *at the expense of* the countries that became subjected to imperialism and colonialism: in his totally ignoring this crucial aspect of the economic historical process Rostow commits his basic error. Far from the subject countries of the Third World remaining in some way outside history as 'traditional societies', they were moulded by the impact of imperialism into societies as historically unique in their own way as the industrial countries were in theirs. I shall deal here with the more strictly economic aspects of this, leaving till later consideration of the important social and political implications.

Let us go back to the period before the West started moving inexorably along the path of economic development in the modern sense. As we noted above, trade in non-renewable real resources at this point was insignificant. But significant changes in the patterns and nature of trade were taking place nevertheless from the onset of the age of European expansion onwards. Most importantly, Britain showed the way in commandeering the primary products of captive and dependent economies in order to process them domestically and re-export them to overseas markets. It is unnecessary to trace here the steps by which the fossil fuels, for centuries

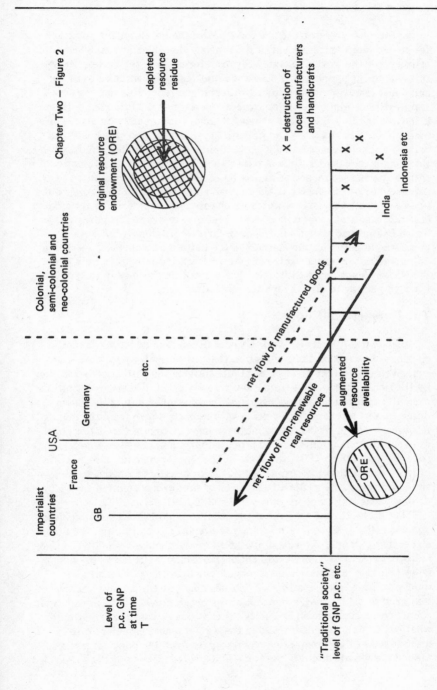

Chapter Two — Figure 2

depleted resource residue

original resource endowment (ORE)

Colonial, semi-colonial and neo-colonial countries

X = destruction of local manufacturers and handicrafts

Indonesia etc

India

Imperialist countries

GB    France    USA    Germany    etc.

Level of p.c. GNP at time T

net flow of manufactured goods

net flow of non-renewable real resources

augmented resource availability

ORE

"Traditional society" level of GNP p.c. etc.

in the form of coal, came to the forefront of the development process —
for an economist's assessment of the crucial role of coal, written last
century, see the work of Stanley Jevons referred to in the bibliography to
this chapter. It happens that the first countries to industrialise were, by
and large, relatively well-endowed with the non-renewable real resources
appropriate to industrialisation; where this was not the case — and Japan
is the outstanding example — the deficiencies could readily be made good
by a combination of trade and imperialism. Even so, it very quickly
became apparent that no country could hope to industrialise and to provide high living standards for at least a substantial part of its population
without having secure access to non-renewable real resources that
happened to be obtainable in the requisite quantity and quality *only* outside the home borders. It is worth emphasising this point, for it is precisely
here that we locate the roots of what I refer to as overdevelopment, and
which I subject to analysis in the next chapter. Gradually, but with
increasing impetus, a trade developed the pattern of which was markedly
asymmetrical: non-renewable real resources started moving in bulk from
the poorer countries to the richer. There is nothing strange in this, but it
is worth pausing to give the matter more attention.

## The Unrepeatable Model

Much conventional economic wisdom in the field of 'development'
continues to work on the assumption that the presently poor countries
can, given the correct policies, belatedly traverse the path already trodden
by the rich countries. But from quite an early point in their evolution, the
currently rich countries began systematically supplementing their own
domestic real resource endowments with imports drawn from the real
resource endowments of economically weaker (more backward) or politically subordinate countries. The process continues at an ever-increasing
pace. From 1928 to 1965, the share of the developing countries in world
iron ore production rose from 7% to 37%, in bauxite from 21% to 69%,
and in oil from 25% to 65%. Basic primary products accounted for 59.5%
of world seaborne trade in tonnes in 1962, but 67.8% in 1972.

What do those who talk about there being a 'model' of economic development make of this? Are the countries presently intent upon attaining
higher living standards really supposed to model themselves upon the first
industrial countries? This would entail their annexing colonies the non-
renewable real resource endowments of which are as yet virtually untouched. Aside from whatever difficulties might attend annexation, all
that need be said is that, as a result of the development of the already rich
countries, no such untouched areas exist in today's world. Furthermore,
what has taken place historically in the way of a net movement on a
massive scale of non-renewable real resources from the poor countries to
the industrialised cannot be reversed. True, some metals might be re-cycled

and made available for export from industrialised countries to those striving to embark upon industrialisation. But this could only ever be a tiny fraction of what has moved over the centuries the other way, and in any case could not include energy resources which — in accordance with the Entropy Law — cannot be re-cycled. In any case, the circumstance is hard to envisage as a realistic possibility.

With demand for non-renewable real resources still rising voraciously, it seems certain that high commodity prices are here to stay, and the secular trend can only be upwards as scarcities continue to develop. This being so, the industrialised countries will clearly jealously husband whatever they have and grab whatever they can get elsewhere. As the present oil crisis is making clear, prices will settle around what the richest buyers are prepared to pay, without consideration for the poorer. In short, the problems facing the poorer countries are different in kind from those that faced the now rich countries a couple of centuries ago in this — as in many other — directions. *They are starting with already depleted non-renewable real resource bases and that in a world where cheap raw materials are a thing of the past.* This circumstance on its own, leaving aside any other consideration for the time being, guarantees that what lies ahead for the poorer countries, whatever else it may turn out to be, cannot and will not be but a belated replica of what the rich countries have already wrought.

Returning to figure 2, the other point it seeks to make is that the other aspect of the expansion in international commerce that accompanied the industrialisation of some countries was the destruction — in part deliberate, in part merely the inevitable outcome of the contact of increasingly unequal economic forces — of many activities in the non-primary sectors in the colonial and semi-colonial countries, precisely those activities that might well have otherwise provided the starting points for autonomous and balanced economic development. In a very real sense, the countries subjected to imperialism were being forcibly *de*-developed, as their indigenous textile industries fell before the assault of the cheap machine-made goods of Europe, their sea-going mercantile fleets before the competition of superior Western fleets (backed by political and military power), and as their nascent metallurgical industries withered through inanition. The list could be much extended, but the trend, varying though it did from one colony or semi-colony to another in respect of specific manifestations, was clear. Certain measurable socio-economic changes have hitherto invariably accompanied development  (as conventionally understood) and growth. It is not difficult to demonstrate that during the colonial period in the subject countries many of these indices were moving in the opposite direction to that associated with development. For instance, the percentage of the population in the primary sector frequently rose, as in Java. Or literacy rates fell, as in Burma under British rule. Or calorie and protein intake per capita per diem fell; this was quite common, if not universal.

Now an interesting point about this is that nobody disputes that, generally speaking, actual output per head of population in the colonial and semi-colonial countries rose. This is undoubtedly what is meant when reference is made to the achievements of Western imperialism. By increasing production, and depressing the consumption of the producers, the colonial powers were able to increase economic surplus which, through the economic and political power they wielded, they were able to divert to metropolitan purposes. The concept of economic surplus is a useful one in this context and it is worth looking at it for a few moments.

We may distinguish between *actual* and *potential* economic surplus. The first consists of the difference between a society's *actual* current output and its *actual* current consumption, the second of the difference between the output that *could* be produced in a given natural and technological environment with the help of employable productive resources and what might be regarded as essential consumption. Many complex and contentious questions arise (2), but for immediate pedagogic purposes let us operate with as simplified a formulation of the concept as possible. As a first step, I shall treat actual economic surplus as the difference between what a society produces and what the producers of that output consume (including everything necessary to maintain the productive process).

Discounting catastrophic circumstances, all societies generate some economic surplus. The interesting question is: to what use is this surplus put? It can appear in the shape of elaborate temple buildings or other forms of monument, and as the support of classes of non-producers such as priests, soldiers, concubines, courtiers, and so on, as well as in a variety of other ways which do not enhance the productive powers of society. Alternatively, it may appear in the form of additions to the productive powers of society, that is as net investment (gross expenditure on capital formation minus the amount required to replace worn-out and obsolete plant and equipment). A society may what we might describe as stagnate for long periods of time — generations — merely adding to its ceremonial buildings and the munificence of upkeep of its non-productive classes. But no society stagnates, or, to put it in other words, succeeds in maintaining ecological-demographic-economic-social stability, for ever. Rise and fall are ineluctable. Rise of course entails adding to the capital stock, fall its reduction.

Before arrival of the European imperialist powers in Asia, Africa, and Latin America, and — in some parts of these regions — for a considerable time thereafter, it seems clear that part of the economic surplus was being devoted to enhancing the productive powers of society. Some political units were naturally in decline while others were in the ascendant, but then this was true of Europe too. In such activities as ship-building, the casting of cannon and production of iron implements, and textile production we can discern the seeds from which further diversification and economic progress might well have sprung had political sovereignty and economic independence not been first eroded and then totally lost. The experience of Japan, so strikingly different from that of the rest of Asia, underlines the crucial importance of independence. To put it in terms of economic surplus, we may say that Japan's leaders set about optimising it and devoting as much of it as possible to increasing the productive powers of Japanese society, while elsewhere in Asia the imperialist powers certainly set about increasing the magnitude of economic surplus — but in order to divert it to enhancing the productive powers of the metropoles and increasing the consumption of the metropolitan masses.

One might isolate any number of striking cases in the Asia or Africa colonial era to illustrate this — Burma, for example, or French Indochina — but probably the most stark instance is Java. If we go back to, say 1830 and survey the island of Java, we find an island of six million inhabitants, working a soil the fertility of which was prodigious and seemingly perpetual (and largely based upon periodic emission of sulphur from the many volcanoes dotting the island), possessing (or having ready access to, from nearby neighbouring islands) a number of valuable non-renewable real resources, and occupying a geographical situation and having geographical characteristics ideal for conducting an immense and far-reaching international trade. Japan's population at the same time was probably about twenty million, but on an area roughly three times as extensive as Java's, thus giving a similar population density. However, only 16% of the total area of Japan is at all cultivatable, compared with some 58% of Java's. Moreover, Japan is proverbially poor in non-renewable real resources, including all of those essential to sustain industrialisation (except sulphur). An imaginary peripatetic economic historian of the early 19th century, acquainted with both territories, would probably have hesitated to predict that within 150 years Japan would be within sight of qualifying for the epithet 'superstate' (and challenging even the United States of America in certain economic magnitudes), while Java languished as one of the most notorious sinks of poverty in the world, with a population growth rate falling off only through the sheer Malthusian pressures of starvation, malnutrition and disease inexorably pushing up death rates.

How are we to account for this extraordinary divergence? I do not think one need look further than the very different socio-political situations in which the two found themselves from the 1830's onwards. Java became victim to Holland's infamous 'Culture System', while Japan was simultaneously entering into the three to four decade period which established the 'pre-conditions' for the Meiji Restoration and industrialisation. On the one hand, the Culture System, in its heyday, epitomises extortion of an enhanced economic surplus by an imperialist power; on the other, the Japanese experience testifies to what other Asian countries might have achieved had they too been able to turn economic surplus to the task of autonomous national development.

Van den Bosch, architect of the Culture System, quite consciously set out to raise the production of Java in order to rescue Holland itself from desperate economic straits. He succeeded — at the expense of the people of Java, whose labour he 'turned into capital' so well that the time left at their disposal for food production became insufficient and starvation stalked the land. When the State-run Culture System faltered, it was replaced by a highly cartelised business structure no less efficient at inflating exportable economic surplus. One might express the process diagramatically: see figure 3 overleaf.

Apart from that portion of it expended on maintaining the traditional Indonesian aristocracy in some luxury in order to enlist their aid in ruling the colony, the enlarged economic surplus was almost entirely devoted by the Dutch to metropolitan purposes: constructing railways, improving port facilities, and in general building up social capital in Holland and relieving the Dutch exchequer and Dutch taxpayer. The tragedy for Java, for Indonesia, was that this immense effort on the part of the people to hugely expand the available (and investible) economic surplus was, from their point of view, in vain. Surely no one can doubt that, had the Indonesian people had command over their own destinies through this crucial period (1830 to 1914), they would have been well on the way towards the end of it to something recognisable as economic development? Instead, while population multiplied more than five times over, average food consumption per capita was falling, and indigenous economic life was effectively demoralised and stunted. Yet from 1867 to 1912 value of exports per capita increased three fold.

The contrast with Japan could hardly be more poignant — and pointed. The Japanese elite, once the decision had been taken to secure the country's independence in an Asia succumbing to Western imperialism, harnessed every resource of the state to transforming the economy. Foreign investment was excluded (an important point to remember when foreign investment is recommended to poor countries as a way to development), and every fibre strained to become as quickly as possible self-supporting in technology and industrial know-how. From 1870 to 1913, GNP grew by about 2.7% per annum (i.e. doubled and doubled again), and by roughly 1.7% per annum in per capita terms. The rate of investment remained high, and current consumption low. But there was this signal difference from the Javanese case: the enhanced economic surplus was being ploughed back with conscious intent to industrialise the nation and raise the productivity of its agriculture. Factories could turn out improved agricultural tools, fertilisers, and other products useful to the rural sector, while an improved agriculture provided both labour for the manufacturing sector and a market for its goods. The fact that the country was unusually poorly endowed in terms of real resources mattered little once the export sector proved capable of earning the wherewithal to purchase requirements from abroad — and the army

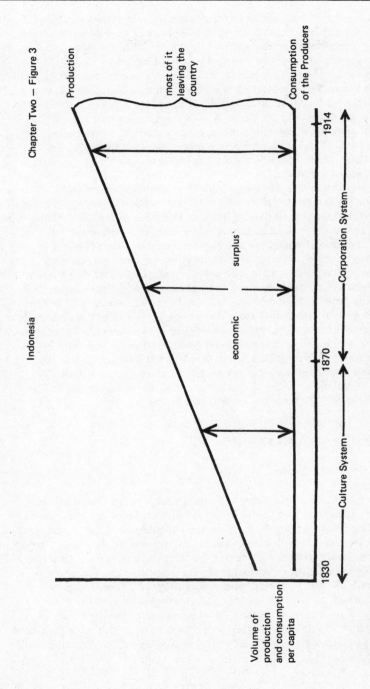

Chapter Two — Figure 3

Indonesia

Production

most of it
leaving the
country

Consumption
of the Producers

economic surplus

Volume of
production
and consumption
per capita

1830

Culture System

1870

Corporation System

1914

(The weight of exports per capita rose sixfold from 1867 to 1912; average annual rice consumption per capita in Java and Madura fell from an 1856-70 average of 114 kgs. to a 1936-40 average of 89.0 kgs.)

proved capable of conquering territories holding out some promise of making good at least part of the deficit.(Japan thus became a premature 'overdeveloped' country as measured by the extent of its dependence on outside sources of supply of essential industrial inputs.)

There are, to be sure, important differences between Java and Japan in respects relevant to economic development: climate, for instance, and social values and traditions. It would be impossible to make anything like a satisfactory allowance for these. What we can do is to summarise the ultimate outcome of the two contrasting processes. The divergence is so marked that, whatever allowance one might make for these factors, clearly their effects could barely modify the broad picture.

See Table I overleaf.

The conclusion is surely inescapable: Indonesia's present 'under-development' is a consequence of her prior subjection to alien imperialist domination. Later I shall develop another antithesis — India and China — suggesting the way out of such post-colonial underdevelopment.

The next thing to consider is, however, the role of the state in the development process in a broader perspective and more general way. It has been ideologically convenient, and economically expedient, for Western development economists to stress the leading role of private enterprise in generating growth. Such evidence as it has been felt necessary to adduce has been drawn (selectively) from the economic history of the already rich countries and from the juxtaposition of such alleged 'miracles' of capitalism as, say, South Korea, and the abysmal growth records of allegedly 'socialist' countries such as Burma. It is worth devoting a few paragraphs to counter-ing this approach, which actually constitutes more a rationalisation for present economic activities than a serious analysis of the past and of historical implications for the present and future.

## POLITICAL IMPERIALISM

### The Role of the State

Britain had many advantages as an industrial pioneer. Nevertheless, it would be quite incorrect to overlook the important role the state played in enabling private enterprise to make the contribution it did. Admittedly, direct government intercession in manufacturing was minimal (aside from military-related activities such as ship-building and ordnance production, though these had clear repercussions in the private sector: for instance, Wilkinson's method of boring cannon was ultimately turned to good account in the making of steam engine cylinders). But in at least two directions state action was critical to inauguration of the development process: first, in establishing effective protection of British interests against actual or potential rivals; and, second, in deploying sufficient military and

TABLE I

|  |  | Comparative indices: | |
|  |  | Japan | Indonesia |
| --- | --- | --- | --- |
| 1. | Infantile mortality rate | 15.0 (1967) | 87.2 (1964) |
| 2. | Life expectancy | 70.0 (1967) | 47.5 (1960) |
| 3. | People per physician | 900.0 (1967) | 41,000.0 (1967) |
| 4. | Literacy per cent | 98.0 (1967) | 43.0 (1967) |
| 5. | Secondary school teachers (000's) | 11,125.0 (1967) | 754.0 (1967) |
| 6. | Miles improved road (per 1,000 square miles) | 4,300.0 (1967) | 60.0 (1967) |
| 7. | Motor vehicles (000's) | 7,169.0 (1967) | 300.0 (1967) |
| 8. | Per cent manufactured exports | 92.0 (1967) | 0.0 (1967) |
| 9. | Population (millions) | 98.9 (1966) | 106.9 (1966) |
| 10. | Annual growth rate of population (%) | 1.0 | 2.3 |
| 11. | Density per square mile | 690.0 (1966) | 190.0 (1966) |
| 12. | Area (000's square miles) | 143.0 | 576.0 |
| 13. | Agricultural land (% total area) | 19.0 | 12.0 |
| 14. | Acres per capita | 0.2 | 0.4 |
| 15. | GNP (US $ million) | 84,560.0 (1965) | 10,450.0 (1965) |
| 16. | GNP per capita (US $) | 863.0 (1965) | 100.0 (1965) |
| 17. | Power p.c. (KWH p.a.) | 1,820.0 (1967) | 19.0 (1967) |
| 18. | Calories p.c. per diem | 2,325.7 (1971) | 1,750.0 (1970) |
| 19. | Total protein p.c., p.d. (grams) | 78.4 (1971) | 38.2 (1970) |
| 20. | Animal protein p.c., p.d. (grams) | 34.7 (1971) | 5.2 (1970) |
| 21. | Cereal consumption p.c. (milled rice equivalent kg/year) | 150.0 (1960-62) | 128.0 (1960-62) |
| 22. | Rice consumption p.c. (kg/year) | 116.0 (1961-63) | 85.0 (1961-63) |

NOTE: The sources drawn on for this table are varied, and the result is not entirely satisfactory for this reason. However, the overall picture is unmistakable, and it is important to realise that the situation in Japan's favour and to Indonesia's disadvantage has worsened in the roughly ten years from the mid-1960's to the mid-1970's. For instance, the latest World Bank Atlas available to me at the time of writing gives the following GNP per capita (figures for 1971): Japan 2,130, Indonesia 80 (both in US $) (these are admittedly calculated on a new basis — see appendix Note to the Atlas — but the continued divergence is not in dispute, only how to measure its magnitude and rate).

diplomatic power and influence to guarantee unimpeded economic access around the globe. Protection, as Arghiri Emmanuel points out, (3) has always been crucial, economic theory notwithstanding. Even in the British case, free trade cannot be said to have been prevalent with the exception of the few decades from 1846 to (at latest) 1914. And no one would dispute that the key steps were taken long before that, during the era of mercanitilism, in fact. Who can doubt, moreover, that it was British feats of arms that really consolidated and gave impetus to British manufacturing and British commerce and industry in general?

However, it is when one comes to the countries that followed Britain's lead that one really begins to appreciate the vital role the state has to play in launching economic development. Mention has already been made of the Dutch Culture System in Indonesia — made inevitable by Holland's falling behind Britain (despite some initial economic advantages) in industrialisation. But, peculiar to the Netherlands though the Culture System was, it does illustrate the need for active government intervention in one way or another to redress the advantage others more advanced already enjoy. Among the first acts of the new independent United States of America was to erect a tariff barrier which, although primarily directed at raising revenue, had a distinct protective hue. Among interests benefiting were the steel and paper mills of Pennsylvania, the brewers of New York and Philadelphia, the glass manufacturers of Maryland, and the iron workers and rum distillers of New England. Later still, the US tariff became avowedly protective, and has so remained, American rhetorical commitment to global free trade notwithstanding. The Federal and state governments also played an active part in numerous ways in such fields as banking, transportation, land disposal, and ordnance orders.

Nevertheless, it would be mistaken to assess the state's role as in any way comparable with that it assumed in Germany and Japan. Friedrich List, in his notable book *The National System of Political Economy* (4) made the strongest possible case for protection and state intervention to enable countries embarking upon industrialisation to catch up with those that had gone ahead. The German state both intervened directly — as in nationalising the Saar coal-mines — and bolstered private industry not only by affording it adequate protection but also by extending it financial subsidies. In such matters as developing a system of technical education and mobilising capital the state helped propel German industry into self-sustaining growth, to use Rostow's term. In Japan, too, it can readily be demonstrated that the state role was decisive at the crucial juncture. As is well known, the Japanese government assumed the responsibility of founding and running certain key industries until they were viable enough to be entrusted to the aspiring industrialists whose education the state itself had carefully supervised.

In general, the more backward a nation the greater the role the state has had to play in order to mobilise and make effective its human, technical, political and diplomatic resources and potential. In the absence of active state initiatives and intervention, opportunities are pre-empted by nationals and agents of powers already more developed, or simply lie dormant. The challenge and the problems were, however, very different in the earlier round of 'take-offs' from those posed to and faced by poor countries today. And this is not just a question of the magnitude of the technico-economic gap between leaders and laggers, real though this aspect of the matter is, for it is also a question of *political* freedom of manoeuvre. Germany and Japan had to strive strenuously to catch up on Britain, but at least they *were* free to take the key economic decisions required because they were politically unimpeded. Today's neo-colonial third world countries do not have this degree of choice (allowing that most of the current leaders lack the motive or will to assert aggressively nationalistic economic ambitions against their imperialist supporters), for erosion of economic sovereignty *via* foreign advisers, the IMF, and conditional aid effectively circumscribes it.

The case of Russia is an interesting one. In some ways, Russia's experiences act as a bridge between the earlier cases and the later. The state had tried to haul up the snoring bear from its slumbers for a couple of centuries before the revolution, but with limited success. Foreign capital had obtained an important hold in the industrial sector which had arisen, and foreign loans implied a degree of foreign influence in policy making. In the event, it proved essential to overturn the entire existing social order to force open the road to full industrialisation. This revolutionary prelude signalled the end of the road for 'peaceful transition' to capitalism. On the other hand, Soviet state planning, as it took shape, simply represented the logical extension of what had gone before: statism — state intervention in economic life — reached its absolute apogee.

Not that Russia was backward in the same sense as we might use the term with reference to numerous African or Asian countries a couple of decades ago, or even in some instances today: in 1913 the Russian Empire stood fifth in the world league table of industrial power. To be sure, this position owed more to the country's sheer physical scale and population and much cried out to be done to bring the giant into line with the industrialised countries to the west. Not without some historical continuity, the decision of the Bolsheviks was for maximum centralisation: as Alec Nove has pointed out (5), as early as 1925 one finds in planning documents such attestations as the following: 'The industrial plan must be constructed not from below but from above'. As we know, growth in total product, and in the industrial sector in particular (and within this sector heavy industry especially), was rapid, but this statistical triumph was achieved at the expense not only of consumer satisfaction (and economic rationality) but also of anything reminiscent of economic and political democracy. A vast and inefficient bureaucracy *(see over) sat astride the population, cynically devoted on the one hand to evading the wrath of superiors for failing to meet the arbitrarily imposed production targets, and on the other to making as much as possible for itself and thus reinforcing its ossifying formation as a new hereditary class or caste. Not surprisingly in such an arbitrary despotism, slave labour played an inestimable part in meeting output objectives. Statism had come to the inevitable sul-de-sac where necessary means nullified expressed ends.

It is of great interest and significance, therefore, that the leaders of the embattled Communist Party of China early perceived the dilemma and paradox. As Jack Belden, the shrewdest and closest Western observer of the pre-1949 Communist leadership, reported of them (6) they spoke quite openly of the mistakes — as they saw them — of the Russians, and indicated that they would certainly take a quite different path. This they undoubtedly have done, even if not without oscillations, for there were many Chinese cadres deeply imbued with Soviet influence. In essence what the Chinese have tried to do (see chapter four for a fuller account) is to accentuate decentralisation and local initiative, maximise centre-periphery agreement on goals and methods by interconsultation, and minimise the central bureaucracy. Moreover, sorting out means from ends, they have from the beginning placed due emphasis on producing consumer goods so that those upon whose labour the whole burden of heaving the economy up from the trough of poverty depended were assured of seeing a steady accretion to the fruits of these labours. Visitors who have seen stores in both Russia and China know what different consequences for the ordinary consumer the two courses have entailed.

## Class Structure, Tradition and the Imperial Impact

The next step to be taken is to examine whether a connection can be detected and established between the timing and type of development process, on the one hand, and class structure on the other. In a sense, these

* The rapid and cancer-like proliferation of the USSR's party, state and local bureaucracies can be seen as a kind of forced or hothouse 'tertiarisation'. The tertiary sector developed only slowly and at a comparatively late stage in the evolution of the earlier capitalist and industrialising experiences. It was undoubtedly made possible by the proceeds of colonialism and imperialism, which so vastly increased the scale of economic surplus available in the metropolitan countries, and made possible the luxuries of welfarism, leisure amenities for the mass of the people, elaborate administrative supervision of every aspect of an increasingly complex social and economic life, advertising, and so on. It is tempting to see Russia's forced march tertiarisation as something made possible by intense 'internal colonialism' exerted on the rural sector and on the empty lands by slave labour on a huge scale.

matters are embedded in the core of Marxism, and — with the present spate of reprints of the classics of Karl Marx, Friedrich Engels, V.I. Lenin and others, and of new commentaries, interpretations and analyses — it is unnecessary to give specific references here, merely to remark that some familiarity with this corpus is an *essential* element in a social science (or indeed any other) education. Attention is, however, drawn to the recent work of Barrington Moore (7), who makes a number of interesting points, but goes — like many another commentator without a specific interest in, knowledge of, or sympathy for, China — wildly astray when he comes to consideration of the Chinese case. But the reader himself may correct any wrong impression thus gained by digging more deeply into the available literature (see bibliography to chapter four).

Reverting for a moment to the hypothesis of some fairly homogeneous 'traditional society' in the different parts of the world prior to the onset of the processes that were to lead to modernisation, in at least part of the contemporary world, we should ask whether there were not, in fact, very important differences from one part of the world to another, differences with implications for the entire future pattern of evolution. The point at issue here is whether the same forces (historical, ecological, economic,etc.) acting on societies with differences so great and significant as to call into question the permissibility of their being all lumped together under the category 'traditional society' would have ultimately produced the same results because of the necessities inherent in these forces, or alternatively whether they would have propelled some societies forward while blowing themselves out in vain on the inhospitable rocks of others. Unfortunately, there is no way of answering the question, though many have speculated upon it (for it has marked political and racial implications). Once one group of formerly 'traditional societies' (the Western) began pulling away from the others in certain key respects, that group was able to impose itself on the others with profound consequences for the original ('tradit-ional', if you like) social structures of these, disfiguring them beyond recognition in due course, and producing as end product something which — if still stagnant in some respects — certainly bears no resemblance to the original. The forces which acted first on Europe never acted in the same way upon any non-European society (with the intriguing exception of Japan, of course) precisely *because* they had acted first upon Europe. We cannot go back and conduct a controlled experiment upon, say, India to see whether in fact, remaining independent of colonial rule, she would have built on the economic foundations she had already established in pre-colonial days, responding to the winds of economic and social change from out of Europe, or to the potential of her own resources to move for-ward along the path of autonomous, balanced, national economic develop-ment. In other words, once colonialism was underway and the dominant force in the world, it obliterated the chances of all its victims to pursue a similar course and guaranteed that, even if one day they might achieve equality, it would not be by the same path.

Two simplistic points that are sometimes made in this connection should be dealt with briefly here. The first asserts that the failure of Western technology to transfer to other parts of the world except under Western auspices (with the usual exception of Japan, where some Westerners using this argument would say that the Japanese simply 'imitated') proves that only Western culture and society are adapted to modern technology. The point raised is an interesting one, because of course it is true that in the pre-colonial period cultural innovations did tend, with time, to spread from the point at which they had been made to all other suitable parts of the world (the windmill, paper, gunpowder, etc.). But the key lies not in the alleged unsuitability of the societies or people of the Third World to adopt modern technology, but in the existence during the relevant period of colonialism and neo-colonialism. Modern technology in the hands of the imperialist powers was a tool of exploitation, not to be allowed to pass, except under tight supervision, restraints and restrictions, into other hands. During the entire colonial period, modern industry stayed in the 'mother-countries' (except to the extent that specific components might be more profitable when geographically situated in a colony), and local people were restricted to the lowest mechanical operations, anything more complex being kept in European hands. Neo-colonialism in many respects perpetuates this kind of situation. What a country freed by revolution from dependence and inferior status can achieve has been shown by the performance of China since 1949, with several technological and scientific firsts already to her credit (and work currently going on in all the most advanced fields). It should be noted, too, that China and Japan both shut themselves off from the rest of the world at the critical juncture in the 17th century.

The other 'explanatory' notion often put forward is that Eastern (or African or Latin American) religion is the real barrier to progress. There are many variants, but basically it is alleged that while the values of Western Christianity (especially in its Protestant form) are eminently compatible with the development of science and technology and of capitalism-industrialism, 'other-worldly' or 'mystical' religions are not. Therefore. it is implied, it is a waste of time to expect or to encourage Western-style development in countries such as India (Hindu) or Burma and Thailand (Buddhist). Actually, this argument puts the cart before the horse. It would be hard to imagine a religion apparently so hostile to capitalism as, for instance, European medieval Christianity. Nevertheless, when the productive forces had developed to the point where it was essential for a rationalising ideology to ease the transition from ideational medieval homeostasis to worldly dynamic capitalism, it appeared in the shape of the protestant ethic, particularly in certain formulations of it. To look at this from the other direction, where business interests strive to flourish in an orthodox Muslim context, reformist tendencies more favourable to the necessary business ethics will appear. Every world religion, indeed, embraces so many trends and is hospitable to so many interpretations, that there is no doubt at all that each and every one of them is quite able to accommodate to whatever socio-economic change or impulse requires it.

It is worth making these points because there have been attempts to argue that only Western and Western-style societies *could have*, colonialism or neo-colonialism, grasped the chances that offered and established the kind of free societies they did (8). Marx himself and Marxists after him have much concerned themselves with the concept of a specifically Asiatic mode of production, requiring considerable modification to any strictly unilinear model of social development (slave society-primitive communism, feudalism-capitalism-socialism-communism). The discussion became embroiled in the Sino-Soviet dispute, but what really was at issue at the outset — and intellectually still is — was whether countries like India could, on their own, break out of the constraints made necessary by their mode of production and tending towards centralism, bureaucratism, despotism, social and economic atomisation in self-sufficient villages, massive conscription of forced labour for the upkeep of the hydraulic systems essential for irrigation and transportation, and historical homeostasis rather than metamorphosis. Marx wrote a good deal about Asia, although very little about Africa, and the scholar can find quotations to suit his own purpose. But his writings show that he did grasp two fundamental things, which are not, as some commentators have tried to make out, at all incompatible: first, that the tremendous and shattering impact of colonialism-imperialism on the countries of Asia, Africa and Latin America shook them irrevocably from the grooves geography and history had worn for them before; and, second, that the colossal forces thus released might well become in time the arbiters of the destinies of the 'advanced' Western countries themselves.

Let me now try to go to the heart of this question. Were I to try to generalise for the entire Third World, regional specialists would be afforded the opportunity to point out with scorn all sorts of specific exceptions to the suggested typology (which would not, of course, invalidate its applicability in general). Although I shall, therefore, restrict myself to consideration of South East Asia, the region with which I am most familiar, much of the pattern I shall outline could equally be applied to African Colonisation.

Still, it is as well to recall that there were great differences, for instance between the mainland (Thailand, Laos, Cambodia, Vietnam) and the maritime part (Malaya, Indonesia, the Philippines), and between hill peoples and plain peoples. The peasantry was naturally everywhere the most numerous social class, and the village, with its headman, the primary social unit. At the other extremity sat the ruler, known as God King, Sultan, or by some other honorific title depending upon the area and era. The court-cum-administration was seen to by members of the royal family (typically very numerous) and members of a handful of hereditary elite families. Religion was entrusted to specialists of one kind or another, depending upon persuasion. There was a large class of slaves of various kinds. Craftsmen provided for the luxury and semi-luxury requirements of the rich and powerful. Soldiers protected the *status quo*, or alternatively (from time to time) substituted one ruling line for another. Mercantile activities of the bigger sort, including international commerce, would be carried on by a cosmopolitan community, resident in the biggest ports, and consisting of, among others, Arabs, Chinese, and Indians. These would include moneylenders. Commerce between villages, and handicrafts, were normally adjuncts of domestic economy, but there might be some full-time specialist handicraftsmen — and even a few villages specialising in the manufacture of some particular good and subsisting by exchange. It will be seen that there were some similarities to class structure in the European Middle Ages, and some differences — notably the absence of an independent class of burghers with their distinctive institutions and organisations.

What did Western colonial penetration eventually do to this pristine structure? In the first place, as we noted above, indigenous commercial and manufacturing enterprise was destroyed or reduced to the less important interstices of the economy. We do not know how local enterprise would have developed had it been able to fight off Western competition and political domination, but Hicks, in his theory of economic history (9), postulates that South East Asia was possibly the only other place in the world — besides the Mediterranean — where all the circumstances favouring development of an advanced trading system (prefiguring the rise of capitalism) existed.

Next, the greater part of the ruling structure was absorbed into, and adapted to the needs of, colonial administration, thus totally changing its relationship to the mass of the people. In a sense this *volte-face* left a vacuum, which the religious leadership, understandably alienated by the arrogant intruders of another religion, moved to fill: Buddhist priests and Muslim religious teachers alike figured prominently in rebellions against the colonial authorities. Their assumption of leadership of and great influence on such manifestations of popular resistance was facilitated by another important change: conversion of the village headman from being a spokesman for the village to central authority, to that of being the representative of central authority in the village. The peasantry and displaced handicraft workers supplied plenty of recruits to resistance, and rebellions erupted frequently throughout the area. Peasant grievances were very real, for many lost their land through the operations of Western land law and money economy, new innovations working together as powerful social solvents. For this, see the classic work by Ngo Vinh Long cited in the bibliography.

If old classes were being radically altered, new ones were arising. Of these we may note: an urbanised, Western-educated intelligentsia ranging

from members of the professions down to clerical staff in Western enterprises and offices; a small proletariat employed in the few essential industrial activities performed locally, the products or services of which could
not be imported from the imperial 'mother country'; a much larger body
of plantation workers poised in status between proletariat and peasant
inasmuch as wages were earned but the work was rural and indeed for
many part-time, alternating with work in subsistence peasant agriculture;
a compradore bourgeoisie class (including a much enlarged resident alien
community) serving the purposes of Western business; a Western-trained
military serving the purposes of Western imperialism (and frequently
drawn largely from a minority community of the colony); a new class of
small indigenous businessmen striving on a small-scale to produce the same
kind of goods as were imported from the West — a group often referred to
as the 'national' (as opposed to compradore) bourgeoisie; and an urban
'lumpenproletariat' drawn primarily from the rural dispossessed.

## Bourgeoisie, Proleteriat and Peasantry

It should be noted that I have used such Western-derived words as
'bourgeoisie' and 'proletariat'. This is common practice in many discussions of colonial and post-colonial class structure in the Third World. I
would like now to dispute the  competence of this terminological application, so confusing and misleading in its connotations.

Take the term 'bourgeoisie', for instance. What it conjures up in the
European context, at least in the heroic pioneering days of the industrial
revolution, is, *inter alia;* hard work; frugality; accumulation of capital for
productive investment in manufacturing industry, transport, or mining;
and intense patriotism and nationalism shading into jingoism. Now what
on earth does the so-called 'bourgeoisie' of the present day neo-colonial
Third World have in common with this? Whether compradore or national,
it is the easy way that is sought: the exclusive licence to import or produce
locally, the government contract, lucrative collaboration with rich foreign
companies, and a multitude of other practices to make maximum money
for minimum effort. There would be some excuse for this — not much —
were the funds thus accumulated funnelled into local productive enterprises, but this is not generally the case, as is well known. The only point
of the exercise is to attain as quickly as possible a flashy meretricious
Western-style way of life, with big air-conditioned cars, vast showy gadget-
infested suburban villas, children at school and university in America,
Australia or Europe for the sake of ostentation, and so on; and, of course,
to build up large bank balances in Switzerland or elsewhere, 'safe' for the
day the wheel of fortune might turn (deposits made domestically are likely
to be with branches of big Western banks: Bank of America, etc.). It
should already be clear that the patriotism and nationalism of this 'bourgeoisie' are to say the least rather peculiar measured against the standards

of the class for which the term was coined. But much more can be said on
this score. The business henchmen of the former Thieu clique in Saigon
and of the ex-Lon Nol clique in Phnom Penh are certainly at one end of
the spectrum for venality and treachery, but it is only a matter of degree,
for from Thailand all the way through to the Philippines (and in many
sovereign states of Africa, too) we can see this eagerness to serve foreign
interests. There are two clear reasons for this: one is quite simply that it
is with the multinationals and the giants of the industrial world that the
big money lies, and it is in faithfully serving their interests (or alternatively
milking them) that the biggest fortunes can be made most quickly (especially since the entire national incomes of most third world countries are
smaller than the annual turnovers of many of the top multinationals); the
other is that today's world is a vastly different one from that of 150 years
ago in terms of the threat of revolution.

Let us consider this. It is true that in 1848 Marx and Engels had opened
the text of *The Communist Manifesto* with the words 'A spectre is haunting
Europe — the spectre of Communism'. But their prognostication was premature, and the European bourgeoisie was — with some scares — able to
look after itself until the Russian Revolution of 1917 (when the bourgeois
ruling classes of other Western powers rushed in panic to fling their armies
against the Bolsheviks). One reason, undoubtedly, was that the Western
working classes were able, by their struggles, to wrest some improvements
in living standards — concessions their rulers were able to make in part
from the 'export of poverty' and 'export of exploitation' to the colonial
and semi-colonial countries. Today, the international revolutionary land-
scape and vistas are transformed. The successful revolutionary convulsion of
China, the irresistible momentum of the revolution of the Indochinese
peoples, and the Third World-wide eruptions of revolutionary violence and
armed liberation struggles aimed against the ruling order, have brought
the spectre to the very foot of the beds of the bourgeoisie of Asia, Africa,
and Latin America. For very survival, the ruling groups of the 'free' world
empire have no option but to submerge the interests of their own peoples
to the imperative of attracting and securing the economic and military
support of the rich capitalist powers, whose interests in their survival
happen to coincide with their own. Rhetorical 'patriotism' and 'nationalism' mask, then, an eagerness to act as heavily armed satraps of the
imperialist powers — the very powers enthusiastically engaged in exploiting
their resources and inhabitants. Their job, in short, is to suppress their
own people for the benefit of foreign interests — a curious form of
'nationalism' indeed!

We should, though, add a few words about the possible positive roles of
capitalist and business classes in the revolution, at certain stages and in
certain circumstances. One thinks notably of Mao Tse-tung's New Democracy formulation, which permitted him to welcome to the ranks of the
anti-Japanese resistance, and subsequently of the anti-Chiang Kai-shek

civil war, small and even large businessmen whose patriotism and disgust at the corruption and inefficiency of the KMT led them to ally themselves with the communists, intellectuals, liberals, workers and peasants rather than with Chiang. In pursuit of this policy, Mao held out safeguards to such proven 'national' bourgeoisie, and restrained ultra-leftists from splintering by revolutionary 'purism' the broad coalition — 'uniting the many to defeat the few' — thus effected. The Vietminh and subsequently the NLF and PRG also strove, successfully, to integrate all patriotic elements, including small and big businessmen, into the widest possible coalition to isolate the anti-national Saigon clique. A similar pattern was followed in Laos and Cambodia. In recent years there have also been other instances, as in the Philippines immediately prior to the Marcos coup, where quite distinct lines of demarcation divided those in the business community favouring action to limit foreign economic control and domination and those prepared, for the high rewards it brought, to promote foreign interests. Such cleavages are obviously of some political interest. But just to make one relevant point from the nationalist movements of the 1930's to the 1950's: united in a common cause (for example, the winning of political independence), very broad class coalitions can be welded together and work effectively. Such co-operation does not, however, obliterate the separate class interests of the components. It was obvious even before the seal of international recognition had been put on Indonesian independence, for example, that class differences were already disrupting the disparate forces that had joined under elite leadership to fight and oust the Dutch. After independence, unchecked by a principled and disciplined party, the various elements went their own ways, the rich landlords and compradore and national bourgeoisie to profiteer and the poor to knuckle down again. The more prolonged, intense, and politically conscious Chinese and Vietnamese struggles, carrying forward social as well as national revolutions, made such an outcome impossible, even though patriotic landlords and businessmen were allies in struggle. The important point is that such patriotic non-working class elements are unstable and vacillating, and leadership must be vested in worker and peasant representatives with ultimate authority.

Before leaving the question of the role of the bourgeoisie in underdeveloped countries, we should say something about the new 'bourgeoisie': the rich capitalist farmers thrown up by the green revolution. It is undeniable that these 'kulaks' and absentee businessmen-farmers already wield considerable political influence in the countries where the green revolution has been extensively pursued. Their new found wealth commands respect, both because of the contribution it can make to party coffers or to the careers of politically ambitious individuals, and because their consumption has become a major factor in shaping markets and thereby investments. Their production, exchange and consumption needs entail a far closer articulation between rural and urban elites than ever before, and a relative relegation of the interests of the older feudalistic landlord class, whose requirements could, and often did, clash with the aspirations of the urban commercial-industrial bourgeoisie.

The emergence of a numerically strong new class with a very powerful and direct interest in preserving the sociopolitical *status quo* was naturally a result not unwelcome to the imperialist capitals of the world. Nor was it an unexpected or unplanned-for result. Increasing agricultural production by means of rewarding and enriching big and (in market terms) successful farmers, and by sucking idle capital out of urban hoards, was obviously an excellent tactic. That it widened rural inequalities and jettisoned numerous poor peasants onto the scrapheap of total redundancy was a consideration of little or no moment. Rural labour thus 'released' became 'free' labour, free to swell the ranks of the industrial reserve army of unemployed and thus ensure the maintenance of pitifully sub-minimal wages wherever labour was required by those with capital.

The basic reason behind the green revolution's so blatantly favouring the strong lay in the costs involved in switching from traditional to new strains. The HYV's required expensive outlays on fertilisers, pesticides, and other inputs if they were to be made to succeed. Only the richer farmers had the wherewithal in their own financial resources to afford these, or had the credit worthiness (or collateral) to attract the necessary capital from those able to supply it. The poorer farmers had neither. They accordingly sank as the others rose. The 1973 oil crisis delivered the *coup de grace* to all but the better-off cultivators, for rising oil prices spelt fertiliser prices soaring out of sight.

However, there is another side to the coin. The green revolution undoubtedly heightened class consciousness in the rural areas where it had an impact. Militancy on the part of lower middle and poor peasants, and among landless labourers, rose sharply, and spilled over into insurrection, as in India in the Naxalbari rising in 1967 (and subsequent armed struggles of the rural poor, with worker and student support, continuing to this day). This is a tendency which cannot be reversed, and which carries within it the seeds of the future all across the spectrum of Third World countries exposed to imperialist techno-economic interference and manipulationism.

So much for the use and misuse of the term 'bourgeoisie'; what of 'proletariat'? Marx used the term to describe the class that, in his day, was the most numerous in Western industrial societies, and the one that was the 'focal point of all inhuman conditions'! The proletariat of South and South East Asia, the Middle East and Africa is comparatively small — in some of the countries almost non-existent — and numerically overshadowed by the peasantry. In addition, the proletarian in employment typically has an income above that of the poor peasant, and he may have some kind of organisation and/or some kind of legislative protection (for example, minimum wages). His position, in short, while from all points of view often deplorable, is *relatively* a 'privileged' one (which admittedly does not say a great deal).

Far worse is the lot of the lumpenproletariat of the slums, the poorest landless peasants, rack-rented sharecroppers, and other rural deprived — here indeed we see the 'focal point of all inhuman conditions' (10). A final word on the lumpenproletariat: this volatile mass was, in the industrialisation of the West, a kind of reserve army for absorption either permanently (with economic advance) or temporarily (as cyclical necessity arose) into the employed proletariat; if the Chinese experience offers any precedent at all for the rest of the Third World, this Third World lumpenproletariat, on the contrary, is a dispossessed peasantry *awaiting return to agriculture* — but to an agriculture totally transformed as a result of successful socialist revolution in the countryside.

This brings us to the important question of the role of the peasantry in the revolution which, we shall argue, alone holds out the promise of true national economic development bringing real benefit to all. Mechanical Marxism, despite everything, still clings to the theory of the vanguard role of the (white Western) proletariat, the peasant peoples of the Third World being, according to one recent Trotskyist writer, sunk in 'disillusionment and apathy', their only hope 'change and revolution in the industrial world'! It is a very good job for the Chinese peasants that they did not wait for revolution in the industrial world, for they would be waiting yet, more than a quarter of a century after the revolution that transformed their lives. In overwhelmingly peasant societies, it must be the peasantry that carries the brunt of social transformation. It is true that urbanisation is now proceeding apace in Third World countries, but it is an urbanisation totally unlike that of the industrial countries, for while there is some industrialisation associated with this hyper-urbanisation, the main contributory cause of the vast and seemingly endless expansion in numbers is the continuing hopeless flight from the rural areas (sometimes as refugees). These are pre-industrial cities, their populations soaring at three or four times the rate of respective national population growths, absorbing now sometimes a third of the whole (as compared with a few per cent fifty years ago), a quarter of more of them in slums and shanty towns (even in such prosperous examples as Malaysia's Kuala Lumpur or Kenya's Nairobi. But political control of these inflated urban masses is easier than it is in the rural areas, and besides they have shown themselves both inflammable and volatile politically, rampaging at the behest of racist demagogues and religious fanatics as well as throwing their weight behind strikes and anti-imperialist actions.

There are several excellent accounts and analyses of the role of the peasantry in the Chinese revolution with Mao's own works as an indispensable source. It can hardly be denied that they carried the brunt of pushing the revolution through, and the relation between this circumstance and the shape of Chinese development since is discussed below in chapter four. But more generally, it seems clear that the peasantry of 'free' Asia, the most numerous class and the class whose sufferings are most severe, intractable, and deteriorating, will have the key role to play in providing the manpower, support, and bases for the revolution. The long-drawn out Vietnamese and the less protracted Mozambique revolutions have demonstrated precisely how such a struggle has to be rooted in the rural areas, with the support of the peasantry, and recruitment from their ranks. With this kind of integration, no power on earth can crush the revolution, short of annihilating the country totally with nuclear weapons.

There are also the fascinating examples of Cambodia and Laos, countries characterised by minute, and in the latter case virtually non-existent, pro-letariats. Yet in both countries successful liberation struggles have been waged while at the same time major steps to elevate the living standards and all round morale of the people have been undertaken. (See references in bibliography.) Elsewhere, where armed liberation struggles are already being waged, we see the same kind of phenomena in embryonic form appearing: from Thailand, Malaya, Zimbwabwe and Ethiopia, with relat-ively well-developed struggles under way, through Indonesia where, for all the disadvantages, the PKI (Communist Party of Indonesia) has survived and created at least one secure base area (in north west Kalimantan — Indonesian Borneo), to the Philippines and South Africa, with long tradi-tions of guerrilla war and present tense struggle. Again in South Asia and in Southern Africa the people are on the move more palpably now than at any previous time. Clearly, the inevitable revolutionary convulsions on the Indian subcontinent will dramatically change the entire international situation; and upon whom can such a movement be based but upon the teeming, poverty-stricken peasants?

## The New Spectre

We have already essayed a comparison between Indonesia and Japan, arguing that the experience of colonial oppression was crucial in contorting and depressing Indonesian economic growth and development, while, in contrast, the fact that Japan retained her sovereignty was the key factor in enabling her to embark upon autonomous and balanced economic growth. I would like now to make some kind of comparison between India today and China today. This is of great relevance, because it seems to me to demonstrate, if indeed any demonstration or proof were required, that thorough-going economic and social revolution today is the *sine qua non* of any secure, independent, and just development process holding out promise of tolerable and steadily rising living standards and levels of culture for the generality of the people. Whole volumes might be devoted to the comparison, and there are many qualitative factors which stark indices cannot convey. It is hard, for instance, to demonstrate the degree of inequality or its implications economically, politically and socially. No statistics can convey the difference in the outlook of a people assured of their future as against that of a people sunk in misery and despair.

Nevertheless, with all these and other reservations (including those concerning the reliability and comparability of the statistical data), I think it worthwhile to draw the sketch:

TABLE 2

*A comparison between Chinese and Indian economic performance since 1950*
*(1950-51 = 100)*

|  | India | 1970-71 | China |
|---|---|---|---|
| Agricultural production | 190 |  | 192 |
| Food | 202 |  |  |
| Grain |  |  | 174 |
| Industrial production | 324 |  | 676 |
| Cotton cloth | 124 |  | 340 |
| Electricity (generated) | 930 |  |  |
| Electricity (assessment) |  |  | 1,318 |
| Nitrogen fertiliser | 2,904 |  |  |
| Phosphate fertiliser | 2,081 |  |  |
| Chemical fertiliser |  |  | 10,571 |
| Exports | 233 |  | 330 |
| Imports | 264 |  | 367 |

Source: Debesh Bhattacharya 'A Comparative Study of Economic Development in India and China since 1950', Xerox, 1973, p.20.

Dr. Bhattacharya concludes that the average annual growth of national product per cent over the period 1952-72 was 5.0% to 5.5% for China and 3.6% for India, and per capita 3.2% for China and 1.3% for India. He also points out that global calculations make no allowance for important matters such as equality v. inequality of incomes and consumption; foreign exchange independence v. international indebtedness; full employment v. mass unemployment; and a large number of other variables in China's favour, some of which we will discuss in chapter four below.

Dr. Bhattacharya estimates Indian Domestic Investment as a % of N.I. as 5.5 in 1950-51 and 11.3 in 1970-71, and Chinese Net Domestic Investment as a proportion of Net Domestic Product as 19.8 in 1952 and 18.0 in 1965. (12)

Striking though these bare figures are, it is as well to re-emphasise that behind them lie qualitative realities best grasped by following what has been written descriptively about the two countries in recent years, by keeping abreast with press reports and articles of all kinds, or, best of all, if impracticable, by visiting the two countries and making one's own observations and judgements (as I have been fortunate enough to do).

Similarly striking comparisons could be, and in other places have been made between North Korea and South Korea (11), and between North Vietnam and pre-liberation South Vietnam. In some respects these comparisons provide even sharper and more persuasive arguments for the case I have been making, because racial, religious and other variables are automatically eliminated, leaving us with the variable of alternative growth and development strategies.

It is hard to dispute that, in the form their evolutions have actually taken, it was certainly Western impact that jolted the countries of the Third World into the trajectories they took (partly as direct consequence, partly in reaction). From this perspective we may understand what Marx was getting at in suggesting that, for all the accompanying atrocities and violence to the Indian way of life, the British imperial presence was an objectively revolutionary force, considered in the long term, through enforced changes such as the building of railways, the consequences of which could not thereafter be nullified by the hand of tradition but which must needs, in conjunction, shatter the old and hold out prospects for the new. In the same way, brutal as they were, the Opium Wars which forced China open in 1842 set in motion social and economic currents in China which were to culminate in the accession to power of the Communists and the inauguration of New China, which all its attainments and promise.

It is not to be thought, though, that the flow of influence continues in the same direction. Orthodox 'development' theory, and many liberal-minded individuals, still profess to see things in this light, with our advanced countries giving 'aid' and a further helping hand to the backward nations. Much left-wing theory also subscribes to this variant of Europocentrism, either in the form of social democratic parties calling for even more 'aid' to the poorer countries, or in the form of mechanical Marxist parties claiming that the poor countries are incapable of carrying through socialist revolutions and therefore must await salvation from the revolt of the (white Western) workers of the industrialised countries.

On the contrary, the tide of history is on the turn. Although the illusion of Western initiative lingers on, a cool impartial look at post-war history demonstrates without question the growing impotence of the imperialist countries, headed by the United States of America, to attain their desired ends. The Kolkos (see bibliography) have analysed and documented this in great detail. America, for all her overwhelming power at the war's end, was unable to 'save' China for the 'free' world, and it was China's liberation which provoked in panic reaction the whole series of U.S. interventions — notably in Korea, French Indochina, and Formosa — designed to shore up an 'impregnable' anti-communist defence perimeter for the Pacific region so central to her concerns and interests. ('Only on the lands west of the Pacific,' minuted the influential Stanley K. Hornbeck, the State Department's Political Advisor for Far Eastern Affairs in December 1940, 'and especially on southeastern Asia is our dependence so vital and complete that our very existence as a great industrial power, and perhaps even as an industrial state, is threatened if the sources [of raw materials] should be cut off.')

The long-drawn out Indochina war illustrated again and again the new reality: namely, that politics and economics in the West will increasingly consist of reactions and adaptations to pressures from the growing initiatives of the countries of the Third World. Far from the mighty US dollar smashing the Vietnamese, it was the Vietnamese who laid low the dollar, and forced an international currency crisis in the 'free' world that has become a permanent part of the global capitalist scene. It was the struggle of the Vietnamese people that elicited the massive mobilisations of workers and students all round the world in protest, sparked off research in depth into the nature of imperialism and encouraged in every country intense anti-imperialist activity. It is impossible to divorce the present ills of inflation, unemployment, and endemic industrial chaos, from the surging tide of people's liberation struggles, spearheaded for so long by the Indochinese peoples. Far from the workers of the rich West coming to the aid of the peasants of the Third World, it is they who are creating the conditions for the workers of the West to liberate themselves. Far from the works of Trotsky enjoying wide currency among the peasants of Asia, it is the works of Mao Tse-tung that circulate among the peoples of Europe, North America, and Australasia. It is no surprise that this should be so, for historically initiative, creativity and energy have alternated between East and West, between one culture and civilisation and another, and today we are living through the era in which the West, so long in the ascendant, is palpably on the wane.

The struggle will, however, be a hard fought one. The weapons in the hands of the imperialist powers in their last-ditch battles are very varied and increasingly adapted, by trial and error, specifically to the twin tasks of keeping 'friendly' regimes in power (primarily by military and economic support) and suppressing 'insurgencies' (primarily by intelligence methods thoroughly tested in Vietnam and by newer tactics and weapons battle-tried there). The works noted in references 41-46 in the bibliography demonstrate how new imperialist weaponry and new approaches to economic 'development' of poor countries combine to make the task of liberation as arduous and long-drawn out as the imperialists can make it while, for the mass of the people, underdevelopment continues to develop.

## The Crisis of Proletarian Internationalism

There is nothing new in the working of the underlying economic laws defining the relationships of richer and poorer, more and less powerful. Over time, the specific forms have modified and the contradictions intensified. Wallerstein (13) has recently demonstrated that from the very beginnings of Western expansion it has been concerned with making good domestic shortages by foisting 'unequal exchange' upon poorer or less powerful territories, in his words expanding 'the territorial base of European consumption by constructing a political economy in which this resource base was unequally consumed, disproportionately by Western Europe.' Overcoming resource limitations in successive directions is also the theme of Wilkinson's book (14), though he underplays the role of imperialism in enabling the rich overdeveloped countries to pass the burden on to the poorer underdeveloped countries. It has been left to Arghiri Emmanuel to articulate with precision and passion the way in which, over the centuries, a handful of countries have been able to construct and benefit — workers and rulers alike — from an elaborate system of unequal exchange condemning the poor of the poor countries to a poverty frequently referred to by Western scholars and liberals as 'hopeless' but nurturing within it the stuff which the Chinese and Vietnamese revolutions set aflame ; 'a single spark can start a prairie fire', as Mao expressed it.

Emmanuel, seeking to account for the lack of commitment of the workers of the overdeveloped countries to anti-imperialist struggle, and therefore for the collapse of 'proletarian internationalism', develops the following, by no means absurd, supposition:

'Let us suppose that a major defeat brings the United States down to the level of an underdeveloped country. Leaving out of account the material losses suffered during and as a result of the event itself, the American capitalist will not find himself any worse off. The members of the liberal professions and the highly skilled workers will experience at worst an insignificant decrease in their incomes. (Despite the huge disparity in general wage levels, an engineer, a manager, or a lawyer in Egypt or in India earns nearly as much as his counterpart in one of the richest countries.) The laborers and the ordinary skilled workers, however, will be hurled into an abyss. It is even hard to imagine how, in the event of such a catastrophe, an American worker who today earns three dollars an hour could survive on a wage of a few cents *a day*. And this is no arbitrary and fantastic speculation. Something of the kind has already happened in Algeria. When the threat of independence became immediately real, big financial capital as a whole adjusted itself to the idea of Algerian Algeria. Provided Algeria did not take the path of socialism, the capitalists had no privileges at risk. Their only privilege was their capital itself, and as long as national independence did not threaten this, they had no reason to oppose it, any more than had the real labor aristocracy, those who earned the wages or salaries of their trade or profession, not those of their nationality or race. Individually, these people made different decisions, conditioned by the ideological superstructure, but as a class they refrained from acting against the Algerian people. It was the European proletariat of Bab-el-Oeud (previously a stronghold of the Algerian Communist Party) that mobilized in defense of French Algeria and supplied the OAS killers. For them it was a question of life or death. *Their* privilege was their quality as Europeans or whites. Algeria as a French dependency guaranteed them European, or French, wages in an underdeveloped country. They earned in a few days what an Algerian earned in a month. Without this privilege they were materially, objectively, unable to live. "La valise ou le cercueil" — the suitcase (for an escape to France) or the coffin — was the saying that related to *their* problem alone.' (15)

In this passage, properly understood and extrapolated, you have in a nutshell the explanation for the prolongation of neo-colonialism and underdevelopment. It is only now, with the assertion of their rights and power by the raw material producers and exporters, as exemplified by OPEC, that the vulnerability of a world structure so beneficial to the rich of both rich and poor countries and to the working class of the rich ones is being rudely exposed. If the falling living standards to which sections of the Western working class are now being subjected stimulate militancy, against whom will that militancy ultimately be directed?

As I pointed out earlier on in this chapter, the economic surplus of the rich countries has been continuously augmented from that of the poorer, while conversely the economic surplus of the poor countries has been continuously depleted to the benefit of the richer. This is a situation that cannot continue indefinitely. Nor is it one that can be corrected solely by raising the living standards of the poorer peoples of the world. As I shall seek to show in the following chapter, the rich countries are 'overdeveloped' in precisely this respect: that they must be net importers of some of the most essential components of a high standard of living, as conventionally understood, such as proteins and the heavy hydrocarbons. As far as the first is concerned, to revert to Wallerstein's observation quoted above from the earliest period of European expansionism and imperialism, we should note that today an international system of 'unequal consumption' exists, a kind of protein imperialism, whereby the peoples of the rich countries in a literal sense take the food out of the very mouths and bellies of the poor and replace it with low quality *foodstuffs*. This may be vividly illustrated by the following extracts from the first of Ingrid Palmer's books cited in the bibliography to chapter one.

'Africa exports its high protein groundnuts when it has been said that a handful of groundnuts per person per day would solve the African protein problem. Africa is a net exporter of meat — mainly from South Africa. This continent is also a bigger net exporter of peas and lentils than the whole of North and Central America together. At the same time Africa is a net importer of high-carbohydrate foods [foodstuffs - M.C.]. Asia is a net importer of high-carbohydrate foods [foodstuffs - M.C.] and is a net exporter of high-protein foods. Although Latin America is a substantial net importer of vegetable proteins it is a net exporter of grains and meat. It is hardly necessary to point out that the big exports of animal protein from Latin America do not affect the low income countries' total protein intake.'

Why? Because, of course, Latin America meat exports go almost exclusively to the rich, overdeveloped countries, to the problems of which the next chapter is devoted.

## REFERENCES

1.   E. Mandel, *Marxist Economic Theory*, Merlin Book Club Edition, (1971) pp 443-445.
2.   Cf. P.A. Baran, *The Political Economy of Growth*, Monthly Review Press, (New York, 1957).
3.   A. Emmanuel, *Unequal Exchange*, NLB, (London, 1972).
4.   F. List, *The National System of Political Economy*, Longmans, Green and Co., (London, 1922).
5.   A. Nove, *An Economic History of the U.S.S.R.*, Penguin, (London 1972).
6.   J. Belden, *China Shakes the World*, Monthly Review Press, (New York, 1970).
7.   Barrington Moore Jr., *Social Origins of Dictatorship and Democracy*, Penguin, (London, 1969).
8.   K.A. Wittfogel, *Oriental Despotism*, Yale University Press, (London, 1964).
9.   J. Hicks, *A Theory of Economic History*, OUP, (London, 1969).
10.   K. Marx, *The Holy Family*, various eds.
11.   Cf. *Journal of Contemporary Asia*, (5.2.).
12.   Cf. also T.J. Bynes and P. Nolan, *Inequalities between Nations; China and India compared 1950-1970*, (Milton Keynes, 1976).
13.   I. Wallerstein, *The Modern World-System*, Academic Press, (London, 1974).
14.   R.G. Wilkinson, *Poverty and Progress*, Methuen, (London, 1973).
15.   A. Emmanuel, ibid, pp183-184.

## BIBLIOGRAPHY

1.   P.A. Baran, *The Political Economy of Growth*, Monthly Review Press, (New York, 1957).
2.   J. Hicks, *A Theory of Economic History*, OUP, (London, 1969).
3.   C.M. Cipolla, *European Culture and Overseas Expansion*, Penguin, (London, 1970).
4.   D.S. Landes, *The Unbound Prometheus*, CUP, (Cambridge, 1969).
5.   I. Wallerstein, *The Modern World-System*, Academic Press, (London, 1974).
6.   A. Emmanuel, *Unequal Exchange*, NLB, (London, 1972).
7.   Samir Amin, *Accumulation on a World Scale*, Monthly Review Press, (New York, 1974).
8.   Geoffrey Kay, *Development and Underdevelopment — A Marxist Analysis*, Macmillan, (London, 1975).
(A selection of volumes, expressing various distinct viewpoints and

approaches, on the development/underdevelopment genesis and symbiosis. These are taken from an immense and constantly swelling literature; there are extensive bibliographies in Amin's two volume work.)

9.    W.S. Jevons, *The Coal Question*, Macmillan & Co., (London, 1866). (A remarkably percipient book, still of interest albeit Jevons, one of the leading economists of his day, was awry on time scales and magnitudes.)

10.    G. Myrdal, *Asian Drama*, Allen Lane, (London, 1968), three vols. (Professor Myrdal's book is in a category of its own as a reference storehouse, but it has glaring weaknesses in analysis and is deeply flawed by omission of China from the scope of discussion.)

11.    C. Day, *The Dutch in Java*, OUP, (London, 1966).

12.    C. Geertz, *Agricultural Involution*, University of California Press, (Berkeley & Los Angeles, 1963).

13.    M. Caldwell & E. Utrecht, *Indonesia Since 1800*, Zed Press (London, 1977). (Three works which throw light on the crucial period of Dutch colonial rule which condemned Indonesia to the poverty still afflicting her.)

14.    G.C. Allen, *A Short Economic History of Modern Japan*, Allen & Unwin, (London, 1972).

15.    J. Halliday, *A Political History of Japanese Capitalism*, Pantheon Books, (New York, 1975).

16.    J. Livingstone, J. Moore & F. Oldfather (eds.), *The Japan Reader*, Penguin, (London, 1976), two vols.. (Three accounts of the great Asian — indeed Third World — capitalist success story).

17.    F. List, *The National System of Political Economy*, Longmans, Green & Co., (London, new impression 1922). (The classic statement of the case for protectionism in countries embarking upon industrialisation and faced with rivals already endowed with established industrial sectors.)

18.    A. Nove, *An Economic History of the U.S.S.R.*, Penguin, (London, 1972).

19.    M. Nicolaus, *The Restoration of Capitalism in the USSR*, Liberator Press, (Chicago, 1975).

20.    C. Bettelheim, *Class Struggles in the USSR*, Monthly Review Press, (New York, 1977).

21.    H. Smith, *The Russians*, Quadrangle, (New York, 1976).

22.    A. Solzhenitsyn, *The Gulag Archipelago*, Collins, (London, 1974 & 1975), first two volumes. (Various looks at Soviet Society.)

23.    J. Belden, *China Shakes the World*, Monthly Review Press, (New York, 1970). (Remains the undisputed classic introduction to an understanding of the Chinese Revolution.)

24.    Barrington Moore Jr., *Social Origins of Dictatorship and Democracy*, Penguin, (London, 1969).

25.   K. A. Wittfogel, *Oriental Despotism*, Yale University Press, (London, 1964).
(Two distinctly different approaches to analysing the respective roots of democracy and dictatorship.)
26.   Ngo Vinh Long, *Before the Revolution*, M.I.T. Press, (London, 1973).
27.   Phoumi Vongvichit, *Laos and the Victorious Struggle of the Lao People Against U.S. Neo-Colonialism*, Neo Lao Haksat Editions, (Hanoi, 1969).
28.   P. Sundarayya, *Telengana People's Struggle and its Lessons*, CPI(M), (Calcutta, 1972).
29.   Nguyen Khac Vien, *The Long Resistance (1858-1975)*, Foreign Languages Publishing House, (Hanoi, 1975).
30.   *Selected Works of Mao Tse-tung*, Foreign Languages Press, (Peking, 1965), 4 vols.
31.   M. Caldwell & Lek Tan, *Cambodia in the Southeast Asian War*, Monthly Review Press, (New York).
(A selection of books on peasants and revolution.)
32.   Lasse & Lisa Berg, *Face to Face — Facism and Revolution in India*, Ramparts Press, (Berkeley, 1971).
33.   Mary Tyler, *My Years in an Indian Prison*, Gollancz, (London, 1977).
34.   Dilip Hiro, *Inside India Today*, Routledge & Kegan Paul, (London, 1976).
(Three glimpses into the seething reality of India under the crust of business as usual.)
35.   U. Melotti, *Marx and the Third World*, Macmillans, (London, 1977).
36.   Shlomo Avineri (ed.), *Karl Marx on Colonialism and Modernisation*, Doubleday & Co., Inc., (New York, 1968).
37.   H.C. d'Encausse & S.R. Schram, *Marxism and Asia*, Allen Lane, (London, 1969).
(Three looks at how Marx viewed the Third World and its prospects.)
38.   R.G. Wilkinson, *Poverty and Progress*, Methuen, (London, 1973).
(A rising challenge and forced response analysis of the 'development' process, relevant to chapter three, too.)
39.   G. Kolko, *The Politics of War*, Weidenfeld & Nicolson, (London, 1969).
40.   Joyce & G. Kolko, *The Limits of Power*, Harper & Row, (New York, 1972).
(Indispensable accounts of the evolution of US policy towards the post-war world, and of the attempts to force reality into the moulds of the American empire.)
41.   M.T. Klare, *War Without End*, Vintage Books, (New York, 1972).
42.   S. Weissman et al., *The Trojan Horse*, Ramparts Press, (San Francisco, 1974).
43.   Cheryl Payer, *The Debt Trap*, Penguin, (London, 1975).
44.   Kim Yong Bock & Pharis J. Harvey (eds.), *People Toiling Under*

*Pharaoh*, CCA-URM, (Tokyo, 1976).

45.　　R. Mortimer, (ed.), *Showcase State*, Angus & Robertson, (Sydney, 1973).

46.　　Peter Dale Scott, 'Exporting Military-Economic Development: America and the Overthrow of Sukarno, 1965-67', in M. Caldwell (ed.) *Ten Years' Military Terror in Indonesia*, Spokesman Books, (Nottingham, 1975).

(The first four works trace various strands in the continuing enshacklement of the poor countries of the Third World in the international capitalist economy; the other two deal with a particularly apposite and poignant example: Indonesia.)

47.　　Ellen Brun & Jacques Hersh, *Socialist Korea*, Monthly Review Press, (New York, 1977).

(A fascinating look at a frequently neglected example of an underdeveloped country transforming itself by its own efforts into a strong industrial state.)

48.　　Hari Sharma, 'The Green Revolution in India: Prelude to a Red One?', in Kathleen Gough & H. Sharma (eds.), *Imperialism and Revolution in South Asia*, Monthly Review Press, (New York, 1973).

49.　　J. Hickson, 'Rural Development and Class Contradictions on Java', *Journal of Contemporary Asia*, Vol. V, no. 3, 1975.

50.　　E. Utrecht, 'Land Reform and Bimas in Indonesia', *Journal of Contemporary Asia*, Vol. III, no. 2, 1972.

51.　　W.F. Wertheim, 'Betting on the Strong?', *East-West Parallels*, W. Van Hoeve Ltd., (The Hague, 1964).

(A selection of discussions of the problems of the impact of rural innovation on rural class structure.)

# OVERDEVELOPMENT

The concept of underdevelopment is a familiar one, made familiar by all the attention that has been paid to it in the post-war period. The general profile of a poor underdeveloped country — low calorie intake, high infant mortality, peasant poverty and landlessness, urban slums and unemployment, and the like — is well known. Disagreements arise when attention is turned from research and measurement to the question of what should be done about it: there are those who purport to believe that foreign aid plus unhindered local and foreign capital investment can do the trick of wiping out the social sores which go to make up underdevelopment; others contend that, on the contrary, only by socialist and anti-imperialist revolution, rejecting capitalism and aid, can the peoples of the poor countries create for themselves the chance to embark upon true self-improvement. In the previous chapter I tried to show *how* underdevelopment had arisen historically, and why — if the diagnosis is sound — only the latter course offers a real way forward for the poor of the third world.

But now we have to deal with another concept: overdevelopment. Until recently the idea that those countries which *have* succeeded in industrialising and, in general, in 'modernising' may not be so much developed as *over*-developed has had much less currency and consideration. I intend in this chapter to discuss the condition of overdevelopment, and to answer questions such as the following. What can we possibly mean by *over*developed? Surely no country in the world has, in absolute terms, too much wealth? How has overdevelopment arisen? What are its characteristics today, its profile? In what ultimate direction and to what ultimate destiny are the overdeveloped countries headed?

I propose to start with a definition of overdevelopment, all the implications of which may not immediately be clear. But the rest of the chapter is devoted to clarification. An overdeveloped country, then, is one in which the forces of production have developed to the point that, regardless of the prevailing relations of production, it must be a net importer of proteins and hydrocarbons over time if it is to maintain or improve upon a certain level and type of consumption per head of its population. Let us consider this.

## OVERDEVELOPMENT AND AGRICULTURE

We began by investigating the role of the fossil fuels in enabling rich countries to sustain hitherto undreamt of standards of living; not universally, to be sure, but for a very substantial proportion of the whole population, and certainly a much greater one than had ever before been possible in history. In the second chapter, we looked into the question of precisely when (over what period of time), and how, historically the now rich countries had succeeded in thus establishing an unquestionably privileged position, and we concluded that the economic surplus of food/foodstuffs available to them had been vastly increased in two ways (both dependent upon securing access to steadily growing supplies of fossil fuels and other non-renewable real resources): one, by raising the production of domestic agriculture *via* stepped-up in-puts of fertiliser, pesticides, machinery, electrically heated or powered installations, and so; two, by importing food on an enormous, previously unheard of, scale. The imported food is obtained on the one hand, by extending high-productivity domestic-style agriculture to certain favoured 'lands of recent settlement' (the USA, Canada, Australia, etc.) which themselves in time became rich industrialised countries, and paying for the resulting food surpluses by the export of manufactured goods, and, on the other hand, by extending imperialist control over the rest of the world and converting their economies to meet the needs (including the needs for fossil fuels, other non-renewable real resources, food and foodstuffs) of the metropolitan economies.

At this point, the reader is advised to go back and re-read the quotation from Quesnay with which the whole book opened. Commenting upon the work of the Physiocrats, the 19th century English economist Thomas Malthus wrote

'[their] great position will always remain true, that the surplus produce of the cultivators is the great fund which ultimately pays all those who are not employed upon the land. Throughout the whole world, the number of manufacturers, of proprietors, and of persons engaged in the various civil and military professions, must be exactly proportioned to this surplus produce, and cannot in the nature of things increase beyond it. In proportion as the labour and ingenuity of man, exercised upon the land, have increased the surplus produce, leisure has been given to a greater number of persons to employ themselves in all the inventions which embellish civilised life. And though, in its turn, the desire to profit by these inventions, has greatly contributed to stimulate the cultivators to increase their surplus produce; yet the order of the precedence is clearly the surplus produce.'(1)

It is worthwhile re-examining the validity of the Physiocrats' basic insight for the 20th century, at this pregnant stage in the evolution of economic theory. We may start with the traditionally accepted factors of production: land, labour and capital. The value of their respective contributions to the value of a society's final output of goods and services can be estimated in a variety of ways, commonly employing monetary or other symbolic notations. Alternatively, we may attempt to express their relative contributions in 'real' terms. The Physiocrats, living in predominantly agrarian pre-industrial conditions, perhaps found it more natural and congenial to think and express themselves in 'real' terms. Their successors, bemused by the seemingly boundless 'miracles' of science, technology, modern accountancy, monetary legerdemain, and increasingly complex economic theory, tended to lose sight of the 'real' aspects behind the veil of money and the mirage of scientific omnipotence. The importance of establishing the truth or otherwise of Quesnay's statements for an understanding of the present international configuration will shortly become apparent.

It is clear that capital by itself, however defined, cannot produce goods and services appropriate to the support of human life. Financial calibrations and calculations are irrelevant in this respect. In real terms, capital simply represents stored previous labour and land outputs rearranged in a certain fashion (such that entropy has been increased — 'free' energy degraded into 'bound' energy). I use the term 'land' here to include nonrenewable as well as renewable real resources (minerals as well as natural fibres and foodstuffs for instance). The accumulation of capital as an historical process represents the application of labour to land in such a way as to increase entropy. The accumulated capital, divorced from labour, is sterile or unproductive. Harnessed to labour, capital facilitates greatly the proliferation of commodities (or, to remind ourselves of Georgescu-Roegen's formulation, the transformation of valuable natural resources into valueless waste).

Labour as a factor of production is also limited in isolation. Labour covers all the human contributions, including innovation and the like. It was at one time thought, as a result of overlooking or misunderstanding the First and Second Laws of Thermodynamics (or more likely — as one pernicious consequence among many of specialisation — through sheer ignorance of their terms and implications) that labour, with an increasingly sophisticated stock of capital, would gradually be liberated from dependence on land (i.e. the originally given natural endowment). This is fallacious. Labour deprived of access to land is as sterile (unproductive) as capital devoid of labour. However vast, complex and technologically advanced the capital at the disposal of an appropriately trained labour force, the conjunction cannot issue in use — or any other — values without land playing a role (in addition, that is, to its embodiment in the fixed capital and the bone, muscle, and brain of the workers).

It is in this sense that the Physiocrats must now be held vindicated as against their detractors of the post-industrial revolution period by the most recent work in economics; work which has been forced by facts and circumstances to take into account ecological, thermodynamic and other factors hitherto unaccountably excluded from consideration. As Quesnay pointed out, the artisan in his own language, which happens to be correct, speaks of 'earning his keep' — he does not say he *produces* it. In exchange for the food from which alone he can obtain the energy necessary for work and recreation, the industrial worker supplies the land worker with some useful articles (clothing, pots and pans, and so on) and many unnecessary ones (strictly speaking, most — if not all — are unnecessary, since Man did without the products of manufacturing industry for most of his history but obviously some are more blatantly unnecessary and useless than others, and others again positively detract from welfare). It should be repeated that there is no substitute for food as the source of human energy; the hoary journalists' chimera of 'synthetic' food ignores the nature of the essential raw material base for such products , the fossil fuels such as coal or petroleum, geologically stored vegetable and animal matter. As for the industrial worker's output, his dependence upon land is self-evident as soon as one inspects what goes into the making of his products, both in the way of raw materials and in the way of the machinery and power he uses. Textiles, for instance, are made up with either natural or synthetic fibres, but the latter constitute one of the byproducts of the petro-chemical industry. Plastic goods, paper, in whatever direction one looks the ultimate dependence upon land is clear. As we have already had occasion to note, moreover, modern 'agri-business' is shackled to the need for a host of inputs related to the fossil fuels. The myriad processes of modern industrial society, in short, cannot be sustained without access to food, fossil fuels, and other products of the land.

If both capital and labour are sterile or unproductive without the co-operation of one or both of the other factors of production, what of land on its own? Clearly, unless one is going to employ contorted and preposterous definitions of 'productive', the land can produce without having labour or capital applied to it, can produce use-values that is. Labour cannot produce without land, but the land would go on producing if all labour was removed from it, though admittedly what was produced would quickly change were cultivation suspended. But we may proceed to look at matters in another way.

The peasant farmer in the subsistence sector of primarily rural countries can readily dispense with the products of the industrial worker, even where some manufactures from abroad (or from a domestic industrial enclave) have become over the years a habitual part of consumption. If necessity dictates — in the form of loss of cash income through market collapse, wartime occupation, or civil strife — former domestic and handicraft industries can be re-activated or new ones improvised. So while the industrial worker is absolutely dependent upon the primary sector, the subsistence peasant has no real need of the industrial worker.

There is, of course, one glaring exception to this: the need in the poorest, most densely populated, underdeveloped countries at the moment for imported fertiliser in a situation where human numbers have soared far beyond the carrying capacity of the soil with even the most intensive trad-itional methods. But it should be nóted that the dilemma is in this instance very precisely an outcome of exposure to imperialism, colonialism, and neo-colonialism, which, while providing conditions in which population swelled, at the same time prevented such developments as would have absorbed the surplus. I return to population problems in chapter four; I would at this point merely like to add that where, as in China, appropriate rural policies are pursued, self-reliance in the rural sector is still possible in poor densely populated countries.

The worker in extractive industry, although like the food producer in being in the primary sector, is as dependent upon the latter as any worker in the secondary and tertiary sectors. Moreover, the modern 'scientific' farmer is as dependent upon the extractive sector, and upon the whole complex of domestic and international exchanges, as is the factory worker, clerk, professional man, and all the others. What we have is a continuum ranging from the hunter-gatherer (with minimal application of human labour and capital to a naturally bountiful land), through the subsistence farmer to the precarious and wide-ranging dependence of developed indus-trial societies on real resource imports from the rest of the world, and par-ticularly from the poor underdeveloped countries, the last circumstance following logically from the accelerating depletion of all original domestic resources in industrial and industrialising countries and the comparatively pristine stocks in the non-industrial and neo-colonial countries.

Anticipating an indefinite prolongation and intensification of depend-ence — a necessary corollary of striving to maintain steadily rising living standards (in conventional terms of steadily rising production of physical commodities) while domestic resources continue to shrink — the leaders of the rich industrial countries have no option but to seek to maximise the geographical extent of the sphere in which they have a relatively free hand to prospect for and extract metals and the fossil fuels, and to skim off valuable proteins (anchovies, groundnuts, vegetable oils, and the like). Two points should be noted. First, although it is to some extent true that the rich countries would have access to the real resources of economically in-dependent powers, to the extent that the latter regarded it as in their own long-term self-interest to sell off non-renewable real resources, the question of pricing is really a crucial one, for the great virtue of neo-colonial control over countries possessing valuable non-renewable real resources is that these can be obtained at minimum cost. As import dependence continues to increase, this will assume a more and more pressing aspect because of its balance of payments implications, exacerbating those problems that will inevitably attend growing scarcity in any case.

The second point to be kept in mind is that modern 'scientific' agri-culture, despite its superficial efficiency and high level of productivity, is parasitic and ecologically unsound. It consumes more energy units than it produces, once account is taken of all inputs and concomitant services. As far as US agriculture is concerned, its apparent technological marvels and its real enough export performance ought not to blind us to the facts. The American farmer burns more calories in the production process than the ultimate product realises. It was fortunate for the States that, until the late 1960's, low-cost domestic oil balanced the cost factors in the agricultural energy equation to a great extent (i.e. the underlying imbalanced calorie exchanges were masked by very low oil prices and government maintenance of prices paid to the farmers for food). This fortuitous circumstance is fast receding. Again, while the American agricultural sector exports gross low quality protein in the form of grain (deficient in some essential amino acids such as tryptophan and lysine), it imports high-quality proteins (fish meals, presscakes of oil seeds, and the like) from the poorer countries. This is what might be called 'protein imperialism', impoverishing the diets of those who can least afford to experience further nutritional deterioration, in order to titillate the obese with forced-fed birds and animals (reared in units run and heated by combustion of fossil fuel).

The overall picture is roughly this. The poor underdeveloped countries as a whole annually send to the rich overdeveloped countries as a whole something like 3.5 million tons of high-quality protein (fish, oil cakes, peas, beans, lentils, etc.), while in return the overdeveloped countries ship to the underdeveloped about 2.5 million tons of gross mainly grain-based protein. Africa exports ground nuts; Peru fish; Mexico, Panama, Hong Kong and India shrimps; in each case at the expense of their own poor, who — the exports retained and fairly distributed — could take a giant stride towards nutritional adequacy. In contrast, as Ehrlich and Ehrlich point out, Denmark imports huge quantities of oilseed cakes and grain to support livestock (for their milk, butter, cheese, meat and eggs); annually, Denmark takes in 140 pounds of protein per head of her population, three times the Danish average annual protein consumption. Here we have the typical prodigality of overdevelopment. It has been calculated that the same amount of food that feeds 210 million Americans would feed 1.5 billion Asians on an average Chinese (that is, in Asian terms, a good, adequate and nutritious) diet. Animals must consume an average of ten pounds of plant protein to produce one pound of meat protein, while for cattle the ratio is as high as 21:1, which means that every pound of steak consumed in overdeveloped countries could (in theory) provide an equal amount of protein for twenty other people.* (See over page) American consumption of meat absorbs an amount of protein equivalent to 90% of the world's annual protein deficiency.

Obviously, howsoever wildly optimistic one may be about the world's agricultural prospects, this kind of energy-intensive, protein-wasteful food production cannot and does not hold out any hope of pointing the right way forward. To generalise it would demand resource inputs far beyond those proposed as possible of attainment by the most euphoric technological optimists. At present, as we noted above, something like 15%-16% of fossil fuels is devoted to agricultural purposes in the rich overdeveloped countries; to allow *all* countries to adopt U.S.-style agriculture would demand, as a minimum first requirement, that 80% of all energy presently available annually go to agriculture. To put the matter another way, striking in its starkness, 'primitive' food-producing methods yeild five to fifty calories of food for every calorie of (human muscular) energy invested, while industrialised food systems use up five to ten calories of (mainly inanimate) energy just to realise one calorie in food.

And now we must bring in the question of forces and relations of production. Once a society has attained the condition of overdevelopment (parasitic dependence, of necessity, upon the rest of the world) as a result of over-development of the forces of production, it is largely irrelevant what relations of production may prevail (i.e. whether capitalistic or socialistic). The socialist government and people of an overdeveloped society might decide to improve the diet of the poorer members rather than continue to over-feed the well-off, and might choose to alleviate the deprivation of the submerged rather than continue to churn out meretricious consumer goods for the generality of the comfortable. Nevertheless, if the mode of production is modern capital-intensive industry plus agribusiness (dependent on the fossil fuels and serviced by an enormous tertiary sector) that society must still, whatever its social priorities, take (net) proteins and hydrocarbons from the less-developed countries. It follows that the levels, regardless of the patterns, of per capita consumption of resources

---

* It is essential to add the 'in theory' because so much well-intentioned liberal and charitable writing on the subject of world hunger gives the impression that, with self-sacrifice on the part of ordinary people in the rich countries, and with sustained pressure on their governments to adopt more 'generous' policies towards the poor countries, 'we' (people everywhere) might achieve more equitable distribution of the goods (including food goods) available in the world. Unfortunately such naivety and woolliness (assuming that at least most of it is not simply cynically aimed at obscuring realities or invoked as a rationalisation for, in effect, doing nothing), distracts attention from all the *real* problems. These are to do with class structure and business interests in the overdeveloped countries, and with class structure and neo-colonial manipulation of the underdeveloped ones. Until we understand who *profits* from prolongation of hunger in the Third World and from extension of agri-business throughout the world, we are in no position to make adequate diagnosis and prescriptions; (2) in the long run, though it won't be 'folks', however well-informed and well-meaning, who will solve the world food crisis; it will be the poor of the Third World countries themselves, by revolutionary seizure of power and implementation of Asian socialist-style agrarian policies.

characteristic of the overdeveloped countries cannot be generalised.

Nor, incidentally, can the process be put into reverse, in the sense of elevating the living standards of the poorer group of countries by progressively impoverishing the richer: much of the wealth of the former has already been irretrievably dissipated by the latter. This point, it should be added, really underlines the ultimate irrelevance of the idea of 'aid', even ignoring for the moment its exploitative character as at present administered. (It would be intriguing to speculate further upon the suggestive parallels between the economic development process as it has taken place globally in the last two or three hundred years and the implications of the Second Law of Thermodynamics.) The mode of production that will ultimately emerge in the economically liberated Third World countries will have to be ecologically sound, of necessity, quite apart from any wise conclusions arrived at on the basis of contemplation of the consequences of Western, including Soviet bloc, industrial hypertrophy. (It is commonly accepted that post-revolutionary Russia has been almost as prodigal and thoughtless of ecological homeostasis as North America and West Europe, and it is now unquestionably challenging the USA as an imperialist power.*)

## PRODUCTIVE AND UNPRODUCTIVE LABOUR

I shall now try to sum up something of what I have been arguing in graphic form. We took note of the definition of economic surplus as the difference between what a society produces and the costs of producing it (above). This may be expressed for underdeveloped countries in another way without violating the analytical spirit and intention of the first definition as follows (and as was done in Chapter Two above): economic surplus consists of the difference between what a society produces and the consumption by the producers. This may be expressed in value or in real terms. For overdeveloped countries, consumption by the producers clearly greatly exceeds costs of production and itself includes a major part of the surplus. In value terms, however, production still greatly exceeds consumption by the producers. In real terms, though, this is no longer so. Consider the following set of figures. The abbreviations used are:

OC = Overdeveloped country
UC = Underdeveloped country
P = Production
CP = Consumption by the Producers
V.p.c. = Value per capita

* I regard both these points as of great importance, but do not on this occasion expand upon them. I do, though refer the interested reader to the bibliography.

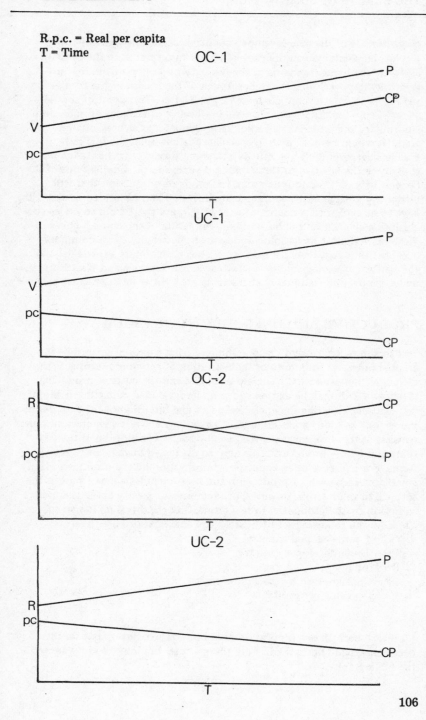

R.p.c. = Real per capita
T = Time

OC-1

UC-1

OC-2

UC-2

A comment on each of these is in order. No importance should be attached to the actual slope of the curves; it is the tendencies, and the difference in these as between OC's and UC's that are of interest and significance.

Fig. OC-1: Should CP be drawn so as to close the gap with P? This refers to the long and complex debate on the 'declining rate of profit'.

Fig. OC-2: The problems of estimation here are obviously very great, at least for aggregate data and for putting dates to the time axis. Clearly, for some articles of consumption — those for which import dependence is greatest — CP is already well above P (where there is any net import CP will be above P). Food is a tricky case: the U.S., for instance, is a net exporter of grain, but a net importer of protein. Perhaps the best procedure here would be to select some number — X — of key resource inputs, disaggregate to produce relevant graphs for each item, and then attempt to sketch a composite figure suggesting shape, magnitudes, and time scale for a diagram such as OC-2.

Fig. UC-1: Requires little explanation: colonialism and imperialism raised production (for export) and reduced per capita domestic consumption, movements broadly maintained under neo-colonialism (and helping to explain the co-existence inside a neo-colonial country of rising production per capita with declining welfare).

Fig. UC-2: The discrepancy here between P and CP may vary in a number of ways from UC-1, depending upon international commodity price fluctuations, whether there are food subsidies, etc.

A word of warning is perhaps prudent. I am well aware that a host of difficult problems, which long baffled economists before the distinction was finally abandoned as too subversive of the established order, plague the division of society into 'producers' and 'non-producers', or productive and unproductive classes. The Physiocrats took the firm position that 'The nation is reduced to three classes of citizens: the productive class, the class of proprietors, and the sterile class', where the first, engaged in the agricultural sector, alone enhance the nation's wealth and support all the activities of the various members (landlords, traders, manufacturers, artisans, etc.) of the other two classes. Professor Alexander Gray remarked that what the Physiocrats were getting at was that to increase the number of cobblers there must first be an increase in the number of cow hides.

Adam Smith had this to say:

> 'The labour of some of the most respectable orders in the society, is like that of menial servants, unproductive of any value. The sovereign, for example, with all the officers both of justice and war who serve under him, the whole army and navy, are unproductive labourers. They are the servants of the public, and are maintained by a part of the annual produce of the industry of other people. In the same class must be ranked churchmen, lawyers, physicians, men of letters of all kinds: players, musicians, opera singers, opera dancers, etc.'

Marx drew an important distinction when arguing that 'Labour may be necessary without being productive', a distinction pursued by Marxist Paul Baran as follows:

> 'what is productive and what is unproductive labour in a capitalist society cannot be decided by reference to the daily practice of capitalism . . . all of it is altogether productive or useful *within the framework of the capitalist order*, indeed may be indispensable for its existence . . . the isolation and measurement of (the) unproductive share of a nation's total economic effort cannot be undertaken by the application of a simple formula. *Most generally speaking, it consists of all labour resulting in the output of goods and services the demand for which is attributable to the specific conditions and relations of the capitalist system, and which would be absent in a rationally ordered society.* Thus a good many of these unproductive workers are engaged in manufacturing armaments, luxury articles of all kinds, objects of conspicuous display and marks of social distinction. Others are government officials, members of the military establishment, clergymen, lawyers, tax evasion specialists, public relations experts, and so forth. Still further groups of unproductive workers are advertising agents, brokers, merchants, speculators, and the like?

Baran draws attention to the fact that in overdeveloped societies, social welfare would actually be increased by putting a halt to the activities of a considerable part of the workforce. Mishan has suggested that we draw a distinction between 'goods' proper and what he has dubbed 'bads': unproductive workers would then be those engaged in the production of 'bads' (i.e. goods or services demonstrably detrimental to social welfare).

The problem is somewhat easier of solution in the underdeveloped societies, both in principle and in practice, because of a simpler and starker class structure and of the nature of the production upon which the vast majority of the population is engaged.

Needless to say, our decision on these questions of what constitutes productive labour and what unproductive will effect the graphs considerably. It may be remarked further that the case I have argued graphically above does not, in my view, conflict with Marxist analysis of the unique role of labour in the generation of surplus value; Marx's analysis is ultimately couched in notational (book-keeping) terms rather than real terms (in the sense I have used the phrase); though he was perfectly well aware, of course, of alternative approaches from his thorough acquaintance with the history of economic thought, his primary purpose was in the final analysis a *political* one, namely substantiation of the reality of exploitation of labour under capitalism (which is not denied here). The primary purpose of the present book is to stress the dependence of the overdeveloped countries upon the maintenance of a net flow of non-renewable real resources and other raw material inputs for manufacturing industry from the underdeveloped countries, for the populations of which this represents an obstacle to their autonomous national development. (In the next chapter I turn to consideration of alternative models, actual, as in the case of China, and theoretical.)

## The Social Profile of Overdevelopment

When discussing economic development, the economist has in mind secular improvement (movement in one direction) in a number of indices taken to measure or reflect improvement in the welfare of the population involved. Among these are: expectation of life; infantile mortality rate; literacy rate; percentage of the labour force in the secondary and tertiary sectors; calorific and protein value of the diet; percentage of consumer income spent on food; productivity per man hour; number of doctors, teachers and so on per 10,000 of the population; ownership of durable consumer goods (cars, TV's, washing machines, and the like) per household; and hours worked per week and weeks worked per year. Obviously no listing of this kind can be complete. Indices are preferred that can be compiled fairly readily from available data easily reducible to figures. Intangibles, important as they are, do not lend themselves to statistical recording in the way, say, the infantile mortality figures do. Of course we can compile figures purporting to reflect such aspects of economic change as the quality of life; for instance by finding ways to measure pollution level, traffic congestion, access to 'getting-away-from-it-all' holidays, and a score or more of other possible factors contributing to the more qualitative facets of quantitative growth. I shall have something to say in what follows on both the quantative and the qualitative aspects.

But let us start with the simpler facts and figures. Once industrialisation was securely launched, and the working class of the pioneering countries had begun to gain some benefit from it (partly by means of their own struggles; partly as a consequence of international unequal exchange), a number of key indices edged upwards. Improvement was not uninterrupted, by any means, nor was it at all evenly distributed throughout society. The fact that we still encounter malnutrition, homelessness and other indications of gross poverty in the richest countries of the world is proof enough of that. Nonetheless, on average, and smoothing the trends, we can see that over a long period in the richer countries of the world there have been improvements in the standard of living of the population as a whole. This shows up clearly when one looks at long term series of figures for infantile mortality rates, expectation of life, and the other figures we listed above. All have improved significantly in the rich countries over the last century and more.

Now it was natural to assume two things from this undoubted conjunction between industrialisation as it had historically taken place and general improvement in indices taken to reflect welfare. The first was that the former was responsible for the latter, and that therefore further doses of one assured further improvements in the other in the richer countries. The second was that industrialisation along the historically-determined pattern only needed to be extended to the poorer countries to start indices of welfare there moving upwards too. 'Economic development', or more simply just 'development' or 'modernisation', was the name given to the twin accomplishment.

Now, we have seen that both industrialisation and gains in living standards in the earlier group of industrialising countries depended upon imposing colonialism and imperialism upon the rest of the world, and — in the process — impoverishing them. We have argued, therefore, that the first path to development is, if for no other reason, not open to the masses of the poorer countries, now striving to take revolutionary power and to transform their own destinies. But there is another interesting point to which we ought now to turn: a large number of the conventional indices of development have begun to reverse direction in recent years in the rich countries. This is a highly significant indicator of profound economic change taking place in the rich countries themselves. And I believe we may take these shifting indices as providing us with a useful profile of over-development. Since evidence is accumulating all the time that the shift is no temporary matter, no stutter on the long secular sweep upwards, I have made no attempt at a systematic presentation of facts and statistics in what follows. It is much more important that the attention of readers be drawn to the phenomenon; they may then accumulate more substantial evidence from their own reading, research and experience.

## Life Expectancy

It is logical to start with expectation of life, for few changes in the last 150 years have been as spectacular and universally experienced as the greatly increased average longevity of people everywhere. To begin with, it was general amelioration in living conditions that contributed most to the improvement, and therefore the change was restricted to the industrial countries. Since the second world war, however, giant strides in medicine and public health have made possible improvements in life expectancy even in countries where general living standards are virtually stagnant. * But for some time now further advance has been effectively stalled. There are two reasons for this. In the first place, death rates have ceased falling in some of the most desperately poor countries such as India, Bangladesh and Indonesia as chronic malnutrition and malnutrition-related diseases take their toll; also relevant is the reappearance of former scourges such as

* 'A Latin American lives longer than a Western European of 1938, with a standard of living half as high. An Asian lives longer than a Western European of 1900, with a standard of living five times lower. An African lives as long as a European of 1880-90, with a standard of living three or four times lower'. (3)

malaria, the vectors having survived assaults by new miracle drugs and sprays and adapted accordingly. In the second place, people — particularly males — are beginning to die at a younger age, on average, in the richest countries than has been the case in the recent past. There are complex reasons for this, which I discuss below, but it is worth while looking at the figures first.

In the Soviet Union, life expectancy for men reached its peak, 66.3 years, in 1964-65; by 1972 it had declined to 65.0. For females, life expectancy has stagnated at 74.2 since 1966-67. In the United Kingdom, male expectation of life in the period 1968-70 was 68.5 — compared with 68.7 in 1963-65. Over the past decade, male longevity has declined perceptibly in Australia, while the US Senate Select Committee on Nutrition and Human Needs was recently told that the 'life expectancy of the American male is actually decreasing.' Yet for so long we have assumed that enhanced life expectancy was one of the almost automatic boons of economic development, and one of the surest indices of its accomplishment.

The latest estimates suggest that in some of the richest countries of the world even the infantile mortality rate is on the increase. The persistence of dire poverty and inadequate social services (despite the constantly swelling army of bureaucrats and social workers) help to account for this.

Such trends are inseparable from changes in diet and general health. I do not propose to engage upon an exhaustive survey of the complex issues involved here; I content myself with a few salient general considerations.

## Diet

Engel's law is as good a place as any to start. It was in 1857 that Ernst Engel, director of the Prussian Bureau of Statistics, published the paper that was to give his name to a basic principle of economics, namely that, with given tastes and preferences, the proportion of income spent on food diminishes as income increases. (Obviously, a starving man will spend every penny he can earn on food while equally obviously the multimillionaire, however extravagantly he eats, can spend but a tiny fraction of his income on food; in between, there is a pretty consistent relationship between level of income and that portion of it spent on food.) You may look at things in a slightly different way and see the operation of Engel's law socially as reflecting the growing productivity of agriculture and the support out of its surplus of an increasing number of people in activities outside the agricultural sector.

But since the great economic sea-change hingeing on 1973, and the resulting cumulative surge in food prices, the observed historical relationship is ceasing to hold. While incomes continue to rise, in other words, the share devoted to food is rising more than proportionately. And even inside this apparent reversal of Engel's law we observe a growing tendency on the part of consumers in the overdeveloped countries to revert to cheaper foods. In some cases this results in a lowering of the nutritional value of their diet (for instance, the calorific value of the British national diet in the first quarter of 1974 was 7% lower than in the last quarter of 1973). Alternatively — and paradoxically — by switching to cheaper but equally nutritious substitutes consumers may merely hasten spread of price rises to these in a 'knock-on' price effect (for example, a prevalent move from meat to peanuts and pulses may simply shove up the prices of the latter in a dramatic fashion). Looked at in another way, the reversal of Engel's law mirrors the contra-trend expansion of the primary sector globally, a phenomenon with which I deal below.

In Great Britain, it was estimated that the food value of the national diet fell in 1974 to its lowest level since 1953, when rationing was still in force for many foods. In 1975, rickets, a deficiency condition, was spotted among school children for the first time on any scale since the 1920's and 1930's. In a mere twenty years British consumers have inadvertantly doubled their intake of food additives, mostly in what food scientists call 'rubbish food' (instant soups, desserts, some soft drinks, many snacks, and some confectionery); more than 40% of these additivies had never even been tested for their secondary effects before being put into use, but it has been shown that migraine, eczema, dyspepsia, ulcerative colitis and many other common ailments can be traced to certain of them. Consumption of sugar in the UK has soared to an *average* of two pounds a head a week (compared with four or five pounds a *year* before the industrial revolution); yet sugar in these modern quantities is demonstrably detrimental to health in a variety of ways besides the obvious dental and obesity problems to which it contributes. Dr. Taylor, a former professor of medicine, observed (in relation to the extraction of wheat for flour): 'I suspect that animals are better fed than we are.' Animals receive the valuable wheat extracts that are removed from the flour, making the bread whiter, but lethal. Between 1965 and 1970, the daily energy value of the average British diet fell from 3,130 calories to 3,100, and its protein content from 86.5 grammes to 85.4.

These matters have, as one would expect, been much researched in the United States of America. It is worth looking at the American situation, since the USA was the first country to attain what is now known as the affluent diet, characterised by high consumption of fats and decreasing consumption of fibres such as raw vegetables and unmilled grain foods. Since the end of the second world war, American consumers have reduced their intake of dairy products, vegetables and fruit by between 20% and 25%, while increasing consumption of sugary snacks and soft drinks by between 70% and 80%. 'Convenience' foods have predominated. Not surprisingly, a nation-wide Federal survey concluded in 1970 that a 'significant proportion of the population was malnourished or was at a high risk of developing nutritional problems'. Large numbers of Americans were found to suffer from marginal deficiencies of vital nutrients like iron, riboflavin, and vitamins A and C. Between 8% and 10% of middle- and upper-class children had zinc deficiencies; they were lighter and smaller than other children and had a poor sense of taste. Iron deficiency, also widespread, was responsible for decreasing the attention span ('the time during which they can pay close attention to the teacher'). Among adults, 40% were technically obese but simultaneously malnourished.

Among the American poor worsening trends in diet have also been recorded in the 1970's. A 1974 special report stated that, despite billions of dollars poured into ever-expanding food programmes 'five years after President Nixon's promise to end hunger in America the nation's needy are hungrier and poorer'. Austin Scott commented in the *International Herald Tribune* (20/6/74) as follows:

> 'The report claims that even though spending for federal food programs jumped from $1.6 billion fiscal year 1970 to $5.1 billion in fiscal 1974, and participation rates in most programs increased, inflation more than cancelled the help those boosts were able to give. From December, 1970, to March, 1974 food stamp allotments for a family of four rose 34% and welfare allotments rose 14.7%. But the cost of food in the government's lowest priced "Economy Food Plan" jumped 41.7%.'

It should be noted that the US Department of Agriculture freely admits that its 'Economy Food Plan does not provide adequate nutrition over an extended time.' Furthermore, with all its shortcomings, the food stamp relief programme only reached about one third of those eligible for participation. The report, presented to the Senate Select Committee on Nutrition and Human Needs, argued that poverty and not lack of food was the crux of the matter (one recalls the astonishing sights when food hand-outs were arranged as part of the abortive attempts to obtain the release of newspaper hieress Patricia Hearst). Two key extracts follow:

> 'In a nation in which the wealthiest 1% possess more than eight times the wealth of the bottom 50%, in which the percentage of national income going to the lowest fifth of the population has remained the same for 45 years, and in which 40 million people remain poor or near poor, more than a food stamp or child-feeding program is at issue. The food programs cannot end their poverty, and fundamentally people are hungry because they are poor.' 'We have not asked, for instance, whether people buy some kinds of food at the beginning of the month and other kinds, or no food at all, at the end of the month when resources run out. There is no difficulty in finding people who cannot feed themselves or their children adequately during the last few days or week of each month . . . We have not collected enough information on the kinds of trade-offs low-income people are forced to make in their family budgets between medical care and food or food and rent.'.

Ironically, the cost of the 'Economy Food Plan' went up in 1974 faster than the costs of the 'moderate-cost' and 'liberal' plans, both of which allow for more meat, fresh fruit, and vegetables.

Diet leads to, and is indeed inseparable from, the question of health. Just as it was taken for granted not so long ago that 'progress' entailed a steady improvement in the calorific value and protein content of the day-to-day diet of the generality of the population, so it was assumed that *pari passu* the health of the people would continually improve, propelled in part by modern medical 'miracles'. Alas, the truth here again is slightly different from expectation, so much so that one is at a loss to know where to begin.

Bleached and refined wheat products and their like by eliminating fibre (roughage) from the diet induce major intestinal diseases like cancer of the intestine and rectum, now the second most common cancer killer in the United States. The manufacturing process involved in turning out 'instant mashed' potatoes removes the vitamin C otherwise so richly present in potatoes, and contributes to a variety of conditions, from heart disease to the slow healing of wounds, lower resistance to disease in general, and decreased absorption and utilization of nutrients. Many food additives have been shown to be carcinogens. Sugar, as well as rotting teeth, makes a major contribution to all the 'diseases of civilization' such as diabetes, coronary thrombosis, hypertension and appendicitis, gall bladder complaints, cancer, and other conditions prevalent in 'affluent' societies, but hardly ever met with in underdeveloped countries. Scientists have demonstrated that sugar attacks the pancreas and liver, lowers protein utilization, and impoverishes the blood. In the United Kingdom, cancer deaths went up from 111,700 in 1960 to 131,100 in 1970, with lung cancer rising by nearly 50% in the decade. Australia has one of the highest death rates from heart disease in the world — 464 per 100,000 persons, compared to 180 before world war two (the US rate, for comparison, is now 361). Conversely, when patients are put on low-fat, low-cholesterol diets as a preventive against heart disease it appears to reduce incidence of colon and rectum cancers as well. The correlation between the affluent diet and major killers has been corroborated over and over again.

## Pollution

Then there is the whole field of environmental pollution with its impact on health. Apart from spectacular manifestations, such as Minamata disease and Itai-Itai disease in Japan, there is a *general* danger, due to accumulation in the soils of the planet of all kinds of toxic substances which then enter the food chain. Both nuclear tests and peaceful uses of atomic energy pose hazards. Linus Pauling claimed in his Nobel Peace Prize lecture in 1963 that as a result of radioactive pollution caused by nuclear bomb tests two million people then living would die five, ten or 15 years earlier than they otherwise would have done. A decade later he warned that if safety standards for nuclear power stations were not made more stringent America would suffer 90,000 additional deaths from cancer yearly, 60,000 more pre-natal deaths, 2,000 extra cases of leukaemia, and 12,000 additional births of children with gross mental and physical abnormalities. The incessantly expanding and densening miasma of chemicals and radioactive fall-out in which we live is now believed to account for 85% of all cancers, according to the Worth Health Organisation.

Dr. E.C. Hammond, vice-president for epidemiology and statistics of the American Cancer Society, and Dr. I. Selikoff, professor of medicine and community medicine at Mount Sinai School of Medicine in New York City, in an appeal for more research, reported in the *International Herald Tribune* (23/3/74), said:

> 'Our world is changing, and, especially in the past 40 years, the environment in which we live has been altered to an extraordinary extent. The air we breathe contains gases and particles that never before entered the human lung. Our food has chemicals designed to improve its taste, freshness, appearance — but which are strange to our intestines, livers, kidneys, blood. We touch, ingest, inhale, absorb an ever-increasing number of synthetic materials and, in other circumstances, agents which have existed on earth but were never part of the immediate human environment. Cancers which we are seeing now had their origin 15 to 35 years ago, and cancer agents being newly introduced into our environment will not show their effect for decades. There has been and continues to be no pre-testing of materials for cancer or other serious disease. Examination is for serviceability, saleability, utility. Whether cancer will result is hardly considered.'

By a coincidence, further down the column, there was a report that the US government was considering banning exposure to the chemical vinyl chloride (an essential in most plastics) since it has now been linked to a rare form of liver cancer which has begun killing workers in the plastics industry.

## Drugs

Again, there is the whole field of drug abuse. After years of ill-informed euphoria, it is now clear that marijuana has complex and cumulative harmful effects, including damaged chromosomes, lower production of sex hormones, greater vulnerability to disease, disruption of the transfer of information from short-term to long-term memory, cancer, brain atrophy, psychosis, bronchitis, and prolonged cognitive impairment in young people. Heavy pot consumption overlaps with the so-called 'hard' drugs in two respects: one, the effects of a high dose of one resemble those of a low dose of the other; and, two, users of one are far more likely to be users of the other than non-drug takers. The percentage of those in England who *only* smoked pot (that is, did not use any other drug) fell from 80% in 1965 to 11% in 1970; all English heroin addicts also smoke pot. The connection between drugs and suicide is too well known to require comment; in Australia, which has the second highest suicide rate in the English-speaking world (South Africa having the highest) at 12.4 deaths per 100,000 persons, more than half are related to drug abuse.

Drug abuse shades into the related fields of pill consumption and alcoholism. In rich overdeveloped countries barbiturates, analgesics, and countless other drugs are swallowed wholesale, causing infinitely more pain, suffering, illness and disease than they were ever supposed to alleviate or cure: 15% of Australians receiving dialysis suffered kidney failure through abuse of analgesic pills and powders; fully a quarter of the persons visiting doctors in Australia in 1970 were dependent upon barbiturates. There are also 300,000 alcoholics in Australia, occupying 10% to 14% of the hospital beds, and costing the nation US $450 million yearly (which gives a per capita figure roughly the same as that in the USA). The connection between alcohol and car accidents, which take an appalling toll in human lives and limbs, and disproportionately among the young and fit, is well-known. Less well appreciated, perhaps, is the monstrous scale of the carnage world-wide; in the United Kingdom alone, over 200,000 people have been slaughtered in road accidents since the war, and this in a country far from having the worst per capita record. Moreover, as Whitlock has shown, there is a remarkable correlation between the traffic accident rate of a country and almost every other index of social pathology such as the rates of suicide, homicide, crime in general, divorce, abortion, and drug addiction. (4)

## Health

This is by no means the end of the catalogue of those factors in over-developed societies leading to declining health and longevity. The first generation of women put in youth on the contraceptive pill is now passing through the child-bearing age, and discovering yet another unpleasant side-effect besides the other well-advertised ones (such as serious birth defects in subsequent pregnancies): a percentage of long-time pill users have been rendered unfertile. Modern medical techniques are enabling overdeveloped societies to keep people alive and in active circulation who otherwise would have died or, in the case of some categories of mental patient, been institutionalised, thus to some extent frustrating the evolutionary process and ensuring the survival of the less-than-fittest, with long-term consequences we are only dimly beginning to discern. The cancer rate in rich societies, despite prolonged and increasingly expensive research programmes, is still rising, and many scientists believe it still has a long way to go as the consequences of prolonged exposure of the human population to radioactive fallout and thousands of chemicals in food, medicines, and other agents with which we come into contact in our daily lives work their way out. In the words of the American scientist Professor Sternglass, the overdeveloped countries are experiencing, and will go on experiencing, the unpleasant explosion of a cancer 'time bomb'. West Germany's hospitals are now treating one sixth of the population annually, an alarming measure of the general state of health in this prosperous and booming economy. Average height and weight of young people in rich societies has stabilised, having gone up for several generations as a result of improvements in diet and public health provision.

Ironically, the economic recession and soaring food prices have had one beneficial consequence: more and more people are regressing to growing their own vegetables, keeping their own poultry, and making their own bread. In 1974, sales of canned meat, fish and poultry in the United States fell between 25% and 60%, depending on the particular item, while frozen food sales dropped 16%. Consciousness of healthy eating patterns has never been more widespread. The governments of Norway and Sweden have both, in fact, embarked upon serious official programmes to reduce consumption of calories, fats, sugar, and alcohol and to encourage people to take more exercise. Interestingly enough, research in Soviet Georgia, renowned for the longevity and excellent health of its inhabitants, has shown that their average daily calorie intake is below medically recommended levels; unleavened wheat or corn cakes are preferred to bread, and vegetables to meat, and consumption of cheese, sour milk and low-fat milk is high. But perhaps the most telling indictment of health in overdeveloped societies is the report that Japanese Lieutenant Hiroo Onoda, who survived thirty years of primitive living in mountainous Philippine jungles before finally surrendering, was

> 'one of the healthiest 52-year old men in Japan today. During his stay in hospital he astonished the Doctors who performed about 200 tests on him. Despite his ordeal, he had few defects and was, indeed, in far better physical and mental shape than Japanese living in modern urban affluence with its pollution and nervous strains.'(5)

It is an interesting dimension of overdevelopment that we can only improve health now by back-tracking to patterns of eating and living we thought we had left behind for ever in the promised paradise of instant meals, deep-freezers, mechanised transport and other tools for living; progress can no longer be made by more and more medical research, medical provision and other such factors, improvements in which historically accompanied the development process.

## Literacy

The trend of literacy rates in the overdeveloped countries is unclear, and in any case much depends upon the criteria employed. To take one obvious example: if today a measure of literacy has to include the ability to programme computers and to read computer print-outs then any slight decrease in literacy calculated by reference to orthodox reading and writing skills would certainly be out-weighed by the rising level of computer skills. Nevertheless, there has been a profound change of attitude towards formal education, and it is as well to try, at least, to sort things out since undoubtedly an increasing literacy rate has always been considered an integral component of the gains to be derived from economic development (and conversely a high rate of illiteracy has always been seen as integral to the profile of underdevelopment).

It has for long been taken as axiomatic that it was for the good of individual children and of society that full-time education be prolonged for all to the maximum extent attainable. Recently, and more and more insistently, this dogma has been questioned. In addition, there is growing scepticism about the relevance of literacy (in the traditional sense) in affluent societies dominated by media other than the printed page. Perversely, however, faced with evidence of obvious decline in average reading and writing skills at school and college, educationalists in half a dozen overdeveloped countries, and notably Sweden and America, have launched a counter-attack on the once prevailing orthodoxy of modern progressive teaching methods, which stressed creativity and voluntary co-operation and participation on the part of students. Swedish findings on declining standards of achievement in children since the introduction of modern maths and project work and the abolition of grammar from language lessons have led to the reintroduction in schools of grammar and traditional multiplication tables. In the United States, awareness of plummeting levels of proficiency in simple composition among students at university level has started a boom in remedial writing instruction classes, with a Ph.D. in rhetoric (almost unheard of only a few years ago) now the best bet for those intent on an academic career in a shrinking market.

Which of the two contrary impulses will prevail is uncertain. In the end, whatever educational opportunities society provides, the issue will be decided by general social attitudes to formal education, social requirements for formally educated people, and, perhaps above all, by the positive or negative attitude of young people. As far as the last is concerned, there are again contrary indications, as the fashion for dropping or opting out of the formal educational process seems to have yielded, in many of the rich countries previously hit by the drop-out phenomenon, to a new concentration upon winning a more secure place in a less secure society by accumulating the necessary credentials for entry to the prized occupations and professions.

It is, however, worth making a couple of fairly speculative observations. If, as I surmise, we are to see an expansion of the primary sector and a considerable re-absorption of population into the rural sector, with accordingly more difficult access to forms of entertainment and relaxation available in towns and cities, the printed word, the book, will assume added importance as a source of both (and of course as a source of information). It may be objected that living in the country in modern industrial societies does not debar one from enjoying urban amenities; the private car enables one to escape the isolation of remoteness, while TV and radio bring information, entertainment and the best of national talent into the furthest cottage. But it should be borne in mind that it is intrinsic to the projections which emerge from the analysis undertaken in this book that there must ultimately be a decline in the ownership of private motor vehicles. Declining living standards, and shrinking secondary and tertiary sectors, must also in time result in making television sets (in common with all durable consumer goods associated with affluence) scarcer and vastly more expensive. Another consideration of relevance is that at least a portion of those volunteering to go back to the land, and of those responding to incentives to do so, will actively wish to dispense with many of the distractions of modern urban society and of the mass media. (On the other side of the literacy coin it is true that strictly speaking a self-sufficient small farmer or full-time farm worker has less formal, practical, vocational need for reading and writing skills than a paper-shuffler.)

The destiny of literacy rates in the overdeveloped countries is thus opaque. I am, however, inclined to think that, on balance, retreat from overdevelopment will in this instance, as with diet and health, yield an overall improvement in the relevant indices, a kind of recovery from overdevelopment. At the moment, poised as we are between a palpably dying past and an as yet unclear future, it is tempting to simplify and pronounce declining educational standards as yet another manifestation of an inexorably encroaching end of empire (along with bread and circuses, bloated bureaucracies, revolting plebs, and so on), and to abandon oneself to enjoying whatever delights social and cultural decadence and degeneration offer. On the other hand, smaller communities surviving the deluge to come may offer a highly hospitable environment for cultivation of traditional skills, including literacy skills. We must remember, too, that it was precisely the loving husbanding and treasuring of the great cultural achievements of antiquity during the dark ages that ensured the subsequent blossoming of the Renaissance (we specifically noted earlier the significance of the survival of Roman law).

## Culture

It would be illuminating to pursue the suggestion of modern overdevelopment as merely a specific variation of the perennially recurring group of phenomena accompanying and associated with the late-decline phase of a civilisation. I shall resist the temptation to do so on this occasion, contenting myself with two quotations which I believe capture the actual essence of senescent Western culture. Pitirim Sorokin characterises it as

'primarily a museum of social and cultural pathology. It centers on the police morgue, the criminal's hide-out, and the sex organs, operating mainly on the level of the social sewers. If we are forced to accept it as a faithful representation of human society, then man and his culture must certainly forfeit our respect and admiration. In so far as it is an art of man's debasement and vilification, it is paving the way for its own downfall as a cultural value.'

Speaking of the self-styled cultural 'underground' or 'counter-culture', American critic John Aldridge surely caught the feel of it when he wrote:

> 'It is all a matter of soul speaking to soul, lovers passionately sweating skin to skin, blown minds exchanging psychedelic mash notes, non-thoughts floating in non-words between nonentities.'

In such a climate it is perhaps somewhat academic to isolate and speculate upon the single strand of literacy.

## SECTOR DISTORTIONS

In turning to the sectoral characteristics of overdevelopment it is intriguing to note that a vastly top heavy tax-supported tertiary sector (and a state-subsidised secondary sector) have almost invariably been features of empires/civilisations in terminal decline. This being so, the glaringly obvious symptoms which daily confront people in the rich industrialised countries of the world today of cancerous bureaucratic multiplication must be seen as significant to the highest degree. A few figures clearly illustrate the trend. In 1961 the number of people in the public services in Britain made up 16.1% of those in the market sector (industry and commerce); by 1976 the equivalent figure was 27.5, and while the bureaucracy had grown rapidly the productive sector had actually shrunk. Of the total wealth created each year by the British people only one quarter was, by 1976, left in the hands of those who earned it; £60 out of every £100 of national income was by then being appropriated by the Treasury. And, not unexpectedly, as the services sector flourished in number, the quality, reliability and availability of services of all kinds palpably deteriorated.

> 'In American industry,' notes Professor Stavrianos, 'the number of administrators per 100 productive workers has risen from 10 in 1899 to 38 in 1963, but this increase in the administrative apparatus has not been accompanied by a corresponding increase in productivity. The same pattern can be seen in American government. In 1930, when the total US population was 123 million, there were 601,319 federal civilian employees and 2,622,000 state and local employees; by April 1973, when the total US population was 210 million, the number of federal civilian employees had jumped to 2,650,000 and the number of state and local employees to 10,800,000. Thus one person in 38 was a government employee in 1930, and one in 16 in 1973.' (6)

Yet indisputably welfare provision for the poorest had over the same period improved little, while urban decay had proceeded apace.

In Sweden, writer Astrid Lindgren revealed in a case which attained world-wide publicity that the tax authorities were demanding 102% of her income. In West Germany, in another well-known case, bureaucrat Felicitas Strippgen went to court to sue her Housing Ministry employers for more work, alleging that she was being paid the equivalent of

US $286 a week for doing nothing and that, as a consequence, she was putting on weight: 'I have put on 30 pounds because of idleness,' she said, 'How would you like to sit in a small office day after day with nothing to do but look at a few newspapers?' Well, apparently a lot of people do; never has recruiting for the civil service and local government services boomed so hugely, in Britain, in Norway, and indeed throughout the over-developed world. To understand the sectoral shifts taking place we must put them in historical context.

Sectoral distinctions were rudimentary before the adoption of settled agriculture. The fact that farmers were now able to produce more than they themselves could consume meant that there was food available to support other occupational groups such as full-time soldiers, priests, skilled craftsmen, courtiers, merchants, and so. As we say above, the inaug-uration of a world economy upon expansion of the western powers in the last few hundred years initiated a new stage in this direction, for the surplus now at the disposal of the conquerors was vastly augmented. Later still, the introduction of modern scientific agriculture, in conjunction with mass emigration and imposition of command over the entire world's reserves of fossil fuel and mineral reserves, enabled the imperialist countries to expand still further the percentage of their populations outside the agricultural sector.

To begin with, shrinkage of the agricultural population in the over-developed countries mainly contributed recruits to industry, and it was industrial exports which helped pay for cheap imported food. But as society became more complex, and as the laws of motion of industrial capitalism created increasingly obtrusive social problems, it became necessary to divert more and more people into what became known as the tertiary sector. The tertiary sector provides services rather than tangible goods such as food crops or machine tools. Services are intangible, and are often consumed at the same time as they are produced ( as in the cases of the services of a football team, of a telephone speaking clock, and of a teacher in the classroom). Economists up to and including Adam Smith (the great Scottish economist whose classic *Wealth of Nations* appeared in 1776) regarded the tertiary or services sector of the economy as un-productive, and indeed to this day there are special difficulties involved in trying to measure its 'output' and its productivity.

The tertiary sector grew and grew. If the so-called 'labour aristocracy' (comparatively well-paid skilled workers in the imperialist countries) re-presented one emanation of the economic surplus impounded from the poor colonial and semi-colonial countries, undoubtedly the vast and ever-proliferating public and private bureaucracies and diverse services represen-ted another. In 1851, sectoral composition in Great Britain was as follows:

| | |
|---|---|
| primary sector | 26% |
| secondary sector | 38% |
| tertiary sector | 34% |

In 1951 it was:

| | |
|---|---|
| primary sector | 9% |
| secondary sector | 45% |
| tertiary sector | 30% |

But if we exclude the category of domestic and personal services, the 1851 and 1951 tertiary sector figures are 25% and 27% respectively, and if we concentrate upon the public service and the professions the growth is even more striking: from 5% to 15%. Public sector employment as a percentage of total number employed rose from 23% to 25.2% from 1961 to 1970. And to this must be added all those in the private sector who are not engaged in production but in administration, distribution, advertising, public relations, and the like. By 1974 there were 11,171,000 people employed in industry and agriculture in the UK, as against 13,596,000 in non-industrial service occupations. Comparing the situation then with that of as recently as 1961 is most instructive:

| | 1961 | 1974 |
|---|---|---|
| Total employment | 21,789,000 | 22,297,000 |
| Transport | 1,649,000 | 1,483,000 |
| Distribution | 3,356,000 | 3,312,000 |
| Insurance, banking, etc. | 985,000 | 1,532,000 |
| Education services | 960,000 | 1,693,000 |
| Medical services | 779,000 | 1,130,000 |
| Leisure | 897,000 | 1,067,000 |
| Public administration | 1,280,000 | 1,551,000 |

This kind of transformation is not confined to Britain, but afflicts all the overdeveloped countries. Between 1961 and 1974 the ratio of non-industrial to industrial employment rose 33.9% in the UK, 18.6% in France, 15.4% in the United States, 14.2% in West Germany, and 10.3% in Italy.

There are numerous interesting features of this sectoral transformation. I can only draw attention to one or two here. In the first place it is clear that the vast increase in state expenditure as a percentage of total national income has not significantly altered the level of employment (as indeed is obvious from the now apparently permanently high unemployment rates in all overdeveloped countries); all that has happened is that people have been transferred in huge numbers from productive industrial employment to non-productive services (and notably public sector) employment. As noted above, this transfer has markedly *not* been accompanied by any improvement in the services provided. If socialism in China has seen labour being turned into capital, late capitalist 'socialism' seems to consist of supporting idle labour out of capital. It should be pointed out, too, that Soviet-style planning and development, highly bureaucratised, involves what might be called 'premature tertiarisation'; indulging in a swollen tertiary sector before domestic productive forces and overseas imperialist plunder have developed to the point reached by the richer overdeveloped societies of the capitalist West.

In the second place, it is no coincidence that the process has gone furthest in Great Britain. In the 1960's and 1970's the UK recorded the lowest growth rates in output and exports of all the OECD countries. But then the UK was the pioneer industrialising country, and is in many important respects the most overdeveloped country in the world. David Smith has noted in attempted explanation:

> 'the low investment ratio *and the fact that the United Kingdom had by far the smallest population employed in agriculture at the start of the period.* In 1961 the United Kingdom had only 4.0 per cent of its labour force in agriculture while even the United States had 7.9 per cent and Germany 13.1 per cent. Over the past fifteen years the share of employment in the primary sector has fallen sharply in most countries and *maybe a number of other economies might now start to suffer from some of the slow growth problems that have long afflicted us.*' (7)

In the third place, one should note the links with immigration. This is a complex subject, but we have to glance at it, even if only in passing. As the reserve army of labour in the declining rural sectors of the industrial countries dried up, new recruits for industry became hard to find domestically. Therefore immigration from poorer countries was encouraged; in the case of Britain, from the 'new Commonwealth' countries (the West Indies, India, Pakistan, and the rest); in the case of Western Europe from South and South East Europe, the Middle East and North Africa; and in the case of the USA from Mexico, Puerto Rico, and elsewhere. With the assistance of this massive recruitment of cheap labour from the international 'rural sector', the rich capitalist countries were able to generate a long secular boom. But it entailed crystallization of a labour caste system, with certain menial jobs more and more identified with and reserved for immigrant labour. Thus, when recession appeared, and with it unemployment on a big scale, one could observe 'white' unemployment co-existing with 'black' vacancies. It is perfectly natural that upward job mobility is easier to accomplish and accept than downward.

Unfortunately, 'better' jobs are not always more useful or more productive socially than less desirable ones, even though those doing them may feel — quite apart from the more generous rewards and better conditions enjoyed — that they are doing something more important. One consequence of recession, and of the government spending stepped up to counter its consequences, has been 'promotion' of huge numbers into the white-collar public services. In Britain, the net effect over the past few years has been a loss of about a million jobs in productive industry and a gain of about a million jobs in the public sector. And the public sector has a proven record of continuous accretion and of the ability to look after its own. The determination of many 'blue-collar' parents to see their children in 'white-collar' jobs is explicable by much more than mere snobbery; desk jobs *are* generally less demanding than field, factory or workshop jobs. But there is obviously a limit to the proportion of white-collar workers those in the productive sectors can support (i.e. feed, clothe, house, provide with cars, etc.). And that limit appears to have been reached.

At the other end of the scale, the rich countries in recession are having to cope with the dilemma that, while it is easy to 'import' cheap labour, it is virtually impossible to discard and 'export' it when its usefulness has been reduced by economic circumstances. The problems that thus arise are clearly inherent in overdevelopment, where sectoral shifts have left vital job gaps that can only be filled by cheap imported labour.

In the next (and last) chapter I return to the sectoral problem in over-developed countries, and discuss the way out. But it is worth making the point here that the pattern observable in the rich countries of a small primary base supporting enormous secondary and tertiary sectors was made possible by creation of a world-wide economic system dominated by, and operated for the benefit of, the original industrialising countries. That system is now being dismantled by the liberation struggles and liberated countries of the Third World. And as *they* opt for balanced economies, the rich countries will have no choice but ultimately to do the same, and by unco-ordinated and chaotic piecemeal adjustments, or by design, themselves return to balanced economies. It is interesting and significant that already, in some of the most overdeveloped countries in the world, there is already an unplanned (and to most planners an unexpected) move back on the part of labour into the farming sector: in Britain, for the first time in decades, the number of full-time farmworkers is going up, and this quite apart from the steady drift of formerly urban people (often middle class and educated) to rural cottages with smallholdings or small farms. In the United States, the 1977 report *Toward a National Food Policy* recommends government encouragement to small family farms, the break-up of agri-farms into smaller, family-size units, and in general de-centralisation of population and re-ruralisation (to use an awkward but useful term).

It should be noted that trends in productivity follow those in sectoral changes. Those countries, such as Great Britain and the United States, furthest along the path have shown the lowest gains in productivity among the rich capitalist countries since the war. Taking 1961 as the base for an index (in constant 1963 values of output per man-hour), the indices for six of these nations in 1974 was:

| | |
|---|---|
| USA | 154 |
| UK | 166 |
| W. Germany | 199 |
| France | 218 |
| Italy | 236 |
| Japan | 329 |

Source: R. Bacon & W. Eltis, *Britain's Economic Problem — Too Few Producers*, Macmillans, (London, 1976), p.161.

The progression down the list is instructive. Explanation is complex, and no one cause can be isolated. Among contributory factors one might merely mention, without allocating relative importance, the following: diversion of capital from productive industry to military spending and expansion of the public services; disillusionment with the rewards of hard work and, linked to that, leisure preference; the comparative decline in the effectiveness of the threat of unemployment and the whip of hunger in instilling labour docility and compliance; deceleration in technological invention and innovation and subtle changes in the prestige of different occupations. (Where are todays equivalents of the Victorian Great Engineers? It has been suggested they are probably television producers or rock stars). The table does show that there is a rough correlation between a society's rating in such trends and its rate of growth of productivity.

The range of indices at which we might look is limited only by our energy and ingenuity in devising them. Again, secularization — the turning away of people from adherence to traditional religions — has always been assumed to accompany development. But is this the case when societies reach the stage of overdevelopment? Today it is humanism that is on the defensive not mysticism, revealed religion, and faith. I do not intend in this work to pursue these intriguing questions. I want instead to turn to another material facet of overdevelopment: the fact that it cannot be generalized on a world scale.

## LIMITS OF DEVELOPMENT

The conclusion that Western standards of living, and ways of living-cannot be made general throughout the world by any conceivable means under any conceivable social order follows in fact from the historical analysis that has been developed above. It is a logical deduction from the parasitic path of development pioneered by the presently rich countries, for not all countries can be parasitic upon each other for the same advantage. But we can demonstrate it factually too.

One calculation produces the estimate that to raise the world's population to current US levels of per capital consumption would require the extraction of almost 30 billion tons of iron, more than 500 million tons of copper and lead, more than 300 million tons of zinc, about 50 million tons of tin, as well as astronomical quantities of other materials. This means, among other things,

'the extraction of some 75 times as much iron as is now extracted annually, 100 times as much copper, 200 times as much lead, 75 times as much zinc, and 250 times as much tin. The needed iron is theoretically available, and might be extracted by tremendous efforts over a long period of time, but a serious limit could be imposed by a shortage of molybdenum which is needed to convert iron to steel. Needed quantities of the other materials far exceed *all* known or inferred reserves. Of course, to raise the standard of living of the projected world population of the year 2000 to today's

125

American standard would require doubling of all the above figures.' The figures would have to be raised yet further if we were to build into the projection the possible rise in living standards over the intervening quarter of a century in America itself, and yet further again were we to try to envisage a world where all 'enjoyed' the per capita GNP projected for Japan at the century's end. (Japan's Economic Research Centre estimated in 1974 that even by as early as 1985 Japan's output per head could be approaching double that of the United States at that time, US $24,000 to US $14,000; in the context of our discussion of the prospects for generalizing high living standards we should note that other Japanese calculations suggest that by the mid-1980's Japan could be consuming a quarter of the then world production of oil, half of the iron, and *all* of the copper and nickel; an absurdity, of course, but a revealing and instructive one.)

Another calculation shows that

'with existing production facilities the poorer group (of countries — not the poorest one) would need about 500 years to produce per capita quantity of steel in use now characteristic of the US. Although production levels in the poorer group are increasing fairly rapidly (close to 50% per decade on a per capita basis) many decades will be required, even in the absence of any major upheaval, before the amounts of steel in use can enable those nations to feed, clothe and house their populations adequately.' (8)

But minerals cannot be mined and worked without energy. There is an almost linear correlation between high standards of living (or to put it another way high per capita consumption of minerals) and energy consumption per capita. At present world consumption of man-made energy is in the region of 6.6 million megawatts. Supposing one assumed that in fifty years, say, the rest of the world were to attain the *present* scale of U.S. energy consumption, and that the then world population were in the region of ten billion, total requirements of man-made energy would be 110 million megawatts a year — a seventeen-fold increase. It is hard to see this kind of target being attained. Mineral supply factors and energy problems, in other words, interlock.

We should add that projections such as these given above are, illogically enough, based upon the assumption that overdeveloped 'development' along traditional lines can go on more or less as before while underdeveloped countries slowly catch up along the same track. Such an assumption is, as we have seen, unsound. On population projections I have something to say in chapter four which follows. Nonetheless, inspection of the magnitudes makes clearer the fallacy of expecting all the world, in due course, to do what the West has done by adopting Western-style methods of production, distribution and consumption. Another way of illustrating this is by means of tabulating production and consumption of bauxite/aluminium (1970), copper (1968), and wolfram (1971) in each of three groups of countries (in percentages of world totals):

|  | 1<br>Capitalist<br>industrialised<br>countries | 2<br>Third<br>World | 3<br>Planned<br>economies |
|---|---|---|---|
| Production of<br>bauxite | 17.4 | 63.5 | 19.1 |
| Consumption of<br>aluminium | 72.8 | 5.9 | 21.3 |
| Production of<br>copper ore | 44.0 | 36.0 | 20.0 |
| Consumption of<br>refined copper | 75.0 | 3.0 | 22.0 |
| Production of<br>wolfram ore | 27.5 | 23.0 | 49.5 |
| Consumption of<br>wolfram concen-<br>trate | 50.9 | 1.2 | (47.9)+ |

+Inferred; source of table: *Kommentar*, no.11-12, (1972).

The pattern of parasitism is self-evident. None of the economists who have derided the pessimistic projections of writers concerned with looming mineral scarcities has offered to demonstrate, one, that such parasitism was not integral to the industrialisation of the presently rich countries, and, two, that *either* it can be reversed without affecting living standards in such countries (and without prolonged war) *or* that all countries can be parasitical upon each other for the same (finite) minerals. Those who extol the Western 'model' of development, and press it upon developing countries, have failed, in other words, to explain how the magnitudes in columns one and two in the table, are at some future point, to be transposed to the benefit of the poor neo-colonies of the Third World without damaging the interests of the rich capitalist industrialised countries.

One should also note from the table the comparative self-sufficiency of the planned economy group of countries (at the time the table was compiled consisting of the Soviet bloc, China, North Korea and North Vietnam). This is a highly interesting statistic, suggesting as it does that planned economies, unlike capitalist ones, are not dependent upon relations of economic parasitism with the poor countries. But when we break down the group into its components some interesting points emerge. In the first place, while it is perfectly true that the USSR houses the world's greatest treasure store of non-renewable real resources (and in that respect is the wealthiest country in the world), it is at the same time economically still a backward country compared with the richer capitalist countries. Production and ownership of such symbols of affluence as private automobiles, washing machines, hi-fi's, and the like still lag behind that of the rich countries, on a per capita basis. If Swedish standards, say, were ever attained nationwide, Russian mineral and energy resources would not appear as inexhaustible as they now do. In the second place, the USSR lacks the capital and technology adequately to exploit these resources. As a result, its leaders are desperately wooing technologically more advanced and richer countries like Japan, the United States and West Germany in order to persuade them to bring in their technical knowhow, their specialists, and their capital to work some of the vast dormant or near-dormant fields, such as the Siberian oil fields. In the third place, the high costs of production of raw materials domestically motivate Russia's leaders to seek alternative sources of supply both in her Eastern European satellites, and further afield, where they actively cultivate imperialistic neo-colonial relations with countries responsive to their blandishments. Soviet academic economists and Soviet spokesmen at international economic conferences have made clear Russia's interest in expanding still further its exports of finished goods in exchange for raw materials. (It is true that this must help bid up primary product prices internationally, but again the USSR frequently engineers barter type agreements, holding down the exchange value of the raw materials sought by hard bargaining backed up by threats and bribes.) At the 25th Party Congress in 1976, for instance, Premier Kosygin reaffirmed Soviet interest in and intention of 'having its co-operation with the developing countries take the form of a *stable and mutually advantageous division of labour*' (emphasis added). The very language is so familiar that further elaboration would be redundant.

The problems of North Vietnam during the protracted war with the United States were of course special ones. But both China and North Korea have actively pursued self-reliance and eschewed 'social imperialism' of the Russian kind. China's chosen path and prospects are discussed more fully in the next chapter.

This book has concerned itself largely with the 'real' aspects of international inequality, as opposed to international inequalities as reflected in disparities in per capita GNP between this country (or group of countries) and that in international capital flows; though, in truth, the latter merely mirror in a complex way the former (money, in Pigou's term, being a 'veil' behind which lurks the reality of wealth). Reverting to the table above, it might be thought that the enormous transfers of primary products, such as those recorded there, from the countries of the Third World to the rich industrialised countries must generate income for the poor countries. But mining, processing, and traffic in industrially required minerals is mostly in the hands of giant Western, Japanese, and multinational corporations, who therefore cream off whatever gain is to be got from trade in them. In the case of some internationally traded minerals control of and returns on production are shared with local state or private companies run by, and for the benefit of, local elites. Where Third World governments attempt to go further, trying to eliminate imperialist interests altogether (except as purchasers), they are likely to be overthrown by intervention master-minded in Washington (as in the cases of Indonesia and Chile).

Government and institutional (IMF, World Bank, Inter-Governmental Group on Indonesia, and the like) 'aid' to poor countries is often connected to raw material extraction. It helps the multinationals by paying for prospecting; for road, railway and harbour building; and for infra-structure provision generally, in the poor countries. In total value it is heavily outweighed by the final 'reverse flow' of profits, dividends and other remittances to private interests in the 'aid' providing countries. Consequently, the final net flow of value is in the same direction as the net flow of real resources, that is, from the poor countries to the rich. Far from the rich countries 'donating' capital to the poor, the poor still provide capital for the rich. For instance, from 1950 to 1965, US direct investments in the Third World totalled about $9 billion, while income on this capital transferred back to the US totalled about $25.6 billion and over the same period US-held assets in the Third World rose from $5.8 billion to $15.0 billion. Between 1961 and 1970, on an outlay of $28.8 billion, American corporations abroad reaped a *net* $35.3 billion. By 1980 it is estimated that the *annual* net return on US overseas investment will be approximately $20 billion.

I make these points because they underline yet again, in another form, the total inapplicability of the Western model to the poorer countries of the world. The fact that the rich countries are sustained by exploitation of the poorer is integral to overdevelopment, as it has been to all previous stages of capitalist development. The point that this chapter made at the outset, and which is worth repeating in conclusion, is that overdevelopment has this further dimension, namely that even with substitution of socialist for capitalist relations of production and social priorities, an overdeveloped country must remain parasitic if the method chosen to generate wealth is a combination of capital-intensive industry and capital-intensive agri-business, the whole presided over by a grossly inflated private and public bureaucracy and service sector. In the next chapter I look at the prospects of transcending overdevelopment.


## THE INEVITABLE SHIFT

Transcend the impasse of overdevelopment the rich countries must. Prospects along the trajectory of the past are bleak. Nonetheless it is reasonable to assume that every effort will be made to continue as before, despite the mounting evidence of accumulating intractable problems. Economists and government advisers of all kinds are trained along conventional lines. Those who benefit from the present dispensation are naturally stubborn and violent in its defence. Politicians who have come up by the old procedures and the old promises cannot be expected to knock the ladder out from under themselves by embracing radical reforms and abandoning the golden carrot of material affluence for all. Nor can we expect change to come as a result of an appeal to reason based upon deep research, convincing analysis and persuasive logic, helpful though such a contribution may be. On the other hand, we can see that great changes in the international economy have an inescapable logic of their own, a logic from which there can be no escape and which must ultimately prevail, however strong and well-entrenched the class interests in the rich countries arrayed against its working out. On this we may make a general point, and a particular one related to the post-1973 position.

The history of capitalism has been the history of tying a large group of poor countries to a small group of rich countries in a symbiotic relationship of overall economic inequality, whereby wealth was moved from the poorer to the richer. In this process, great changes took place in the social and economic structures of both. In the imperialist countries, the primary sector shrank proportionately, while the secondary and tertiary sectors expanded *pari passu*; in the colonies, semi-colonies and neo-colonies the primary sector expanded, the indigenous secondary sector was largely replaced by foreign imports (and latterly by foreign-owned firms located in the Third World as well), and the tertiary sector grew absolutely and relatively.

Now it could be argued that the tertiary sector in the overdeveloped countries does contribute something to popular welfare (leaving aside such activities as entertainment, advertising, and the like), most notably in ad- ministering distribution of, and providing, the forms of social support and advancement such as direct benefits and educational opportunity. However, even this is hardly a strong argument, since the working classes fortunate enough to live in welfare states by and large pay enough in taxes and contributions to more than cover every benefit and service provided (and often enough, despite this, have to suffer indignities in extracting their entitlement, or, as in the case of education, are subjected to the ideology of another class, the ruling class).

But there is another consideration of greater moment, and that is that relatively high working class living standards in the capitalist countries have historically been made possible by transfer of value (by various means) from the underdeveloped countries. In turn, non-productive tert- iary sector employees have, one way or another, appropriated a consider- able portion of this wealth for their own support, whether as pop stars or bureaucrats, with the bureaucracy in particular emerging as a group pecul- iarly well able to preserve its gains, add continuously to its numbers, and in general oppose any attempt to reverse this trend. There seems very little room for doubt that the working classes of the overdeveloped countries would be considerably better off if the tertiary sector were to be really drastically pruned (given that this was done by a radical socialist govern- ment, *not* by a conservative, liberal or social democratic one).

But that is to see things in an unreal isolation. Let us turn therefore to the underdeveloped countries. The leaders of the peasant guerrilla in

Cambodia were quite correct to detect that those in the tertiary sector in unliberated (neo-colonial) countries are almost entirely, if not wholly, parasitical upon the workers and peasants of these countries, taking much and giving nothing in return, waxing fat by helping alien capitalist corporations to plunder the wealth and labour of the countries they control (often as a result of alien intervention and/or support). They are, in fact, part of the servicing of that transfer of value of which we have spoken, and which, apart from contributing to the enrichment of the few, contributes to the comparative comfort and welfare of the many in the overdeveloped countries. In post-revolution Cambodia, the tertiary sector was quite simply eliminated at a stroke. Those who had flourished in it while all hell engulfed the peasant masses either fled the country or were absorbed into agricultural production, for the first time in their lives helping to produce their own keep.

Let us suppose that other countries once liberated from enmeshment in the net of international capitalism opt for a development strategy as radical as that of Cambodia. The channels by which value has been transferred historically will dry up. Let us merely enumerate a couple. As each liberated country restricts export of its primary products (diverting them to domestic purposes), a further continuous rise in their general price level will be inevitable. Moreover, many of the manufactured goods presently marketed in the unliberated Third World will become completely unsaleable there (or saleable only on a very much smaller scale), either because demand for them will have evaporated (luxury consumer goods) or because the newly-liberated countries will have begun substituting home manufactures for imports (necessities of life and simple consumer goods). This will necessarily intensify competition among the overdeveloped countries themselves for each others' markets, provoking trade war characterised by reciprocal protective restrictionism of all kinds (quotas, high tariffs, import controls and so on). The terms of trade will shift, steadily lowering the real wages of the working class in the presently rich countries. To the unproductive in the still swelling tertiary sector will be added more and more unemployed (partly from loss of overseas sales, partly from further automation, computerisation, and other such examples of 'progress'). As overseas sales contract, the ability of overdeveloped countries to buy essential imports of food, energy, and industrial raw materials will contract more than proportionately (as prices of the latter group will be rising while frantic trade warfare holds down export prices of manufactured goods).

It is apparent that if the majority of liberated countries in the Third World do pursue the attainment of balanced economies, free of unequal entanglements with the contracting capitalist world (and they certainly will: vide China, North Korea, Vietnam and Laos in addition to Cambodia), sooner or later the presently rich countries will obviously have no choice but to do the same. Western prosperity was founded upon creation of a world-wide economic system dominated by, and operated for the benefit of, the original industrialising countries; it is now being dismantled by the liberation of country after country in the Third World, against their stubborn and brutal resistance. But the resistance is ultimately futile.

In this context we should assess the significance of the oil crisis of 1973. But, while it is useful to pinpoint a specific date (and 1973 has already become a universally-accepted shorthand notation for the dramatic economic upheavals that have distinguished the 1970's, and that constitute a watershed between a past culminating in the 1960's and a future beginning to take shape), it is important to note that what hit the general public with spectacular force in and immediately after October that year had been building up for some time.

As far as oil itself is concerned it may be conceded at once that there was collusion between the oil majors and the oil sheikhs in jacking up the price in order to derive super-profits from consumers right round the world. But the ability of the unholy alliance of the two successfully to pull off their *coup* rested upon an underlying real change: the onset in the oil industry (and the energy industry in general) of increasing costs (diminishing returns). The quadrupled oil prices of 1973 stuck precisely because it has not proved possible to evade them by turning to alternative energy sources. The explanation is quite simple: expansion of production of such alternatives drives their unit cost upwards to match that set by the oil interests (in terms of energy efficiency per currency unit expended).

But, *via* the integral role of fossil fuel energy in modern agriculture, rising oil prices were quickly reflected in sharply rising food prices. Agriculture, in turn, faced increasing costs on a world scale. The impact of high oil prices, in fact, was felt throughout the entire primary sector, for the metallurgical industry consumes huge amounts of energy, and consequently throughout the international economy as a whole. Rates of inflation of an alarming magnitude gripped all countries in the capitalist world. To check inflation, governments resorted to credit restriction and unprecedentedly high interest rates. Serious recession had set in by 1974-75.

Now it is true that recession, through depressing demand (by people for finished goods, by factories for raw materials), eased primary product prices, including even oil prices. Planners and politicians in the overdeveloped countries heaved a sigh of relief, feeling that, after all, 1973 was not a portent of the end of the world as they had known it. But as soon as some recovery became apparent in 1975 in the stronger capitalist nations, such as West Germany, Japan, and the United States, primary product prices at once rallied, threatening to choke the new-born recovery off in its infancy. The explanation is clear: only when the level of economic activity in the industrialised countries is so low that primary product stocks build up, and their production is accordingly cut back, can the secular trend of rising primary product prices and the switch in the terms of trade towards the primary producing countries be arrested; as soon as a higher level of industrial production is achieved by expansionist government policies the inexorable movement of raw material prices is resumed, as stocks fall and production breaks new limits, further pushing up costs and prices. Industrial recovery is aborted by re-accelerating inflation and recalcitrant balance of payments problems. There are, therefore, both choke-off and ratchet effects, for industrial recovery produces its own limiting factor in shoving up raw material prices, while at the same time, to the extent that each limited recovery edges world production past previous peak levels, it ends up by depositing raw material prices on a new high plateau, from which they may partially retreat during the quickly ensuing recession, for that high to be itself surpassed and left far behind as soon as another recovery is effected. What we are experiencing, in fact, is the onset of diminishing returns (increasing costs) on a world scale.

Now it is perfectly true that human history has not been a record of uninterrupted progress. There have been innumerable setbacks, both on the broad canvas of the rise and fall of whole civilisations, and on the scale of the day-to-day warp and woof. It is equally true that there have never been lacking prophets who detected and proclaimed that the end of the world was nigh, only to be belied by facts (though it is interesting that the more intelligent and perceptive Jeremiahs have usually proved quite right as far as their own particular worlds were concerned). So, there have been ups and downs in the past, and those who have mistaken a temporary or local downward turn for a permanent and universal one have hitherto invariably been proved wrong. But is it as simple as this comforting formulation would suggest?

Every kind of human society of which we have knowledge has employed methods for regulating population numbers in such a way that the environment can support that society indefinitely with the food obtaining techniques available to it. Of course a sudden shift in climate or other such act of God can violently disrupt a homeostatic pattern such as that suggested. And this has frequently happened in the past, leading to the disappearance or precipitate decline of hitherto balanced societies. In societies larger and more complex than hunting and gathering tribes there is also a 'long wave' cycle of vitality-ascent, maturity, decline, all the dynamics of which are not fully understood.

However, let us here concentrate upon the population-resources aspect. Men naturally prefer the familiar and the less arduous to the unfamiliar and the more arduous. Hunter-gatherers could provide for the needs of themselves and their families with comparatively little labour. Only when population (for whatever reason) rose to the point at which, given the land at their disposal, it was no longer possible so to provide would a hunter-gatherer group reluctantly embark upon the more demanding food-obtaining method of settled agriculture. Each successive innovation, up to and including the present fossil-fuel based agri-business, was made necessary by the pressure of population upon the preceding food obtaining technique. But settled agriculture introduces a second causal factor which has to be taken into account: class divisions and exploitation. Nevertheless, surplus extraction by a ruling class is still circumscribed by the ecologically possible within the territory at its disposal and given the population control methods and food-obtaining techniques available to it. With capitalism yet another complication intrudes, for, as we have seen, there emerges an international division of labour and an international 'class' system whereby the sheer ecological pressures are felt at several removes from the locations where new food-obtaining techniques are made the subject of research and of subsequent investment and innovation. Again, though, the total number of people who can be fed is, as it must be, determined in the final analysis ecologically — that is by the overall carrying capacity of the land and fossil fuel available. (In other words, there are objective natural limits regardless of the type of social organisation of production and consumption favoured).

Now we come upon an interesting feature of the present conjuncture, seen in this light. After the second world war, sensational advances in medicine and public health made possible, even in the poorest countries of the world, quite unprecedented jumps in population numbers. It quickly became apparent that agriculture would be hard pressed to keep pace with the rising tide of people. A revolutionary method of food production was therefore called for; and, as one would expect from the historical record, one was forthcoming. But it had a characteristic that had not previously attached to 'improved' food-obtaining techniques: it could not be universally replicated. In all previous crises of ecological equilibrium, the transition to a more intensive form of food obtaining could, as it became more generally necessary, be generally adopted. *All* (or nearly all) hunting-gathering groups could, at need, turn to settled agriculture. All seats of settled agriculture could, at need, greatly increase production to keep abreast of rising population by steadily intensifying the production process through more and more scrupulous and systematic application of methods already known or readily borrowed and incorporated. But the move to modern agri-industry (heavily dependent upon the fossil fuels) which has been made in various countries of the world and in segments of the rural sector in most other countries of the world, cannot be universally followed. It is, therefore, a wrong turning in the evolution of food production world-wide. Moreover, even where adopted, it can only be but a temporary expedient (because stocks of fossil fuels are finite). We have, therefore, to look in another direction for methods of food obtaining and social organisation promising establishment of durable and generalizable population-food-resource homeostasis. We explore possibilities in the next chapter.

# REFERENCES

1.  T. Malthus, *Essay on Population*, 2nd edition, (1803).
2.  S. George, *How the Other Half Dies*, Penguin, (London, 1976).
3.  A. Sauvy, *Zero Growth*, Basil Blackwell, (Oxford, 1975), p53.
4.  F.A. Whitlock, *Death on the Road*, (London, 1971).
5.  *International Herald Tribune*, 22/4/1974.
6.  P. Stavrianos, *The Promise of a Coming Dark Age*, W. H. Freeman, (San Franciso, 1976) p84.
7.  D. Smith, National Westminster Bank *Quarterly Review*, November 1975.
8.  *Scientific American*, September, 1970.

# BIBLIOGRAPHY

1.  R. L. Meek, *The Economics of Physiocracy*, Allen & Unwin, (London, 1962).
(A full scale study of this important school of economists.)
2.  Barry Commoner, *The Poverty of Power*, Jonathan Cape, (London, 1976).
(Sub-titled, 'Energy and the Economic Crisis', Commoner's latest book concludes that 'the capitalist economic system which has loudly proclaimed itself the best means of assuring a rising standard of living for the people of the United States, can now survive, if at all, only by reducing that standard.')
3.  A. Glyn & B. Sutcliffe, *British Capitalism, Workers and the Profit Squeeze*, Penguin, (London, 1972).
4.  J. Gillman, *The Falling Rate of Profit*, Dobson, (London, 1957).
5.  J. Steindl, *Maturity and Stagnation in American Capitalism*, Monthly Review Press, (New York, new ed. 1976).
(Three analyses of the tendency of the rate of profit to fall in capitalist economic systems.)
6.  G. Borgstrom, *Hungry Planet*, Collier-Macmillan, (Toronto, 1967).
7.  G. Borgstrom, *Principles of Food Science*, Collier-Macmillan, (New York, 1968).
8.  G. Borgstrom, *Too Many*, Collier-Macmillan, (Toronto, 1969).
(It is convenient to bracket these three works by one of the most distinguished contributors to the whole field of food and population at this point.)
9.  P.R. & Anne Ehrlich, *Population, Resources, Environment*, W.H. Freeman & Co., (San Francisco, 1970).
10.  D.L. Meadows et al. (eds.), *The Limits to Growth*, Earth Island Ltd., (London, 1972).

11.    J.W. Forrester, *World Dynamics*, Wright-Allen Press, Inc., (Cambridge, Mass., 1971).
(Three of the books that sparked off the public debate on the adequacy of real resources to sustain development; reference 10 is the famous Club of Rome report.)
12.    A.D. Sakharov, *Progress, Co-existence, and Intellectual Freedom*, Penguin, (London, 1969).
13.    *Problems of Communism*, November-December 1974.
14.    *Problems of Communism*, November-December 1976.
15.    Andrei Amalrik, *Can the Soviet Union Survive until 1984?*
16.    A. Solzhenitsyn, *From Under the Rubble*, Little, Brown & Co., (Boston, 1975).
(Some further references to the USSR to add to those noted in the bibliography to chapter two; Sakharov shows the extent to which even this distinguished dissident is wedded to the pursuit of high mass consumption after the American pattern; *Problems of Communism*, November-December 1974, carries three articles on Russian 'overdevelopment', while that for the same months in 1976 has an interesting article on Soviet imperialism; Amalrik and Solzhenitsyn review various aspects of Russian backwardness and chronic inefficiency. The present author attempted a case study in Soviet imperialism in his contribution to U. Davis, A. Mack & N. Yuval-Davis (eds.): *Israel & the Palestinians*, Ithaca Press, London, 1975.)
17.    US Senate,   *Hearings Before the Select Committee on Nutrition and Human Needs*, U.S. Government Printing Office, Washington, D.C., 1973, 1974.
18.    Frances M. Lappe, *Diet for a Small Planet*, (New York, 1973).
19.    R. Mackarness, *Not All In The Mind*, Pan Books, (London, 1976).
20.    J. Yudkin, *This Nutrition Business*, Davis-Poynter, (London, 1976).
21.    M. Pyke, *Success in Nutrition*, John Murray, (London, 1975).
(A mere sampling from the rapidly expanding helping of books on modern diets, health, food adulteration, maximising human food off-take from a given area of land, and related topics.)
22.    F.A. Whitlock, *Death on the Road*, (London, 1971).
(A fascinating analysis of the impact on society of the car as a lethal weapon.)
23.    P.A. Sorokin, *The Crisis of Our Age*, Dutton & Co., (New York, 1945).
(Despite its vintage — or perhaps because of it — this remains, in my view, the most incisive description and analysis of the decline of the West. It condenses much that is contained in his *magnum opus*, *Social and Cultural Dynamics*, Bedminster, Englewood Cliffs, N.J., 1962, a work in four volumes which originally appeared between 1937 and 1941.)
24.    Carlo M. Cipolla (ed.), *The Economic Decline of Empires*, Methuen, (London, 1970).

(This collection of essays on the declining phases of such empires as the Roman, the Ottoman and the Chinese is introduced by the Editor with a typically cogent and lucid survey of the topic in which he points out that the economic difficulties of declining empires show striking resemblances. Readers in the present overdeveloped countries will feel a shock of familiarity in much that is recounted in the book.)

25.   K.W. Kapp, *The Social Costs of Business Enterprise*, Spokesman Books, (Nottingham, 1977).

26.   E.J. Mishan, *The Costs of Economic Growth*, Staples Press, (London, 1967).

(Kapp's pioneering work, which originally appeared many years ago, has now been re-issued, enabling us to appreciate its stature as an original and far-seeing contribution to economics. More recently, Professor Mishan has kept up the attack in a spate of books and articles, of which the one noted is his best known.)

27.   C.R. Hensman, *Rich Against Poor*, Allen Lane, (London, 1971).

28.   H. Magdoff, *The Age of Imperialism*, Monthly Review Press, (New York, 1969).

29.   Teresa Hayter, *Aid as Imperialism*, Penguin Books, (London, 1971).

30.   Joyce Kolko, *America and the Crisis of World Capitalism*, Beacon Press, (Boston, 1974).

31.   M. Barratt Brown, *The Economics of Imperialism*, Penguin Books, (London,1975).

(Five well written books which present a clear picture of the mechanics of modern imperialism.)

32.   E. Mandel, *Late Capitalism*, NLB, (London, 1975).

(The leading theorist of current Trotskyism undertakes in this lengthy volume a thorough analysis, abundantly illustrated statistically, of the current phase of capitalism, in an historical context. Although the present author has come to quite different conclusions from those arrived at by Mandel — see my review of this book in *Race & Class*, Vol. XVIII, no.1, Summer 1976 — the book is to be strongly recommended for the numerous facets of 'late capitalist' society upon which it sheds light.)

33.   F. Hirsch, *Social Limits to Growth*, Routledge & Kegan Paul, (London, 1977).

34.   R.S. Scorer, *The Clever Moron*, Routledge & Kegan Paul, (London, 1977).

(Two very different books from Mandel's, both deal with aspects of what I have called overdevelopment. Professor Hirsch points out that, while economic growth can extend and deepen ownership of material goods, there are some 'goods' which are in absolutely limited supply, 'positional goods', those the scarcity of which cannot be lessened by any means whatever, because not everyone can achieve the upper part of any ordinal ranking, whether in terms of position in a hierarchy or in terms of general desirability of situation; no matter how greatly we extend and improve education, in every social direction there can only be a few who reach the top, and there is no way of giving everyone a conveniently placed home in an adquate garden near his or her work and a short walk away from lonely deserted countryside. Professor Scorer believes that our present crisis, caused by our moronic cleverness, has no solution, only an outcome; in this respect, overdevelopment differs from the declining phases of previous civilisations.)

35.    Ivan Illich, *Medical Nemesis*, Calder & Boyars, (London, 1975).

36.    Ivan Illich, *Deschooling Society*, Calder & Boyars, (London, 1972).

37.    Ivan Illich, *Tools for Conviviality*, Calder & Boyars, (London, 1974).

38.    Ivan Illich, *Energy & Equity*, Calder & Boyars, (London, 1973).
(Essential reading for all those who wish to obtain a pellucid insight into the deep malaise of overdeveloped societies).

39.    R. Gilpin, *US Power and the Multinational Corporation*, Macmillan, (London, 1976).
(A useful survey of the international economic situation which faces us, and of the alternative ways out proposed by conventional liberals, marxists and mercantilists.)

40.    G.C. Hildebrand & G. Porter, *Cambodia — Starvation and Revolution*, Monthly Review Press, (New York, 1976).
(The first book-length *sympathetic* account in English of this extraordinary revolution which prefigures the future in a way scarcely considered by Gilpin in reference 39.)

41.    Joe Stork, *Middle East Oil and the Energy Crisis*, Monthly Review Press, (New York, 1975).

42.    M. Tanzer, *The Energy Crisis — World Struggle for Power and Wealth*, Monthly Review Press, (New York, 1975).

43.    Jean-Marie Chevalier, *The New Oil Stakes*, Allen Lane, (London, 1975).
(Three good introductory texts on the background to 1973 and its implications; the work by Professor Chevalier is more analytical and profound than the two others.)

44.    Ester Boserup, *The Conditions of Agricultural Growth*, Aldine, (London, 1965).

45.    Colin Clark & Margaret Haswell, *The Economics of Subsistence Agriculture*, Macmillan, (London, 4th ed. 1970).
(Two standard works, to be read in conjunction with Wilkinson's *Poverty and Progress*, cited in the bibliography to chapter two.)

# TOWARD HOMEOSTASIS: TRANSCENDING UNDERDEVELOPMENT

It is logical that we should conclude with a consideration of social forms which suggest themselves as alternatives to underdevelopment, on the one hand, and to overdevelopment, on the other. In this chapter I look accordingly at new models of development (China, North Korea, Vietnam, Laos and Cambodia) which differ strikingly not merely from both first and second capitalist paths but also from the Soviet model. Then, taking Great Britain as an extreme example of overdevelopment, I raise the question of whether such a country can transcend its overdevelopment and attain some degree of homeostasis (sustainable eco-economic equilibrium). The Chinese model has, as one would expect, most direct relevance for those underdeveloped countries with conditions reminiscent of pre-revolutionary China (countries like India, Pakistan, Bangladesh and Indonesia). But it may have lessons for the overdeveloped countries as well, in the field of environmental planning for example.

In the future, as in the past, there will be complex interaction between events and developments in the poorer countries and those in the richer. Behind the liberation struggles in the Afro-Asian countries lies a determination to terminate the international division of labour which worked to enrich the imperialist countries. If most in due course follow the example of the Asian socialist societies at which we shall be looking, as they surely will, it cannot but make it extremely difficult, if not impossible, for those developed countries most dependent upon trade (such as Great Britain) to continue along the old lines. This is one of the interactions which I take into consideration below. But first let us look at the Asian socialist countries, starting with China as the biggest and most visible social experiment in the world today.

## THE PEOPLE'S REPUBLIC OF CHINA

In the whole world there are only two areas of really intense human agricultural transformation of the 'natural" environment with a history of millenia rather than centuries, and these are Western Europe and China. Of the two China is the more remarkable in many respects since the Mediterranean-related societies of the West enjoyed and enjoy many natural advantages of soil and climate denied to the Chinese, while — despite her vulnerability to foreign invasion — China has much the longer record of a recognisably continuous socio-cultural tradition. It is worth looking for a moment at Chinese history in order to put the Communist achievement into perspective.

Over several millenia, the Chinese people have expanded to the south, west and north of an original cradle area in the Yellow River valley. But the distribution of hospitable land in the country has dictated where the bulk of this population could settle and thrive. Only about a third of the land mass of the country is used for agricultural purposes, with only 11% of the total land area cultivated. Yet where it is cultivated is is cultivated with an intensity unequalled anywhere else in the world. Rising population over the centuries has made this essential. Today, nine-tenths of the population live on approximately one-sixth of the area of the country. Population densities in the most settled regions are very high — up to 660 people per square kilometre in the Red Basin of Szechwan, for instance, compared with the world figure of 76, and with the United States figure of 21. A plot of land, worked by the most intensive Chinese methods, can support many times the number of people that an equivalent plot could support in the United States or in Western Europe. Rice in particular makes possible ultra-intensive methods. Only 27% of the cultivated land is under rice, but from this come 46% of total grain production. The other important food grains are wheat, maize, kaoliang, and millet. Historically, upland farming and livestock rearing have not figured conspicuously in the Chinese agricultural pattern, and before the Revolution much of the hill lands rejected as unsuitable for intensive grain production were simply denuded as their vegetation, trees, bushes and even roots, were stripped for use as fuel or for constructional purposes. The concentration on grain for immediate human consumption is illustrated by the following comparison: American per capita consumption of grain is 2,200 lbs. a year, but of this 2,060 lbs. goes to feed animals providing the meat constituent of the diet; the equivalent Chinese per capita consumption is, in contrast, only 400 lbs. almost all of this directly consumed.

## Traditional Chinese Agriculture

We saw above that the European agricultural revolution (which spread to the Americas and Australasia in due course) was associated with the incorporation of important leguminous plants, such as the clovers, into the agricultural cycle. The British agrarian revolution which led the way was picking up momentum from the 18th century, with 'improving landlords' drafting treatises on the new and better practices. The Chinese agricultural revolution took place in a much earlier period: the 8th to 12th centuries. Better milling techniques encouraged a switch from millet to wheat in northern China, while mastery of wet rice cultivation opened up the warmer south. At the beginning of the 11th century the then Emperor (Chen-tsung) introduced and publicised a fast-growing rice strain from Champa (in what is now known as Indochina); it nearly halved the time taken for a crop to mature, and therefore made double-cropping possible. At the same time, the cultivation of dry-land crops such as wheat, barley, and sorghums was encouraged south of the Yangtse, thus enabling land that was formerly marginal to be used. In this agricultural revolution, an important part was played by observant officials and landlords. Travelling about China, they noted improved techniques and reported these in text-books and pamphlets; the development of printing greatly expedited the spread of advanced ideas. Government offices put up wall posters telling local peasants how best to farm their fields. Four key features of this agricultural revolution were: one, superior soil preparation, improved tools, and enhanced use of fertiliser; two, improved seed strains; three, a 'great leap forward' in hydraulic control and irrigation techniques; and, four, extension of the national commercial network making possible wider growth and marketing of cash crops, the cultivation of which could be integrated with the cultivation of food grains without detracting from their yields.

After about the middle of the 16th century, another wave of innovations enabled Chinese agriculture to extend once again into hitherto marginal areas. This time it was thanks to the so-called 'American crops' such as maize, sweet potatoes, Irish potatoes and peanuts. These enabled culti-vation to be pushed up into dry hills, mountains and sandy soils too light for rice and the other indigenous food grains. Peanuts, as a leguminous, nitrogen-fixing, crop came to play an important part in Chinese crop rotations. Imprudent land practices in the uplands, while enabling cropping for a time, ultimately exhausted the soil in many formerly tree-clad areas, forcing farmers into a kind of shifting cultivation and leading to the abandonment of many once colonised hill areas in central and northern China.

Nevertheless a growing population was accommodated:

| (In millions) | |
|---|---|
| 1650 | 100-150 |
| 1750 | 200-250 |
| 1850 | 410 (± 25) |
| 1893 | 385 (± 25) |
| 1913 | 430 (± 25) |
| 1933 | 500 (± 25) |

(Source: D.H. Perkins, *Agricultural Development in China 1368-1968*, Chicago, 1969, p.240).

Controversy surrounds the question of China's failure to industrialise in the 16th to 19th centuries, when Europe was thrusting ahead. The issues debated are complex but the penetration of Western imperialism certainly seems to have exacerbated a degeneration and decadence already perceptible in Imperial China under the Manchus.

Traditional Chinese agricultural practices were on the whole homeostatic in ecological terms. Food exported from the countryside to towns and cities was matched by the return of carefully collected night-soil from the urban areas to the farms, where it was used as fertiliser. Wet rice farming was in itself soil-conserving; the technique demanded contour-ploughing and field layout and thus prevented run-off and loss of the fertile topsoil. Fish farming in the flooded rice fields kept down pests and provided much needed protein. Draught farm animals were fed on vegetables of high cellulose content indigestible to human beings. Pigs and poultry grubbed for whatever scraps man did not or could not return to the fields. Pest losses were compensated for to some extent by ensuring that pest corpses and pest excreta were dug back into the soil. Vegetable matter used as fuel provided a fertilising ash. Harsh realities dictated this kind of parsimony. The major defect of the traditional system lay in the inadequacy of social undertakings in the sphere of water control, for although China was the archetypal 'hydraulic society', the construction and maintenance of dams, irrigation, drainage and river banking fell short of what was required to minimise the impact of heavy rains or prolonged droughts the ultimate causes of which were, and always will be, beyond human control.

The Chinese themselves trace the breakdown of the traditional agro-ecosystem to the 19th century penetration of the country by Western capitalism and imperialism, though even before then population pressure had been taxing the available cultivable land at the prevailing ceiling of agricultural techniques, as was shown by rising land prices and the growing frequency of famines, typical end-of-dynasty phenomena. Superimposed upon dynastic decay, with its multiple consequences (such as neglect of irrigation works), there was now also the hectic and unprecedented creation of semi-industrial coastal cities and other inflated urban coagulates. These were predatory upon the countryside. Collection of night soil, integral to Chinese agricultural practices, was now neglected, and the valuable fertiliser was instead flushed down drains and ditches to the sea. The opium habit, encouraged and fed by European traders, undermined physical stamina and economic purpose. Violent anti-foreigner revolts raged across China, devastating whole provinces. The traditional system, for all its faults, had supported a steadily growing population for millenia. Now catastrophe became commonplace.

## Communist tasks

As early as the Chingkanshan-Kiangsi (1927-34) and Yenan (1935-45) days, when the Chinese communists were surrounded by enemies and forced to maintain themselves from the limited land accessible to them, Communist Party leaders, notably Mao Tse-tung, had begun to work out a distinctive approach to agriculture. Central to this is the idea that agriculture is valuable as such, (not merely as a milch-cow for surpluses with which to develop industry). The agricultural sector should, therefore, have its own equilibrium. Furthermore, there ought also to be the maximum possible degree of self-sufficiency, at every level down to the smallest unit of the totality. Clearly this imposes obligations which make mandatory careful husbanding, development and conservation of all natural resources to hand. It should be noted that acceptance of this responsibility by the basic units disposes of the double disincentive of any bureaucratically-inspired mechanical egalitarianism, for the less well-placed will not relax efforts in the expectation of gratuitous help from the better-placed, while the latter will not be discouraged by seeing the fruits of their efforts redistributed to others. The classic example of this is the famous model commune of Tachai which, by prodigious efforts, succeeded in pushing cultivation up the steepest hill sides by moving countless tons of rock and rubble to construct numerous tiny aprons of irrigated field.

So, on the threshold of 1949, the Chinese leaders, with a good deal of hard won experience behind them, embarked upon the monumental task of regenerating the Chinese economy and ecosystem. What were the basic parameters of the problem that faced them?

First, there was the sheer magnitude of the population: at around 600 million it had reached unprecedented heights, despite all the traumas of the preceding century such as peasant risings, civil war, and the Japanese invasion. Second, the available cultivable area was narrowly circumscribed. Third, the enormous problem of flood and drought control had to be met and its virtually unlimited demands on labour and construction materials reconciled with all the other matters pressing upon the new Peking regime. Fourth, the opportunities for improvement in the agrarian sector were already perilously limited, since the passage of time, the application of ingenuity, and human necessity had already edged yields up to very high levels.

Finally, we ought to mention the hardening determination of China's leaders to forego foreign aid; they had done without it throughout the revolutionary process, and were unperturbed at the prospect of foregoing it in the new circumstances (Russian aid, abruptly and unilaterally terminated in 1960, was meagre and grudgingly given; remittances from overseas Chinese were economically more significant). However, this commitment to self-reliance did entail placing yet further responsibility upon the indigenous agricultural sector to produce the essential investible surplus.

The Chinese communists set out on their task with two advantages: Marxism and a peasant backbone. Marx provided a general framework wrought in terms of the contrast between (capitalist) exchange values and (socialist) use values. He was also quite explicit concerning degradation of the environment as a direct consequence of the operations of capitalism which he had demonstrated required expansion to survive. 'Capitalist production', he wrote in Volume I of *Capital*,

> '. . . disturbs the circulation of matter between man and the soil, i.e. prevents the return to the soil of its elements consumed by man in the form of food and clothing; it therefore violates conditions necessary to lasting fertility of the soil . . . Moreover, all progress in capitalistic agriculture is a progress in the art, not only of robbing the labourer, but of robbing the soil; all progress in increasing the fertility of the soil for a given time is a progress towards ruining the lasting sources of that fertility. The more a country starts its development on the foundation of modern industry, like the United States, for example, the more rapid is this progress of destruction. Capitalist production, therefore, develops technology, and the combining of various processes into a social whole, only by sapping the original sources of all wealth — soil and the labourer.'

The Chinese people and the Chinese earth were the riches the communists had at their disposal; they could not have had a sounder guide in their approach to releasing their enormous potential than Marxism married to their own two decades of experience in the rural areas.

The fact that China is a peasant society, and that the Chinese communists, unlike Western mechanical Marxists, were able to perceive not only the revolutionary role of the peasantry but also that their labour must form the base for the transition to socialism, gave the leadership from the outset some powerful advantages. The peasant is hard-working, frugal, and an archetypal conservationist when intensive care of the land entrusted to him rebounds to his own and his family's benefit; his very life depends upon his agricultural practices being ecologically sound. Besides, dependence upon the peasant meant that a Soviet-style approach (squeezing the peasant for every possible drop of capital to invest in heavy industry) could not be contemplated (nor was it considered correct anyway); to enlist the peasant in the necessary transformation of the Chinese earth meant, at a minimum, retaining his support, rewarding his efforts with steady tangible improvements in living standards (including the availability of simple consumer

144

goods); and deliberately enhancing his self-respect, status, and cultural level. (Western palaeo-Marxists were shocked when Mao enjoined urban workers to go out to the countryside to learn from the peasants how to be good revolutionaries.) The Chinese development strategy had, of necessity, to be sensitive to agricultural realities and therefore to ecological realities.

## Communist Policies

The principles which have governed the Chinese approach since 1949 can now be discussed. In the first place it is important to note that China's leaders have consistently sought to combat materialism and consumerism, in marked contrast not only to the whole Western/capitalist value-system, but also to competitive Khrushchevian 'goulash communism'. Growth and economic expansion in themselves have never been the primary objectives of policy (except in interludes when Russian influence made itself felt either directly or via those in China enamoured of the Russian model — notably in the early years and in the Liu Shao-chi period between the Great Leap Forward of 1958-60 and the launching of the Great Proletarian Cultural Revolution in 1966); on the contrary, the transformation of social and political consciousness has had priority. Put in another way, transformation of the relations of production has been stressed above simple augmentation of the forces of production. This is not to say that growth has been deliberately eschewed or that it has not been attained; indeed, the evidence suggests that China has succeeded in maintaining a momentum of economic growth unrivalled by any country at an equivalent stage in the process, and on a par with the best performances of any economy of any stage of its development. According to figures given by the late Premier Chou En-lai at the Fourth National People's Congress in Peking in January, 1975, in the first quarter century of People's China grain production had grown by 140%, cotton production by 470%, and oil output by 630%; in the ten years from 1964 to 1974, he claimed, industrial output had risen by 190% (i.e. nearly trebled). Behind these phenomenal achievements there lies a clear grasp of the relevance of the questions 'how?' and 'for what?' 'how?' — by socialist co-operation and by full social cost accounting; 'what for?' — to raise the quality of life in town and countryside steadily and to move towards obliteration of the distinctions between worker and peasant, town and country, and mental and manual worker.

If the distinction between rural and urban areas is to be obliterated, environmental gains must follow. Giant industrial-residential cities, whether in rich countries or in poor, generate pollution, as well as intractable social problems. The stated policy in China is to reduce big cities and to stabilise medium and small cities.In pursuit of this policy, about twenty million people in China were transferred from urban to rural areas from 1959 to 1963, and as a result of the Cultural Revolution a further thirty million had been resettled in the countryside by 1972. Over the last few years 1.5 million school-leavers a year have left the cities to settle in the countryside — a sharp reversal of the general pattern elsewhere in the world, and one hitherto regarded as the inevitable accompaniment of economic growth and development.

Integration of town/city and countryside involves consciously directing policy so that the urban areas serve their immediate hinterlands, and are served by them. For instance, night-soil collection in built-up areas has been carefully organised so that nothing will be lost that can be and should be returned to the soil. Soiled toilet paper is collected and burnt, the ash being used as fertiliser — obviously a better method of disposal than flushing it away through pipes and drains to the sea. Local industries which cannot be accommodated at the commune level, but the products of which are needed in the surrounding rural areas, are located in regional towns/ cities, In return, the hinterland supplies its urban area with food and industrial raw materials. But food is also grown inside urban boundaries wherever there is a patch of suitable soil, and there will typically be vegetable communes within or abutting on the town limits. Corn and sunflower plants are grown in urban backgardens and backyards.

In most countries the biggest cities, and particularly the national capital, exercise an enormous pull, attracting a self-selected elite anxious to shine in and benefit from the superior educational, cultural, and general social surroundings. In these unregulated primate cities are to be found the most skilful and ambitious doctors, actors, lawyers, professors, and so on. The Chinese leaders have gone to great pains to try to reverse this process, by exhorting the best and the brightest to go out into the rural areas, and by striving to the maximum possible extent to ensure that amenities in even the remotest rural areas will be as good as those in the big cities. Judging by what one can observe in the way of hospital and school provision, for example, in even out of the way communes a large measure of success has been achieved in this respect. This may not have an immediately apparent *direct* impact as far as the environment is concerned, but a moment's reflection will reveal the indirect implications. Urban workers, intellectuals, and cadres are also encouraged, indeed obliged, to spend time working in the rural areas 'learning from the peasant'. It is obvious that the factory worker, let us say, will have a more personal concern with the problem of a toxic effluent from his factory process if he has experienced for himself the importance of a good pure water supply for agriculture. The peasantry, so often in the last couple of centuries branded as the class condemned by history, has been put firmly back on the stage of history.

The emphasis on self-sufficiency is another major component of the overall design. Communes are encouraged to do for themselves whatever they possibly can. Even if, as a result, unit costs of production in conventional terms are higher than they might be by taking advantage of the economies of scale realised by concentrating production of specific goods in huge centralised factories, we must allow against this the huge savings made possible by decentralised production, for instance in the provision of transport facilities (lorries, railway waggons, roads and railroad trucks, storage and handling facilities, refuelling points, and the like). Moreover, for the peasant to master industrial techniques is seen as a very important good in itself, once again helping to blur town-country, worker-peasant distinctions. The millions of urban workers resettled in the countryside obviously have a crucial role to play here in imparting skills to the peasants among whom they find themselves, and in leading the way in establishing and developing secondary industries. By 1970, the local sector (whose output, incidentally, is only partly incorporated in national income statistics which therefore underestimate China's achievements) accounted for 70% of the output of processed agricultural produce; 60% of all chemical fertiliser (these small rural plants produce fertilisers that are cheaper, faster-acting, and less soil-hardening than those produced by huge petro-chemical plants); 64% of all agricultural implements; and 40% of all road-building material. Even high technology production is sucessfully carried out at commune level: the manufacture of very sophisticated electronic tubes, X-ray equipment, and transistors, for example. Often these are turned out by men and women who, prior to their joining in such production,had had no technical training.

There are stringent planning restrictions on new factory building. Before permission is given by the appropriate planning authority to go ahead it has to be satisfied that adequate provision has been made to utilise or neutralise noxious effluents and emissions and to use rather than just dump waste by-products. Factories are sited down-river from population centres, and down from the prevailing wind. In plants inherited from pre-Revolutionary days measures have been taken to up-grade pollution control to acceptable standards. As we shall shortly see, great ingenuity has been exerted to up-grade 'waste' into some useful product. Naturally, as the Chinese themselves readily concede, they have still much to do before they can rest content in the control of environmental pollution, but they are very conscious of the problem and of its multiple inter-actions with economic planning in general.

Two large-scale projects deserve special mention: re-afforestation and water-control. Since 1949 trees have been planted in staggering numbers everywhere. Along city street this is to provide shade, help purify the atmosphere, and beautify. In the countryside tree-planting is an integral and essential part of the drive to transform the Chinese earth and permanently elevate its productivity. Great belts of trees, some of them hundreds of miles long, have been planted as part of the campaign to halt and reverse the creeping encroachment of deserts, to improve climate and conditions thus enabling settled high yield agriculture in formerly marginal or low-yield areas, and to stabilise hill slopes by preventing excessive run-off and soil erosion. Between 1949 and 1960 alone an area twice the size of

Britain was put under trees. The trees thus planted are of all kinds; one must not think in terms of the British Forestry Commission's stereotyped mono-arboriculture. There are trees which yield edible fruit, nuts, leaves or bark; soft wood and hard wood trees; tea and coffee bushes; and so on. In conjunction with reafforestation, the Chinese have re-introduced bird and animal species that had died out with pre-Revolution denudation. Many of these species are themselves useful — for instance fur-bearing mammals. China's forest area had shrunk, before the Revolution, to the dangerously low level of 10% of the total land area (as compared with 30% in both the USA and the USSR); this is rapidly being righted through a most enlightened reafforestation programme which is having manifold beneficial effects on the Chinese environment. One must contrast this most strongly with the situation which prevails in 'free world' countries in Africa and in South and South East Asia, where trees are being slaughter-felled without regard to re-planting in order to supply timber to rich overdeveloped consumer countries, notably Japan and the United States. In some countries, particularly Malaya, the Philippines and Indonesia, clearance has reached the point where alarming leaching and soil erosion threaten many areas with total ecological (and ultimately human) disaster.

In China irrigation and water-control works have also been carried out on a gigantic scale. Flood and drought, the traditional scourges of the Chinese masses, have accordingly been tamed. Since 1949 immense projects have been conceived and carried out to control and harness the huge Yangtse and Yellow rivers, and a host of minor waterways. Every-where dams, canals, river embankments and complex irrigation systems have been created and have transformed Chinese agriculture. Vast expanses of waste land have been brought into cultivation as a result — 2.26 million hectares in 1970 alone (the total area under cultivation was estimated in 1973 as 127 million hectares). Sixty million acres can now double-crop as a consequence of improved water-control and availability. Hydro-electric power production has soared as the number of dams has grown; electricity generated rose thirteen-fold between 1950-51 and 1970-71. In addition to the massive major schemes, millions of smaller canals, reservoirs, ponds and dams have been dug and constructed or consolidated since the Revolution. Former desert areas have been converted into flourishing oases in several parts of China, including vast areas of the north-west in Sinkiang. The mileage of navigable waterways has been vastly extended in a country where boat and barge play a key role.

An extremely important aspect of both reafforestation and water control projects is that they have cost the central government very little. Commune workers, at times of year when agricultural activity is slack, are released in huge numbers to work on these projects. They receive from the commune from which they hail their normal daily wage for as long as they are employed on constructional or tree-planting work. Much of the labour consists of earth-shifting; the great Haiho regulation scheme entailed the moving of 1.9 billion cubic metres of rock and soil, and labour input averaged 45 million man days a year for the principal works alone. Nearly a million hectares of waste land were reclaimed at a total cost to the government of a mere 60 million yuan (US $30 million or £18 million). We have here another example of how conventional approaches by Western economists to China's GNP estimates can, wittingly or unwittingly, under-estimate actual achievement. But the point to note is that the success of the Chinese way of 'turning labour into capital' brings into question the orthodox development planning wisdom that calls for massive capital out-lays by central government, on a scale that a poor underdeveloped country could only sustain with foreign 'aid' guaranteed subtly and not-too-subtly to twist the objects and direction of 'development' along lines congenial to private foreign investment and to foreign purchasers of raw materials and cheaply-assembled consumer goods.

At a different level from the big projects of which we have been speaking, but relevant both to their objective of upgrading the productivity of the soil and to the Chinese attitude to wastes, with which we deal below, is the scrupulous and conscientious enrichment of the soil itself. Green water plants are grown everywhere on waterways (leaving cleared pathways for boat traffic) and on ponds to provide valuable green manure. Tall grasses are cut for compost. River silt is dredged up for application to the fields. Where the soil is clayish, green manure and sand is worked in to it to make it break up more easily and to yield more. Where the soil is sandy, river mud is dug in to raise fertility. Wherever humanly possible denuded hill or gulch sites are deliberately recovered with soil laboriously carted from elsewhere. I saw for myself in the Dragon Well green tea commune south of Hangchow how bare hills had been carefully and painstakingly restored by heaving fertile earth dug up in the process of well and irrigation work elsewhere in the commune and laying it in sufficient depth to sustain the growth and flourishing of tea bushes. With such perseverance and diligence, Land itself virtually ceases to be an immobile factor of production.

## Decentralisation

Two of the slogans governing the Chinese approach to the problems of achieving social and economic development in harmony with Nature are 'Putting politics in command' and 'Better red than expert'. In other words, decisions, at whatever level (from shop floor or production team up to central government) ought to be governed less by a narrow concern for bookkeeping profit or maximum 'efficiency' in an isolated, technical, sense than by broader considerations with social, environmental, cultural and political needs in mind. Moreover, the further slogan 'struggle against the dictatorship of central management' draws attention to the fact that it is not considered enough if decisions satisfactory on the first count are reached by any means: they must be reached by means which involve the

the participation of all concerned — the working class must liberate itself. From the point of view of an impatient manager (whether of the capitalist or Soviet mould) who knows what should be done, and how, to attain maximum production and efficiency, time spent in thrashing out issues thoroughly by general discussion so that general understanding and assent emerge is 'lost' time. In China, on the contrary, such discussion is seen as an integral part of what the Revolution is all about, not only *as important* as the proliferation of goods and services as such, but *more important*. The path forward to Socialism is seen as involving achievement of the goal of social labour (producing use-values) replacing labour for wages (producing exchange-values). It is worth developing this point a little.

People in the capitalist countries are familiar, either intellectually or through inarticulated experience, with what work alienation means, with what it means to live and work in a society in which the major and even the minor decisions affecting their lives are made remotely and without much real reference to the preferences and aspirations of the generality of the population. In the Soviet system too alienation has characterised the production process from the beginning, Lenin and Trotsky alike extolling and calling for 'a military style of work' in the running of the economy, and specifically 'one man management' in the factory. To the extent that workers' participation has developed, notably in Yugoslavia, it has had the objective of engaging the identification of the workers in a given plant with the *profitability* of that plant, a profitability in which they may share by a variety of incentive schemes, bonuses, and so forth. Decentralisation in the Soviet bloc in recent years was forced upon the central bureaucrats by the sheer inefficiency and top-heaviness of centralised planning. It has entailed reducing price planning and an increased emphasis on profitability at the level of the enterprise. The workers have an interest, a direct financial interest, in the success of the particular plant in which they work. Each plant strives against others to make profits. The objective is the creation of exchange-values, not use-values. As the Chinese have long alleged, all this constitutes taking the capitalist road.

Chinese decentralisation has quite different characterstsics and objectives. The emphasis on small and medium enterprises, the breaking-up or strict limiting of giant enterprises, and the run-down in planning bureaucracies at all levels, is motivated by socio-political as well as economic considerations. The smaller the enterprise, the more readily it permits development of *real* as opposed to merely formal worker participation in planning and in decision-making of all kinds. Discussion is not about how that particular production unit can maximise its output, or about how the workers in it can maximise their incomes, but about how it can serve and meet social needs, the social needs of the people who work in it and their dependents, the social needs of the immediate neighbourhood and hinterland, the collective social needs of China, and the requirements for pushing forward the revolutionary transformation of the Chinese people, Chinese social structures, and the Chinese economy in a thoroughly socialist fashion. National planning is both flexible and responsive, on the one hand, and, insofar as direct responsibility is concerned, restricted as far as possible to those key areas where it is essential (foreign trade, production and allocation of important raw materials such as coal and iron, and so on), on the other. 'From the bottom up, from the top down' reflects the process by which local and central objectives are reconciled and harmonised by a process of discussion and accommodation, a constant watch being kept on tendencies to administrative centralism. Where production is so decentralised and dispersed that central planning would clearly be at best futile, it is not attempted; the provision of daily necessities of life and agricultural implements, for example, falls into this category.

## Recycling

But the Chinese also look at the other end of the question. We saw how a Western economist described the process of economic growth as one of 'converting valuable non-renewable resources into waste'. This kind of view has forced itself upon people in the capitalist industrialised countries (and to some extent in the Soviet bloc) by the evidence of their own senses: As the Chinese comment:

> 'Under the capitalist system, because the capitalists seek enormous profits and because of severe anarchism in production, large quantities of waste liquids, gas and slag are allowed to pollute the air and rivers, drain into farm land, affect the people's health, damage marine resources and harm agricultural production. In the United States, Japan, and in many other capitalist countries, industrial wastes have become insurmountable nuisances in society and unsolvable political problems for the ruling class, causing growing dissatisfaction and objection on the part of the working people.' (1)

In addition to modulating production to real needs, the Chinese are determined to eliminate waste both in the production process and in ultimate disposal of the final product. It was noted above that all kinds of vegetable and animal wastes are scrupulously conserved and methodically returned to the land in order to maintain and enhance its productivity on a long-term basis. But the elimination of waste, and with it, inevitably, a major part of environmental pollution, extends through the entire economy.

The Chinese line is that the 'three wastes' should, by imagination, ingenuity, and continual experimentation and innovation, be transformed into wealth. Numerous cases of how this campaign has operated and what it has achieved could be cited, but a few examples will suffice.

When I was in China in 1973, I visited the Hangchow Red Flag Paper Mill. At one time the effluent had been discharged without treatment into the local water network. This had had a damaging effect on agricultural production locally, and had, of course, irritated and angered the peasant farmers affected. Influenced by the Liuist line of putting production first (giving development of the forces of production precedence), the then factory leaders had ignored this side-effect as none of their business; presumably it was up to the peasants, or the district authorities, or the state, to do something about it. But as a result of the Great Proletarian Cultural Revolution, the old managers were discredited, and the workers themselves, after consulting with scientists, perfected a very simple chemical process whereby the harmful discharge could be converted into a useful liquid fertiliser for distribution and sale to local peasants. I saw the rather primitive plant which had been constructed for this purpose. That this process was not, in strictly book-keeping terms, a 'profitable' one was quite irrelevant; by 'putting politics in command' and relying upon their own efforts and resources, the workers and cadres of the factory had turned a 'bad' into a 'good', to the all-round social benefit. We might say that they had applied what would be called in the West 'full social cost accounting', if we allow for the important distinction that the Chinese take into account more factors (such as the important positive factor of the heightening of the workers' socialist political consciousness as a result of their practical experience) than would be allowed for elsewhere.

One more example from my own observations in China before turning to more general comments. At the Wuhan Iron and Steel works, I was impressed by the care that was being taken to minimise environmental degradation. It is true that smoke abatement was not all it might have been, but this the Chinese freely admitted, explaining that they were working on it. But in other directions there was ample evidence of successful coping with potentially harmful or unsightly by-products. For instance, the cinders and slag were being converted into cement and bricks for local house-building, into phosphate fertiliser, and into road metal. The waste water was being treated to neutralise poisonous contents noxious to fish in neighbouring fish ponds and at the same time to derive and abstract useful chemicals with a variety of industrial and other uses. The gas from the coke ovens was being used to make nitrogenous fertiliser. Great emphasis was given to such examples of multi-utilisation.

Other examples abound. For instance, at a Shanghai chemical works, 600 tons of grease salvaged from the city's dishwashing water over a three-year period was processed to yield 3 million bars of pure soap. Another initiative of this plant was to collect cigarette butts, from which enough insecticide to treat 1,500 acres was extracted. The Shanghai city authorities have established a waste and used materials company with many branches which organise 'door-to-door' purchases of wastepaper, broken glass, hair, feathers, bones and even bottletops, which are all processed for industrial or agricultural use — often in ingenious ways.' (2) Film workers in the city of Changchun retrieved 10,000 ounces of silver from the chemicals used in developing films. In the rural areas, thousands of small chemical plants have been built to process such 'waste' materials as cotton-seed hulls, corn cobs, chaff, and sugar-cane residue to make alcohol, fur-fural, acetic acid, acetone, glucose and even antibiotics. These small factories are situated right in the midst of the fields they supply, so that costs of distribution are negligible; fertiliser leaving the plants in the morning can be on the fields by the same afternoon. The ash from the coal brickettes used for domestic heating and cooking makes an excellent fertiliser.

> 'As part of the drive for frugality and diligence the gases from cooking ovens, furnace plants and other industry are also being utilised. For instance, over a hundred chemical materials are now recovered from coke oven gas alone. In the past, factories and plants poured waste gases into the air, dumped slag, cinders and ashes into ravines and ditches and let waste water flow into streams and rivers. But now the workers convert these into useful products such as synthetic fibres, rubber, plastics, detergents, insecticides, drugs, fertilisers, and dyes. The Fushan No. 3 Petroleum Plant pumps all its waste gas into bottles which serves as fuel for home cooking. We have one of these in our flat and they are very cheap and effective'. (3)

Several patterns emerge, but one way or another every fibre is being strained to minimise the impact of the 'three wastes' and to convert them to good use. Sometimes several factories supply all their wastes to one big plant specialising in reduction and conversion of waste. In other cases, waste and scrap collection is entrusted to retired workers, housewives and children who convey it to small-scale re-processing factories. Yet again, there are specialist firms engaged in the acquisition of waste and its re-direction to other factories with the capacity to use or usefully process it.

## Rural Science

One question with which we must deal is that of the possibly pernicious consequences of intensive use of artificial fertilisers. American scientists are currently expressing concern about the long-term effects in the States. US farmers are now approaching, if they have not already attained, the upper limit of what can be done in the way of intensive farming with maximum fertiliser use.

Recent research corroborates that the annual increments of yield per unit area or per animal have been steadily declining since the second World War for such agricultural products as wheat, barley, sugar beet, eggs and milk. Estimates suggest that by the end of the century the present impetus of improvement in production of these commodities will have been exhausted.

Two dangers now loom: the first is that toxic levels of nitrate compounds are being recorded in groundwater in parts of the great American Corn Belt and affected well-water induces birth defects and foetal deaths when consumed by pregnant women or farm animals; the second is that, the road of further intensification on given acreage being blocked, US farmers will increasingly turn to extending acreage by eating into hitherto virgin lands which, unfortunately, readily lose their fertility unless careful conservation techniques are used from the outset (in 1974 alone it is estimated that 60 million tons of topsoil were lost from carelessly farmed new acreage). There are clear warning signals here: the interests of future generations are being sacrificed to present needs.

We have seen the gigantic efforts the Chinese have put into conservation. But are they headed in the wrong direction insofar as their rapidly rising use of inorganic fertilisers is concerned? It appears not; there seems to be an awareness of the problem. As one reporter commented:

'. . . supplies (of inorganic fertilisers) are still inadequate and the present intention of commune members seems to be to keep it always as a complement to organic fertiliser, never a replacement. Many would see a full switch to chemical fertilisation as opting for the "capitalist road", sacrificing the long-term health of the soil for short-term gain.' (4)

I was told in China that extremely careful experiments were constantly being made at commune, production brigade and production team levels to determine which particular 'mixes' of organic and inorganic fertilisers were optimal for a particular soil, crop, climate, exposure, etc., thus matching input to the best long-term interests of the soil. This contrasts with the indiscriminate application of fertiliser too often characteristic of agri-business in the rich industrialised 'over-developed' countries. Incidentally, having developed chemical pesticides and herbicides, Chinese agricultural scientists are now having second thoughts and working towards greater reliance upon biological forms of pest and weed control.

Inorganic fertilisers, pesticides and herbicides are all relevant to the so-called 'Green Revolution'. How have the Chinese coped with the problems associated with the agricultural innovation once paraded as the 'solution' to the world's food problems? Well, to begin with, the social-structural problems associated with its introduction in the context of semi-feudal, semi-capitalist agriculture in 'free' Asia do not arise: the commune, production brigade and production team in China embrace the new methods and strains in order to elevate the general level of social consumption, whereas in the Philippines, Indonesia, India, Kenya and the like it is the rich peasants and landlord who seize upon the possibilities in order to enhance their own production for profitable sale. Besides, in China great care has been taken to develop a multiplicity of the new high-yield strains; at all levels, right down to the cellular agricultural-production units, every effort has been made to evolve varieties optimally suited to the particular local soil and other specific conditions. This is an excellent practice, and has the added merit of containing contagion, which can run unchecked where there is mono-culture of one particular seed derived in a central rice research unit, as has happened in parts of 'free' Asia.

The Chinese have another advantage: their leaders, cadres, scientists, technologists, and skilled workers of all kinds do not despise and disparage the humble labouring peasant. On the contrary, they realise and fully acknowledge not only that agriculture is the base for everything else, but also that amongst the peasantry there is an invaluable inheritance of wisdom bitterly earned over the centuries and an ingrained suspicion of untested innovation. These qualities are nonetheless complemented by a shrewd eye for and ready appreciation and adoption of new ways the peasants themselves can 'see' fitting into the immemorial rural round. Thus, in China, the peasants are not simply objects of experiments, students in rural extension classes, or recipients of directives from political superiors and agricultural 'experts', but are themselves fully involved on an equal footing with cadres and specialists alike. This means that scientific innovations such as the new high-yielding rice and wheat seeds are not just given from on high, but the scientific principles of selective breeding for high yields are explained *so that the peasants can conduct their own trials and devise their own new strains.*

Conversely, the cadres and experts listen to and learn from the peasants. The improvements large and small that ordinary Chinese peasants have pioneered since the Revolution are countless. For instance, peasant-turned-expert Yen Tse-kuei from Szechwan Province in Southwest China gave demonstrations at the 1973 Peking national agricultural exhibition of his method for preparing methane gas. He had built a 12-cubic-metre methane gas generating pit two years before. The gas, produced from a compost of night soil, pig dung and grass is sufficient for cooking and lighting for his six-member family. The resulting fermented dung and grass makes fine fertiliser. The spread of this method helped solve the need for fuel and good fertiliser, and simultaneously serves to kill off insect eggs and bacteria. When a new method of extensive planting of sugar spread to Fengkai county in Kwangtung province white ants and aphids caused serious problems but the peasants devised effective pesticides from materials at hand, including cow urine, salt, and wild plants found in the local hills. Peasants have also pioneered the deliberate breeding of insects known to prey upon given pests; Chinese scientists are now themselves devoting more time to investigating biological as opposed to chemical methods of control, as we noted above.

By and large, peasants and experts work closely together, the former learning relevant scientific and technical skills enabling them to stand on their own feet, the latter working side by side with the peasants in the fields gaining a far deeper insight into problems than they could do in the laboratory. The ability of both is enhanced, and the sharp barriers which typify the relation of urban 'expert' and rural peasant elsewhere in the Third World are lowered and distinctions blurred, in line with Chinese policy. Transcending the division of labour which had sprang up and developed *pari passu* with capitalism was precisely how Marx had fore-seen the way forward to socialism and ultimately communism. The proof of any recipe (of course) lies in the results (see table below).

Yields in tons per hectare, 1971

|  | Rice | Wheat |
|---|---|---|
| China |  |  |
| High stable yield areas | 4.3 | 2.9 |
| Average | 3.2 | 1.5 |
| Japan | 5.2 | 1.8 |
| Taiwan | 3.4 | 2.3 |
| India | 1.7 | 1.3 |
| USA | 5.3 | 2.1 |
| Indonesia | 2.4 | — |
| Bangladesh | 1.5 | — |

(Source: adapted from B. Stavis: 'China's Green Revolution', *Monthly Review*, October, 1974, p.28).

A couple of comments on the table add usefully to the information it provides. First, 1974 was a record year for grain production in China, output exceeding that of 1973, which had seen the previous peak; in a number of places exceptional yields, up to 12 tons per hectare , had been recorded. Second, over the years the central government has been able to build up a buffer stock of more than 40 million tons of grain (for comparison, the Indian government is thought to have 2-3m. tons) while the communes have been made responsible for storing emergency stocks equal to at least 18 months' consumption of their members; for the world as a whole, though, the contemporary outlook was unusually bleak, with reserves of grain at the time the 1975 harvest was ready to come in esti-mated to have reached their lowest levels since global records began in the late 1950's. Not only poor under-developed countries were caught up in this recession, for crops in 1974 were down in the United States, the Soviet Union, Canada, Australia and the Argentine as well.

Why was world agriculture precipitated into crisis in the 1970's? There were a number of reasons. Natural calamities, such as unusually severe droughts, floods and earthquakes, were in part to blame. But underlying trends with much more serious secular implications were also established during this period. Notable among these were growing resistance to technological intensification on the part of yields in the rich countries and steeply rising costs of inputs such as fertilisers (and in particular the important nitrogenous fertilisers). Various estimates by the FAO (UN Food and Agricultural Organisation) and the United States Department of Agriculture suggest that by 1985 there will be a very narrow margin between world food production and demand, even allowing for little improvement in nutritional standards (two-thirds of the human population currently live in countries where the *average* diet is some 95% of theoretical requirements). The World Bank calculates that by 1985 the gap between domestic production of food grains in the developing countries and demand there could be in the order of 77 million tons — a figure which is much in excess of the exportable surplus the major developed food grain producers expect to have available then.

However, none of these estimates allow for the possibility — a very real one — of other presently underdeveloped countries winning liberation in the late 1970's and the 1980's and transforming their agricultural prospects much as the Chinese have succeeded in doing. It should also be borne in mind in assessing these and similar projections that Western and Western-dominated institutional sources (such as the World Bank) invariably underestimate food production in the Asian socialist countries, and — in flagrant contradiction of the evidence — discount the possibility of sustained improvement in per capita food production there in the years ahead. The presumption is that socialism and agricultural progress are incompatible. But there is also the conscious or unconscious bias inevitably induced by the financial attractiveness to the corporate food giants of some over-developed countries — such as the United States, Canada and Australia — of exporting food grains to poor countries that remain dependent. In this respect the contrasting experiences and prospects of India and China are instructive, for although China imports food, it also exports it (and generally exports far more in value terms than it imports — the favourable excess reaching US $595 million in 1973), while India has *never*, since independence, exported food and generally has to rely on vast imports to balance the domestic food budget — imports that have to be paid for by accepting American PL480 food aid with attendant strings attached.

While world harvests were generally more bounteous in 1975 and 1976 than in the preceding lean years, problems remain. In the rich capitalist grain exporting countries pressure is being exerted by farmers' lobbies and by the big grain trading corporations to have acreage restricted and support prices boosted lest relative abundance threaten profits. In the poor countries of the Third World, landlordism, hoarding and speculation ensure that little benefit of Nature's bounty seeps through to the poor and needy. Only in liberated countries like China are bumper crops faithfully registered in a commensurate improvement in general welfare.

## Population

It is impossible to put China's food-growing successes in perspective without looking at what has been happening to her population. In pre-revolutionary China, to father a large family (with sons particularly important) was the ambition of every husband. Yet today attitudes have changed fundamentally. Between 1970 and 1975 the Chinese population growth rate dropped from 1.85% to 1.18% — the most rapid demographic transition on record, according to the 1976 Worldwatch Research Institute report on world population. This remarkable achievement is thrown into relief against other Third World growth rates: the Ivory Coast's 3.8%, Libya's 3.7% Mexico's 3.5%, Liberia's and Syria's 3.3%, Pakistan's and Brazil's 2.9%, Bangladesh's 2.7%, and India's 2.3%, for instance. The immediate objective of Chinese government policy is to reduce the national population growth rate to 0.9% per annum (that is, roughly in line with countries such as 1960's Germany and Italy). It had to be noted, too, that this rapid decline in the rate of growth of population has been accomplished while mortality rates, particularly infant mortality rates, have been moving downwards dramatically in response to the immense improvements in public health and medical provision in People's China. Dr. Lester Brown, in presenting the Worldwatch report, said that China's performance should come as no surprise:

'. . . comprehensive Chinese effort focuses not only on increasing family planning services, including abortion, but also upon reshaping economic and social policies to encourage small families, and on an intensive public education campaign extolling the benefits of smaller families'. (5)

In popularising family planning, cadres stress that its adoption is a major contribution to socialist construction and socialist revolution, consolidating the victories in production, and acting as a major factor in the liberation of women. In urban and rural areas alike, family planning advice is available; operations and contraceptives are free of charge; cadres set an example of small families; outside marriage chastity is seen as a virtue and enjoined, while within it restraint is tacitly approved. Of equal, if not greater, importance is the perceptible relationship between effort and reward; the Chinese masses know from their own experience that their hard work and their restricted families have brought them steadily improving living standards. In any case, as far as the vital rural areas are concerned, collective methods of production have removed any advantage a peasant might previously have gained from having several sons to toil with him in the fields, while parents still have the obligation of saving in order to 'set-up' their children on marriage. In the cities, rates of population growth are already very low: in Changsha 1.1%, in Peking 0.97%, and in Shanghai 0.48%. In Suchiching Commune near Peking, the rate dropped from 1.33% in 1972 to 1.13% in 1973. (6) China appears likely to attain, through conscious policy intelligently implemented, its target of near-stable population by the end of the century.

## Inflation

Price rises of inordinate proportions have seriously alarmed and incommoded the governments and peoples in the capitalist countries in the 1970's. Even the countries of the Soviet bloc have not been left unscathed by the scourge of inflation. Yet again, the Chinese experience is instructive. Since the pre-revolution hyper-inflation was adroitly brought under control by the new Chinese communist leaders, the price level has been kept remarkably steady, with if anything a tendency for the prices of necessities and consumer goods to fall. Paradoxically, perhaps, this has been achieved principally by pursuing a conservative and 'orthodox' financial policy, one that would have brought nods of approval from Gladstonian Chancellors of the Exchequer. Among the main ingredients have been: one, balancing the national budget (which covers a major part of the country's investment programme); two, keeping wage rises slightly in arrears of gains in productivity; three, balancing the overseas account; four, regulating currency in circulation by the operations of the central (People's) Bank; five, encouraging savings; and, six, paying labour for work performed (in agriculture, once a year, in industry, monthly). As in the pre-Hire Purchase Victorian days in Britain, if you want something you work and put aside savings until you have accumulated the needed sum. It is true that China has been greatly assisted in its successful combatting of inflation by the fact that her foreign trade as a percentage of national income is probably the lowest in the world. Self-sufficiency in oil (China exports oil to neighbouring countries such as North Vietnam, Thailand and Japan) has also been of great help. Nonetheless, to keep prices steady in today's world is not something to be written off as of negligible significance.

## Postscript on China

It is too early at the time of writing (early 1977) to assess the full significance and implications of the major changes which have taken place in China in the last eighteen months. Three of the greatest leaders who guided the Chinese people through the ordeal of revolution and the tasks of socialist reconstruction died in quick succession: Chu Teh, Chou En-lai and Mao Tse-tung. Hua Kuo-feng emerged as the new Premier and Chairman of the Communist Party of China, and the retrospectively dubbed 'gang of four' (Chiang Ching, Mao's widow; Chang Chun-chiao; Wang Hung-wen; and Yao Wen-yuan) were arrested and vilified. While continuity with the preceding period was and is stressed repeatedly, particularly with respect to furtherance of Mao's characteristic social, political and economic ideas, some commentators elect to detect a significant shift in emphasis in practice. This shift is alleged to be in favour of accelerated 'modernisation' in industry and the armed forces.

Chairman Hua himself has frequently pledged his loyalty to the ideas of his illustrious predecessor, as in his May Day speech in 1977. But on that occasion he called for sustained efforts to make China a modern industrial power and underlined the need to speed up military modernisation (meaning, according to Western observers, primarily acquisition of 'sophisticated' equipment and a conventional defence/offence capability). Mao did not deny the need for China to become a great industrial power. But he did emphasise incessantly the dangers inherent in placing construction of heavy industry above every other objective. In his 1956 speech on 'Ten Major Relations', which has been published and widely circulated by the Hua government, Mao specifically criticised the Russians for their '. . . lopsided stress on heavy industry to the neglect of agriculture and light industry . . .', resulting in '. . . a shortage of goods on the market and an unstable currency'. The Soviet policy of accumulation for the rapid expansion of heavy industry had had bad effects because of '. . . measures which squeezed the peasants very hard. It takes too much from the peasants at too low a price through its system of so-called obligatory sales and other measures. This method of capital accumulation has seriously dampened the peasants' enthusiasm for production. You want the hen to lay more eggs and yet you don't feed it, you want the horse to run fast and yet you don't let it graze. What kind of logic is that?'

It is obviously reassuring that the new leaders have chosen to nail the banner of the 'Ten Major Relations' to their mast, to the extent that it embodies all that has made Maoist development strategy distinctive. As far as the armed forces are concerned, the emphasis on modernisation need not entail more than adapting basically Maoist strategy to changing tactical imperatives and circumstances. An American visitor, in China at the end of 1976 at the invitation of the Defence and Foreign Ministries, summarised his view of the then state of the Chinese armed forces:

> 'The overall impression is of hard-working, well-trained forces proud of their role. This is balanced in both the air force and the army by the impression that they are preparing to fight a war in the 1970's with the equipment of the 1950's.'

But he himself reported that the officers with whom he spoke continued to adhere to the Maoist credos that 'The role played by the soldier is decisive' and that 'The man who knows why he fights and for what he fights will be victorious'. (7) Replacing older weapons by new ones does not necessarily imply abandoning the Maoist cellular defence-in-depth strategy, whereby territory can be swapped for time, and every part of China can independently maintain resistance to an invader whatever happens to every other part of the country.

Caution enjoins us, therefore, to conclude that it would be premature to assert that China has, with the death of Mao Tse-tung, been wrenched off course and headed in an altogether different and in effect more 'conventional' developmental course. Time alone will tell. Nothing that happens, however, can obscure or diminish the outstanding contributions Mao and his closest comrades made in their quarter of a century in power to fashioning a distinctive development strategy, one more effective in practice, more relevant to the problems faced, more democratic in implementation, and more egalitarian in the result than any hitherto.

# NORTH KOREA

It is worth saying something about the little-known socialist regime in North Korea, the Democratic People's Republic of Korea (DPRK). In the first place, North Korea's leaders have built their development theory and practice round the central concept of *juche*, which is frequently transliterated as 'self-reliance'. In the second place, nowhere else in the Third World is so direct a comparison possible between the comparative economic and social performances of a self-reliant socialist system and a dependent neocolony, as represented by South Korea (the Republic of Korea, ROK).

The North Korean leader, Kim Il Sung, himself describes *juche* as:

'... holding to the principle of the revolution and construction in conformity with the actual conditions at home and mainly by one's own efforts ... We are not engaged in the revolution of another country, but in our Korean revolution. Precisely this, the Korean revolution, constitutes *juche* ... all ideological work without exception must be subordinated to the interests of the Korean revolution.'

Professor Chang Hyok of Kim Il Sung University in another gloss on the concept summed up in the word *juche* has described it as 'using our own raw materials, our own techniques, our own workers to satisfy our needs'. Wilfred Burchett, the Australian journalist who lived in North Korea from 1951 to 1954 and re-visited it in 1967, has defined it as 'the use of national resources for national needs; the development of skills strictly related to these resources and needs; the drive for self-reliance in skills and techniques to the utmost degree ...' (8)

Specifically, the DPRK now exports machinery, some of it to advanced industrialised countries, having set out in 1945 (after decades of Japanese occupation and colonialisation) without a single machine-plant or a single Korean trained engineer. This determination to do for themselves whatever needs doing, while perhaps particularly stressed in the North Korean case, is undoubtedly what the Third World struggle for liberation is all about at heart. And, in my view, it casts doubt upon the realism of some Western socialists who argue that the liberation of the neo-colonial countries need not jeopardize the jobs of the industrial workers of the overdeveloped countries. The argument runs that, for instance, car factories, at present turning our private automobiles for, among others, the elites of the Third World, can be converted to producing tractors for liberated countries embarking upon socialist construction. But liberated countries will seek to emulate North Korea's example in striving to manufacture their own tractors and other such mechanical aids to economic development.

In agriculture, there has been a significant inversion of pre-war circumstances. Then, the southern part of the Korean peninsula was the country's granary, providing grain for the deficit northern part and for the colonial Japanese. Today, it is the North which has shot ahead. Grain production there doubled between the late thirties and the early sixties, and has risen steeply since. By the mid-seventies, the goal was eight million tons of grain a year, and Kim Il Sung made the claim, in a speech on January 15th, 1975, that 'World history has never known such a high tempo of growth in agricultural production.' This has been achieved under socialist co-operativisation, with the close collaboration of an industrial sector capable of turning out huge numbers of tractors and other agricultural implements and of meeting all domestic fertiliser needs. The 1973 population of North Korea was 15 million, giving a per capita grain availability of over half a ton.

The contrast with South Korea could hardly be more marked. Formerly a grain-surplus and exporting region, what is now the Republic of Korea nowadays has to import rice and other foodstuffs. Grain production,which had averaged 5.4 million tons a year in the late 1930's had actually dropped to an average of 4.7 million tons in the first half of the 1960's, by which time the ROK was importing an average of 700,000 tons of grain per annum. Despite imports, there is evidence of falling grain consumption in the rural half of the 33 million (1973) South Korean population: an average peasant family has been reported as consuming 29 bushels of rice in 1964, but only 23.3 bushels in 1970. (9) One bushel = 60lbs, so that the 1970 peasant family had, on this calculation, about 1,400 lbs of rice in the year. Official figures give a per capita rice production for the ROK for 1970 of 123 kgs. (abour 270 lbs.). Taking rice alone, DPRK output in 1975 was estimated to be about 230 kgs. (510 lbs.) per capita.

But to register the magnitude of the economic achievements of North Korea, we should not only pair off leading economic indicators, but also take account of such important factors for the mass of the people as social and economic equality or the lack of it, adequacy of health, welfare and educational provision, standard of housing, and similar indices. On the latter set of criteria there is no disputing the clear and overall superiority of socialist North Korea compared with the capitalist South. The reader anxious to verify this is referred to the bibliography. But even in the arena of the much trumpeted ROK economic 'miracle' — industrial output — the DPRK has a better record: from 1954 to 1970/71, gross industrial output rose by 23.5% per annum in socialist North Korea,as against 15.3% for capitalist South Korea. As of 1970, GNP per capita was estimated to be US $375 in the North, and US $110 in the South.

The importance of this comparison lies in the peculiar circumstances of the Korean peninsula — artificially divided at the 38th Parallel — whereby differences in performance have to be put down to the economic system, since the peoples north and south share basically the same cultural, historical and geographical heritage. What is clear is that, deprived of massive loans, US military propping, and integration into the international capitalist economy, South Korea would collapse, whereas — abiding by *juche* — North Korea can stand independent indefinitely. Moreover,

whereas South Korea has become a dumping-ground for pollution-gener-
ating industrial processes, which are increasingly confronted with effective
opposition and legislative hindrance in the overdeveloped countries such as
Japan and the United States, North Korea has taken firm steps to minimise and outlaw environmental abuse;in the new Land Law adopted in the
DPRK in April, 1977, twenty-four of the eighty articles deal specifically
with 'Land Conservation', while the remainder outline a policy consonant
with the twin aims of development and conservation. The land administration is charged with the task of protecting the land and beautifying the
scenery by creating shelter belts, anti-erosion forests, and 'hygienic, scenic
and water conservancy forests'. Again, in contrast to the uncontrolled
growth of the South Korean capital, Seoul (in which a sixth of the population lives, many in shanty slums, and which has a budget equal to the
combined total of the budgets of all other parts of the ROK put together),
the North Korean formula, as given in the Land Law, is as follows:

> 'In land development and the exploitation of resources the arable
> land should not be encroached upon but be cared for and protected
> by all means. The cities should not be too big in scale, but small
> ones should be built in large numbers.'

## INDOCHINA

An equally instructive contrast can be drawn between the experiences
and achievements of those parts of Indochina which remained in imperialist
hands until 1975 and those parts already liberated by then. In what follows,
I shall deal briefly with the following points: first, a comparison between
North Vietnam (the Democratic Republic of Vietnam — DRV) and South
Vietnam (Republic of Vietnam — RVN) from 1954 to 1975; second, a
comparison between Khmer Rouge food policy and American food policy
in Cambodia from 1970 to 1975; and, finally, a review of post-liberation
policy developments in the three countries of liberated Indochina (the
Socialist Republic of Vietnam, Democratic Kampuchea, and the Lao
People's Democratic Republic).

It should be noted that, although I have chosen to discuss only Asian
cases here, it would have been possible to adduce African examples too.
For instance, in Mozambique the revolutionary Frelimo government is
engaged in a massive programme of rural regeneration, based upon experience gained in the liberated areas during the protracted struggle against
the Portuguese colonialists. Familiar elements in the programme include
the transfer of urban population back to the countryside, the formation
of communal villages, reversal of colonial priorities in the trade sector
(i.e. putting the diet of the people before export earnings), and pursuing
the long-term aim of self-sufficiency (when local agriculture can provide
enough food for all, and local industry can supply rural needs for manufactured goods and process local raw materials).

## VIETNAM

More has been written about the Vietnam conflict than about any other single occurrence in human history. Nonetheless, in this context it is worth stressing the significance for the numerous countries of the Third World of this sharpest of confrontations between alternative paths. From 1954 onwards the illegitimate 'Republic of Vietnam' which had been planned in Washington, and thrust forcibly upon the people of the south in violation of the international Geneva accords of that year, was entirely a creature of United States making, a hollow Frankenstein's monster that duly collapsed and decomposed when the creator's supporting hand was withdrawn. The unquenchable will of the Vietnamese people for national unity and independence found expression in the resistance and ultimate triumph of the DRV and the National Liberation Front of South Vietnam (NLF).

It was basically for economic — that is, imperialist — objectives that the United States became embroiled in the first place in Vietnam, and went on in pursuit of these objectives to commit crimes of war that were to arouse the condemnation of the world. But it is with the domestic economic dimensions of the long conflict that I shall be concerned here. To start with, we should note that, rather as in Korea, it was the southern part of the country which traditionally produced a surplus of food, while the northern part depended upon supplementing its own food output by importing from the south. Overall, Vietnam had been a major rice exporter before the second World War (although it is important to note that exports were maintained at their high level by starving the people who actually grew the rice, the peasants of Vietnam, of whom more than two million died of starvation in the terrible famines of 1943-45). The post-war period saw little alleviation of the people's suffering as the French attempted, vainly, to re-impose the colonial yoke. The negotiated peace of 1954 gave the two segments of a (supposedly temporarily) partitioned Vietnam an opportunity to demonstrate what each would do for the people's welfare. The evidence of the years after 1954 is unequivocal: the revolutionaries cared and were effective; the Americans' mercenaries didn't and weren't.

Indeed, while the DRV succeeded in raising rice yields from a pre-war low of 1.2 to 1.4 metric tons per hectare (one of the lowest yields in the world, and probably considerably below what it had been before the French fastened their rapacious colonial rule on the country) to 5 to 5.5 metric tons per hectare, all that US 'aid' could accomplish in the South, with superior initial conditions, was a raising of average yields to 2 metric tons per hectare. Almost all of this latter rise, be it said, was due to the ingenuity and industry of the ordinary peasant, whose courage and tenacity of purpose largely overcame all the obstacles the Americans put in his way, from stealing his crops to spraying them with toxic chemicals, and including both a land 'reform' which played into the hands of the landlords and the attempted forced sale of expensive and inappropriate US farm equipment.

All of this is well documented, even in American official and pro-government sources.

In fact, as the war went on, that part of South Vietnam under American occupation actually became a net importer of rice, to the tune of 568,000 tons in 1970 (whereas, pre-war, exports amounted to 1.6 million tons annually). US farmers were naturally only too happy to oblige with the needed rice, paid for by the US taxpayer, since by this stage of the conflict the South Vietnamese economy as such had virtually ceased to exist, those living in the American controlled zone living largely on aid or charity, or by pandering to the colonialists' need for services of all kinds, including notably mercenary military service. The enormous Saigon budget deficits which resulted from military and security-related expenditures were plugged by commodity imports (financed by the US tax-payer), so that equally enormous trade deficits resulted. Since no attempt was made to dictate what commodities were imported, they inevitably reflected not the needs of the mass of the people but the purchasing power of the corrupt elite. Two discouragements to local enterprise of a useful kind therefore operated. In the first place, there were such easy profits to be made from importing at an overvalued exchange rate that local business-men abandoned the harder path of production with local labour using local raw materials to meet local needs. In the second place, imports killed whatever domestic industries had struggled to survive; in fact, vast quantities of textiles were being imported while local looms lay idle, local unemployment soared, and locally produced fabrics lay rotting in ware-houses. Anything further from *juche* it would be hard to imagine.

The record of the DRV was very different. While not without its problems and setbacks even before the onset of American bombing in the mid-sixties, by 1965 the standard of living of the people had been very sub-stantially raised from that prevailing in 1954. Rice production and rice yields had been raised, while equitable distribution guaranteed an adequate diet for everyone. Simple consumer goods were in reasonable supply. An excellent welfare and education system had been constructed from nothing. Housing had been improved, and the irrigation system greatly extended. The agricultural cooperatives were embarking along the path of diversifi-cation, operating their own small handicraft industries and machine shops. Imports were restricted to those items essential for development which could not yet be locally produced; as a result, luxury goods disappeared but this was not, of course, felt as any loss by the bulk of the people. In short, North Vietnam was confidently poised for further advance along the path of national autonomous economic development.

The American aerial onslaught forced an abrupt change in economic course, involving thorough-going decentralisation of production and dis-persal of population. Much of the physical construction of the pre-1965 period, such as new houses and blocks of flats and hospitals, schools, factories, bridges, roads, railways and dams was totally destroyed. Vital installations, repeatedly damaged, made incessant calls on huge labour teams mobilised for instant essential repairs. I saw this for myself during a visit to the North in the winter of 1966-67. Agriculture in some of the most frequently bombed areas, such as in the southern part of the country, was severely hampered, and rice imports from China became essential to maintain dietary standards. Many other countries contributed aid of various kinds — military and medical notably.

Although extension of the war to the North, and its escalation every-where, posed very great problems for the DRV, there were also incidental gains. The problems are obvious: diversion of a dispersed industrial capac-ity to military purposes; reduction of the labour force by recruitment of able-bodied men and women into the armed and auxiliary forces; and the added burden on the remaining civilian work force of having continually to make vital repairs to severed railway lines and breached irrigation works. These are only the more visible. Chief among the gains was that dispersal and war-time circumstances generally made decentralisation of decision making unavoidable and indeed essential. Previously, the DRV had begun to suffer from an overly bureaucratic form of socialist planning; the war abruptly reversed this direction. Local cadres and people had to react at once to crises and problems that arose for them and accordingly to improvise. Greater scope was offered for local and personal initiative. The challenge of defying American imperialism and ultimately routing it provided the incentive. And the correct political line of the *Lao Dong* (Workers' Party) ensured the unity and guided the overall direction of the struggle. Proof of the efficacy of the DRV resistance effort in its economic aspect lies in the remarkable fact that right through until 1975, 1965 levels of production were maintained.

The Saigon regime crumpled in a matter of weeks in the face of the final assault of the liberation forces in the spring of 1975. It was a measure of the superiority of socialist self-reliance over almost total dependence upon alien support. Success would not have been possible without the application of effective military, political, and economic policies by the National Liberation Front of South Vietnam in both the liberated areas and the American-occupied areas. Expulsion of the American imperialists and the overthrow of their puppet regime was a *Vietnamese* victory, towards which all sectors of the population of North and South contri-buted.

While the peoples of the world, and above all the peoples of Indochina, greeted liberation in April 1975 with joy, relief and high hopes, the immense problems which faced the victors were and remain enormous. I can do no more here than indicate the direction which policy has taken since them.

Liberation of Saigon, and of the other previously Saigon-controlled areas, confronted Vietnamese leaders with the huge task of re-absorbing millions of people who had for two decades been abstracted from productive labour. Millions of youngsters had grown up in the Disneyland world of Washington-financed imports. Countless others knew no trade but corruption, gangsterism, beggary, prostitution or one or other of the numerous perversions of normal socio-economic life which flourished in the unreal hothouse climate created by the American presence.

In the North, herculean labours of reconstruction had to be set afoot. Industrial production had to be restored and greatly increased. Communications had to be re-established and extended, enabling intercourse to be normalised and speeded up between North and South. Throughout the country, the terrible scars of war had to be erased from the countryside, insofar as this was possible for it is feared some areas most thoroughly saturated with US poisons sprayed from the air may never recover their former fertility. New areas had to be opened to cultivation, considering that the total population of the country had risen from a 1940 total of some 20+ million to 45 million on liberation.

The first unified National Assembly was convened in June, 1976, to proclaim the existence of the Socialist Republic of Vietnam. At the Fourth Party Congress of the Vietnam *Lao Dong*, held in Hanoi in December, 1976, the name of the organisation was formally changed to the Vietnam Communist Party. Of more substance was the shape that was there imparted to economic policy for the remaining four years of the 1976-80 Five-Year Plan. Decisions taken were based upon a realistic assessment of circumstances and prospects. They are worth a review.

In the first place, the leadership accepted that the exceptional aid extended to the country from many sources during the war, most of it in the form of outright gifts, would now have to be replaced by a more realistic balancing of the books. Aid from Russia and the Eastern European countries has already been significantly cut back, and while a number of countries have volunteered reconstruction aid which in total is not insignificant, Hanoi clearly appreciates that foreign assistance must now actively be canvassed from wherever is may be forthcoming, whether it be from other socialist countries, from the West and Japan, from international agencies such as the IMF and the Asian Development Bank, or even from foreign national and multinational corporations prepared to abide by the guidelines laid down for foreign investment and joint operations by Hanoi. It is, however, stressed that all this is to be seen as immediate assistance leading to an accelerated achievement of that independence and self-reliance for which the Vietnamese have fought so long and sacrificed so much.

The next ingredient is an insistence that agriculture and light industry must be given priority over heavy industry. Vietnam is still overwhelmingly an agricultural country, and experience has shown in innumerable cases of socialist planning that the co-operation and enthusiastic effort of the peasants cannot be harnessed unless their enhanced production is rewarded with a return in the form of the kinds of consumer goods which they need and desire. Light industry is also import substituting, and, properly directed, should also earn precious foreign exchange as well as saving it.

We noted that the war forced decentralisation upon the DRV. It is apparent from the programme of the revised Five-Year Plan that decentralisation is now to be built into the planning and administrative framework for the future.

Finally, the problem of the unemployed millions liberated in the southern part of the country was tackled. It was reported that in the first twenty months after liberation some 700,000 people had been moved out of Ho Chi Minh City (formerly Saigon) into farming areas, but Pham Van Dong, the Prime Minister, estimated that from 1977 to 1980 another four million people would have to be similarly re-absorbed.

In a statement to mark the second anniversary of liberation, the distinguished writer, and editor of *Vietnamese Studies*, Nguyen Khac Vien, claimed that, in all, another six million city dwellers would need eventually to be settled in the countryside: 'In the south,' he wrote, 'there are several million people more used to doing business than to working with their own hands. Several thousand shopkeepers, coffee house and restaurant owners and hawkers still spend their time trading, trafficking, speculating, making prices waltz and pocketing substantial incomes. Worse still, many young people shy away from work, preferring to traffic for a living.' He added that more than 80% of the Saigon population provided no useful work for the state, and estimated that only 35% of the people in southern Vietnam lived outside the cities (a triumph for Professor Samuel Huntington's notorious 'accelerated urbanisation', achieved by intensive US bombing of the rural areas during the war). This proportion would have, he said, to be doubled, entailing the ultimate absorption of some seven million former town-dwellers into rural occupations, a complete reversal of the movement which has come to be identified with 'development'.

Great publicity has been given in the West to alleged brutalities on the part of the new rulers of Vietnam. Former missionaries and others, who stayed behind after liberation only to be subsequently expelled, have been responsible for giving currency to these stories. Other reports, however, make perfectly clear that whatever the hardships associated with the change-over (and no one has sought to underestimate these, least of all the Vietnamese) the general situation for the mass of the people has already greatly improved since liberation. Observers have noted, rebutting charges of 'forced' resettlement, that as soon as Ho Chi Minh City was freed, countless peasants, driven into penury and mendicancy there by American bombing, simply packed up, abandoned their shanty-town shacks, and trudged back to their native fields. One thing is evident: re-united Vietnam is on a course promising a prosperous and independent future for its people, whereas imperialism brought nothing but disaster and pauperization.

## Laos

If I say little about Laos it is not because I underestimate the significance of the revolution there or the achievements of the Pathet Lao (the organisation which led the protracted resistance to American intervention and finally presided over the formation of the Lao People's Democratic Republic). On the contrary, I am filled with admiration for the spirit and ingenuity of the Lao people and their leadership. Limitations of space alone dictate brevity. But we should note two characteristic features of the liberation process. In the first place, while those who collaborated with the US eagerly jettisoned their own culture to embrace uncritically a foreign language, English, and the 'American way of life', the Pathet Lao throughout strove to preserve genuinely Lao culture, fostering the language and the arts of the people in every way, as an integral element in the revolutionary struggle for independence and assertion of national identity. In the second place, while the American-occupied zone had become totally dependent upon hand-outs from Washington (the old saying was that 'Laos used to have an economy but now it has an aid programme'), the liberated area, in spite of intensive American bombing, had determinedly worked its way to self-reliance, fighters and farmers uniting to produce and to resist.

Like its Indochinese neighbours, Laos, since liberation, has continued to pursue these two guidelines. The vast Plaine des Jarres, so bitterly fought over and pulverized during the war, has now been re-populated and converted back into a rich farming area. Thousands of villagers, forced to flee by the hostilities, have returned to eliminate bomb damage, to plant crops and to raise cattle and pigs again. Throughout the country, a new energy and purpose inform reconstruction and the thrust to national development.

## Cambodia

Much might be written about Cambodia over the whole of the same period, 1954 to 1975, revealing again the costs of dependency and the rewards of economic independence. But I shall concentrate here upon a particularly poignant example: the contrast between US and Khmer Rouge policies after the *coup* of 1970 which deposed Prince Sihanouk and installed military puppets selected by Washington and headed by General Lon Nol. An understanding of these years is crucial to obtaining perspective upon the concerted chorus of concern for the fate of the Cambodian people which has arisen from the Western media since the liberation of the country in 1975.

We should note that Cambodia had little difficulty in providing for its own food needs right up to 1970 (although this is not to deny that the peasants had grievances arising from indebtedness, land seizures by greedy notables, and other socio-economic abuses: proof of this exists in the fact that a rural guerrilla was already under arms by 1963). Very swiftly after the coup of 1970, the rural areas were liberated, as the peasants rallied to the guerrilla (known to the outside as the Khmer Rouge), with which Prince Sihanouk had at once thrown in his lot on his deposition, becoming its titular head.

Phnom Penh, the capital city, quickly became more or less besieged, in common with a handful of other urban areas. The pre-1970 population of the city had been about 300,000. It swelled to some 2.5 to 3 million as peasants flocked in to avoid the savage bombing which Washington and the puppet regime proceeded to visit upon the open countryside. By bomb rocket, napalm and defoliants, the Americans sought to bring desolation and destitution to the rural areas, with the objects of slaughtering as many of the people as possible and of starving the rest into submission.

As far as the people in the American-occupied areas, principally Phnom Penh, were concerned, Washington gave their welfare, including the supply of basic food, a low priority. When guerrilla action finally closed the Mekong River, the capital could only be supplied by air. The limited cargo space available was largely devoted to military material (and to maintaining the supply of 'essential' luxury items for the elite); such rice as was flown in as often as not disappeared into the black market, or was even corruptly flown back out of the city to attract a better price elsewhere. Long before the liberation of the capital, in April 1975, rice riots, street deaths from starvation, and widespread acute malnutrition-related disease, had become commonplaces of daily life. And when the Americans and their closest collaborators finally abandoned the city by plane and helicopter they left behind hospitals (deprived of electricty and water by last-minute sabotage), overflowing with the sick and the wounded, a couple of million hungry people with neither jobs nor access to land, and no foodstocks.

The leaders of the Khmer Rouge had, however, foreseen the difficulties that would confront them, and had made provision accordingly. Despite the ferocious bombardment to which the rural areas had been subjected, agricultural production had been maintained and even improved. Irrigation works had been built and extended, making double cropping possible over a much greater area than hitherto. New crops had been introduced. Live-stock management had been encouraged. Non-food needs had, as much as possible, been met by handicraft industry and by the primitive manu-facturing plant that could be improvised. The success of the policies carried out may be judged by the results. Not only were the people in the liber-ated areas fed: in addition, a small surplus of rice was made available for export in order to pay for vital imports; the People's Liberation Armed Forces were provided with food; and, most importantly, enough rice was collected and stored to support the two and a half million people of Phnom Penh after its liberation, until they could be put back to produc-tive employment and until the first fruits of their labour were available one full harvest cycle later.

The present President of Democratic Kampuchea, Khieu Samphan, had been studying the economic problems of his country since his student days in Paris. Himself from a humble family, he had concluded that, even in 'normal' circumstances, more than four-fifths of the population of Phnom Penh were redundant, consuming what had been produced by the labour of others and contributing nothing to the social pot themselves. It followed that one of the priority tasks of a liberated Cambodia must be the deployment in productive labour of those hitherto parasitic. There was, therefore nothing unpremeditated about the evacuation of Phnom Penh. Careful preparations had been made in the five years of civil war to ensure that the evacuation would be logistically possible by stockpiling rice at intervals along the routes out into the countryside. We now have the eye-witness evidence of participants in the long trek that progress was orderly, informal and leisurely. While people moved out of the capital city in their hundreds of thousands, key personnel from the guerrilla moved into it (doctors, nurses, engineers) to tend the sick who could not be moved to field stations, and to restore the public services sabotaged by the departing Americans. Workers, too, came; their job was to restore production in the long idle factories of the city.

Careful planning was rewarded by an adequate 1975 main harvest, won by the arduous toil of the people. For many of the evacuees from Phnom Penh it was their first taste of the hard physical labour involved in pro-ducing the food they ate, and those who fled to neighbouring Thailand were to bewail the fate that had overtaken them, and to describe field work as 'torture', not stopping to reflect that they had happily lived on the labour of others in the pre-revolutionary past without giving a thought to alleviation of the 'torture' by planned economic progress. By late 1976, the Thai rice authorities were raising the spectre of Cambodian rice exports 'destabilising' regional and world markets. On the second anniversary of liberation Khieu Samphan was able to announce that agricultural produc-tion already 'far exceeded' that of only a year before: in his words, people generally were receiving anough food to 'take care of their health and fatten them up'. Canals, dams and reservoirs were being constructed throughout the countryside to hasten further progress. 'The cattle and buffalo are our closest comrades-in-arms in the nation-building campaign', he added. 'If our cattle work hard, we can build our country rapidly.'

Rubber production, halted by US defoliation, has also been restored, exports being resumed *via* neighbouring Thailand. A trade mission has now been opened in Hong Kong. Trade delegations have visited a number of countries. Handicraft and light industry have been fostered to meet the people's needs. Medical services have been greatly expanded by adopting a system of auxiliaries, modelled on the Chinese 'bare-foot doctors'.

The aims of the revolutionary regime have been succinctly laid down in the Constitution ratified in 1976:

'. . . the entire people and the entire Revolutionary Army of Kampuchea desire an independent, unified, peaceful, neutral, nonaligned, sovereign Kampuchea enjoying territorial integrity, a society where genuine happiness, equality, justice and democracy exist, without rich or poor, and without exploiters and exploited, a society in which all live harmoniously in great solidarity and join the struggle to do manual work together and increase production for the construction and defence of the country.'

These are ideals markedly different from those which inform conventional development thinking. Widely adopted by liberated Third World countries, they could not but force a reappraisal of economic strategies on the part of the overdeveloped countries.

# TOWARDS HOMEOSTASIS: TRANSCENDING OVERDEVELOPMENT

'I believe there is a danger that, after we have paid off our overseas debt, including the sterling balances, our current account balance of payments will be balanced as a result of an oil surplus *plus* our invisible surplus being offset by a non-oil visible deficit. There is a danger that we shall export less and less, and import more and more manufactured goods. The production and refining of oil, and the production of petrochemicals, provide little employment. As our industries wither away — as a result of our failure to be competitive — unemployment will become greater and greater. It will not be Keynesian unemployment, due to lack of demand. It will be the unemployment which is the result of lack of productive equipment. *And when the flow of North Sea oil and gas begin to diminish, about the turn of the century, our island will become desolate.*' (Lord Kahn, 'Mr. Eltis and the Keynesians', *Lloyds Bank Review*, no. 124, April, 1977, p.12) (emphasis added).

This analysis by a distinguished British economist of the prospects for the United Kingdom is illustrative of the strength and persistence of the identification in our minds of wealth with flourishing trade and good monetary revenues. I hope I have already shown that, in fact, the wealth of any community lies in its '. . . revenue of energy available for the purposes of life. That being given, in sufficient amount and in form being capable of being utilised by the existing knowledge of the time, *everything* requisite for the life of the society can be maintained.' (1) As Adam Smith himself observed: 'When food is provided it is easy to find the necessary clothing and lodging.' Is there any real reason to suppose Britain would be rendered 'desolate' if her trade dried up and her oil and gas ceased to earn foreign exchange? The answer must clearly be no: any suggestion that the British Isles cannot provide from its own soil the wherewithal to feed its present and expected population is nonsensical. Furthermore, granted the unfolding of the Third World liberation process as we have envisaged it, self-sufficiency is precisely what the country will be required to strive towards in the decades ahead.

## British Overdevelopment

In many ways, Britain is a particularly interesting case in this context. It was, in the first place, the pioneering industrial power. At the height of Britain's greatness, in the mid-Victorian period when there was confidence in the future of the Empire upon which the sun never (and, it was thought, would never) set, her rulers consciously chose to pursue a policy of dependence upon cheap imported food for the British worker and imported raw materials for British industry. Agriculture at home was therefore allowed to settle at a level where it could meet only a part of domestic demand (with two spurts of hectic expansion and attention during the two World Wars, in the course of which the vulnerability of overdevelopment was laid bare).

In the 20th century Britain increased her dependence upon the outside world by switching from coal, of which she had huge resources, to oil, of which she had at that time no known domestic reserves. A total blockade of the British Isles, similar to that which paralysed the Japanese economy towards the end of the Pacific War, would demonstrate the extent to which, in her overdevelopment, Britain has gambled on continued access to the underdeveloped countries and on the competitiveness of her export industries for procurement of some of her most vital requirements. The question is how is this kind of dependence to be reduced, How, in other words, is Britain to shape an economic future compatible with the trends discernible internationally towards greater autarky (on the part of liberated Third World countries) and towards altogether higher levels of primary product prices, including food prices? If our analysis is accurate, not only will the volume of world trade contract, but the terms of trade will continue to favour agricultural and mineral products at the expense of manufactures. Britain has been export-orientated for a long time; but is it reasonable to expect her industries to win an ever-expanding share of a shrinking world market? This is what would be required for continuation of the present course to have any prospect of success. I think this is an unrealisable objective, and shall attempt to explain why, and to postulate an alternative more in keeping with likely international realities.

I should interject that while I have constructed the argument of this section around the British case I am aware that an adequate analysis would have to take account of the specific features and prospects of the other overdeveloped countries, for although there are strong similarities in their historical experiences (shrinkage of the primary sector, to take the most striking instance) there are also particulars that enjoin caution in generalisation. But my hope is that others will pick up the arguments deployed here and apply them to the circumstances of their own countries. The sceptical will no doubt bring forward another criticism, namely why the objective of self-sufficiency should be restricted to the level of the *nation:* why not take it down further — to the level of the village community, or the family, or even the individual? The answer is to be found, I believe, in human experience and the outcome of countless historical and geographic vagaries. If I cannot do better than that on this occasion, I ask forbearance; full discussion of the point would require a volume on its own.

The first thing that would strike a perceptive visitor to Britain from a subsistence society would surely be the number of people who do not actually *produce* anything. The dictionary definition of a producer is 'one who produces article of consumption'. In subsistence economies there is little leeway for the support of non-producers, and the great majority of the population in fact labours at growing food and at providing for

themselves, within the framework of the family or of the tribe/clan, their
own clothing, household utensils and the like. In Britain, however, there is
a vast tertiary sector (office workers, salesmen, traffic wardens, security
guards, advertising copywriters, and the like), while even in the secondary
(manufacturing) sector a lot of what is turned out is far from strictly
necessary, and in some cases detracts from social welfare. In 1970, out of a
total employed population of 22,891,000, only 798,000 (3.5%) were
engaged directly in the primary sector (agriculture, forestry, fishing, mining
and quarrying), with 8,911,000 (38%) in manufacturing, and the remainder
in construction (6%) and a variety of services (52.5%). No less than 7%
(1,431,000) were 'paper-shufflers' in the national and local civil services.

> 'From 1966 to 1975 the economy's productive market sector —
> industry and commerce taken together — lost almost 200,000 jobs
> a year . . . Local authority manpower alone rose from 1,250,000 in
> 1960 to nearly 3,000,000 in 1975 . . . By comparing 1961 and 1974
> we see the major shift . . . the non-market sector increased by 45 per
> cent while the market sector declined by 5 per cent . . . the incomes
> of those who do not sell their output must come from taxing the
> incomes of those who do' (2)

The authors of the above quote, Bacon and Eltis, are, of course, working
upon different premises and towards a different prescriptive goal than I,
but their figures nevertheless afford striking confirmation of the rapid
transformation of the British economy in the direction of ever more
distorted overdevelopment, with the majority of the population in non-
productive employment. Marketable output is obviously not necessarily
useful, socially desirable or the result of productive labour; a criminal can
market his loot and a whore sell her services, to take but two examples. I
do not, however, intend to become embroiled in all the complicated issues
and questions which arise from even a fairly superficial consideration of
the definition of productive and unproductive labour. My guidelines here
will be rough and ready ones, owing more to common sense and intuitive
feeling than to pedantic hair-splitting or Linnaean niceties.

Working in a rule of thumb kind of way, let us, then, try applying one
or two tests. At one end of the spectrum, the entire population of a
country could be, let's say, pop singers, P.R. executives or whatever as
long as there was sufficient international demand for their 'products' to
enable them to exchange that product on the market for the food, clothes,
and other necessities without which they could not live. At the other end,
in a totally autarkic economy, deprived of all trade and intercourse with
the rest of the world, it is clear that a very large proportion of the population would have to be employed creating the necessities of life, while
few could be supported in non-essential roles.

Or again, let us try to imagine what would happen to an overdeveloped
country like Britain if this or that category of worker went on indefinite
strike. Obviously, there are groups of workers whose suspension of activity
would very rapidly throw the whole country into severe crisis: farmers

and farm workers; coalminers; and a handful of other occupational groups. (It is important to note — see below — that of these 'essential' categories, many are only 'essential' given the existing socio-economic dispensation.) Conversely, there are many occupational groups whose prolonged withdrawal of such labour as they do normally undertake would have little, if any, harmful effect; cessation of all activity on the part of some such categories (criminals, for instance) would positively benefit social welfare. How long would it take the population at large to feel the effects of a strike of company directors or of university lecturers? In contrast, it would not take long for an adverse impact to make itself felt, in present-day urban circumstances, in the case of a strike of those responsible for the regular collection and disposal of household and industrial refuse. (It will be noted that there is little correlation at present between the usefulness of an activity and its material rewards.)

Let us, though, adopt a more dynamic perspective. A strike of lorry and van drivers today would rapidly lead to great hardship both to individual consumers and to industry, since so much produce is currently road-borne. But let us postulate two possible developments: first, a swingeing tax on road transport, penal enough to divert traffic back to an extended rail network offering a much improved service, the charges for which would be highly subsidised by the taxpayer; and, second, a carefully planned and implemented re-distribution of population, combined with restoration of labour-intensive agriculture designed to make possible local self-sufficiency in basic goods and foodstuffs and other essentials. Such a policy would, over the years, drastically curtail the need for vans and lorries to hurtle about all over the country, and would render redundant all their drivers plus all those who, one way or another, cater to their needs in petrol stations, transport cafeterias, and the like.

Productivity measured by current indispensability is thus subject to political and economic decisions, except in the case of the handful of vital occupations with which no conceivable society can dispense. But at the moment all the existing major political parties in Britain, and most of the minor ones, apparently accept that what I have called overdevelopment is pre-ordained; part of the natural order that has to be accepted without query, or at least historically determined and inescapable. I hope to show that this is not so.

Before I do so, I should briefly indicate here what I believe acceptance of and commitment to the present economic strategy and trajectory will entail over the next couple of decades. It will be seen that this is little more than a recapitulation of much that has gone before; nevertheless, it is worth underlining the key points.

World primary product prices will continue to rise, we assume. As far as food is concerned, competition for food supplies coming on to world markets will increase as population and requirements grow. At the same time food production costs will continue to rise as vital in-puts, such as the petroleum-based fertilisers, pesticides and the like, become more and more expensive. Huge food corporation conglomerates, like Cargill, Continental Grain Inc., Louis Dreyfus and Sons, and Bunge Corp., will, with their political retainers and allies among the American government agencies, go on pushing up prices by cornering and manipulation. Countries dependent upon importing food will have to be prepared to pay higher and higher prices for the privilege of continuing to be so dependent. The same considerations apply to non-food primary products. In addition, there will clearly be determined attempts on the part of raw material exporting countries to achieve 'opecisation', emulating the oil-exporting countries in improving upon natural advantages by cartelisation. Besides, as country after country succeeds in obtaining liberation, entailing their using more and more of their own resources for their own purposes, internationally marketed surpluses will decline. Growing scarcities and the fear of ever-greater scarcities in future must propel prices upward.

It may be objected that the liberation of Third World countries, whatever it may entail for availability of raw materials, is irrelevant to the problem of British food supplies. Pre-war, Western Europe as a whole imported (average of 1934-38) 24 million metric tons of grain, over 60% of which came from the countries of Asia, Africa and Latin America. Four decades later, the picture had changed dramatically: in 1972, Latin America, Western Europe, Eastern Europe, Russia, Africa and Asia imported together 92 million metric tons of grain (Western Europe 21 million), while North America, Australia and New Zealand jointly exported 92 million tons. But a number of points should be made. First, the magnitude of available marketable surpluses fluctuates from year to year and cannot be relied upon, particularly if climatologists are correct in predicting less favourable weather conditions for food production over the next historical period. Second, granted surpluses, the food will go to the customers who can afford to pay the asking price, which will continue to be bid up and to harden; 'afford to pay' means, in the end, exporting to the equivalent value, directly or indirectly. (British machinery sold to China or another Third World country could earn money to be put towards paying for North American grain.) Third, it is the Third World countries which at present supply Britain with high-grade protein for her livestock; the governments of liberated countries will obviously retain such protein to raise the dietary levels of their peoples.

Great changes are also indicated on the other side of the equation, namely the marketability of manufactures. Here we foresee a future of intensifying competition. Countries pursuing the second path to capitalism will increasingly compete on world markets with first path countries, having the advantage of lower wages and absence of effective and autonomous trade unions and independent workers' parties. There will be mounting pressure on the governments of the older industrial countries to adopt protectionist measures — a pressure that is already making itself felt.

Clothing and shoe workers in the USA want cheaper foreign clothes and shoes shut out of American markets; Japan has been forced to resort to re-siting many of her factories overseas in order to beat growing bans on goods 'made in Japan'; British workers in declining industries are demanding tariff protection against competing imports from the EEC. The rapid spread of knowledge about technological innovations lessens the edge held by the most advanced countries. More and more countries also make and export machinery, so there is no longer a monopoly there for the older industrial countries like Britain. At the same time, liberated countries like China consciously work towards self-sufficiency right across the technological spectrum; China's import dependence has declined dramatically since the Revolution.

The chances of Britain carving out an adequate stake in world trade in the coming decades would, then, appear to be bleak. I shall not go into the complex matter of attitudes towards work in Britain and other overdeveloped countries. It is self-evident that great changes are taking place, favouring increased leisure and a less intense striving for job advancement and accumulation of personal capital. Without seeking on this occasion to offer explanations or hazard extrapolations, I shall merely observe that these trends run counter to vigorous and successful waging of trade war in a context of mounting competition.

## The Alternative Future

I should now like to turn to consideration of a radical alternative future for Britain. This must start from the assumption that transcending overdevelopment involves, in the first place, reversing by deliberate policy some of its most prominent features (such as the gross hypertrophy of the tertiary sector). To put it figuratively, we must back-track in order to embark upon a different path, since the one to which we are presently committed appears to lead to a dead-end.

A post-overdeveloped Britain would be based upon an agricultural sector employing a very much higher percentage of the available labour-force; exactly how high would depend upon a number of factors. As a result, Britain would be self-sufficient in food (with the exception of exotic items like tropical fruits). The British diet would be modified, with a smaller meat component. Energy self-sufficiency would rest upon elimination of wasteful uses (such as the internal combustion engine), wider use of solar heating and simple methane-gas appliances using household wastes, and carefully planned husbanding of fossil fuel reserves for essential uses (as in agriculture). The import bill would be much reduced from its present level, thus reducing the need to export. The redistribution of population to rural areas would ease urban problems of all kinds, including those related to housing, traffic, over-large 'local' authorities, and city social pathology (crime, delinquency, addiction, and the like).

The first question that arises is whether the land of Britain is *capable*, given optimum allocation of the other factors of production (labour and capital), of supporting the British population forecast for the future. It should be noted in this connection that one of the most significant trends of the 1970's so far has been the decline in the birth rate, and that by 1976 British population was actually falling for the first time in peace-time since records began almost 150 years ago. Nevertheless, demographic forecasting is a notoriously fallible exercise, and I shall here work with the assumption of an end-of-century maximum population of something in the region of 60,000,000.

The total agricultural area of the UK (arable, permanent grass, and rough grazing) in 1970 was 47,837,000 acres. I shall assume that the present trend towards alienation of agricultural land for urban expansion will be halted and eventually reversed (at present some 30,000 acres a year are being thus alienated). Some currently idle land could be made productive, with appropriate incentives and in-puts of labour and capital. On the other hand, if there is to be reduction in imports of forestry products, more land than at present will have to be devoted to forestry (one projection suggests an advisable rate of new planting of 250,000 acres a year). A family working one acre intensively can, on reasonable soil carefully tended, supply its own vegetable needs. If we leave aside rough grazing, Britain has thirty million acres of agricultural land available. If we assume four members per family, it will be seen that we have the necessary acreage.

But this is far too crude a calculation. Allowance has to be made for the support of essential workers in the non-agricultural sector, and for some livestock. Even so, there is unanimity among those who have gone into the matter in any detail that the transition to self-sufficiency in food can be made in Britain. However, we must distinguish between those who see it being accomplished within the framework of the present system of land ownership, import availability, and capital/energy/intensity, on the one hand, and those who envisage it only within a radically altered framework. The key points at issue between the two camps concern the continuing efficacy and availability of non-human energy in-puts.

The argument of this book supports those who see radical change as a prerequisite. At the moment 90% of the protein concentrates British farmers feed to their livestock is imported from the underdeveloped countries, who need protein desperately for their own poor; Britain, with 1.5% of the world's population, takes 10% of the world's fishmeal, for instance. It is surely unrealistic to imagine such transactions continuing indefinitely. Nor can one assume that there will be any reversal in the secular tendency upwards of fossil fuel prices, which are reflected directly or indirectly in all modern agricultural activities; on the contrary, they will continue to rise (North Sea oil notwithstanding). As far as fertiliser is concerned, nitrogenous fertiliser is energy expensive, and the UK has to import phosphate; there is, however, enough domestic potash, and natural manure, both animal and human, is at the moment wasted in most prodigal fashion.

If energy inputs of these kinds become continually dearer and more difficult to obtain, the whole present basis of farming in Britain will just have to be changed. Enough grain is already grown, but 70% of it is fed to livestock; converted directly into human food, it would yield a better diet than most people in the world presently have. A drastic reduction in low-land livestock farming would free land for grain production and horticulture, with some pig and poultry raising for manure and meat. Protein concentrate imports could be curtailed. Per acre, good nutritious vegetables like the cabbage and the potato yield many times the energy and protein yielded by beef cattle, sheep or pigs.

We should recall at this point that while modern agriculture, as practiced in Britain, North America and Western Europe, is efficient in *economic* terms in the sense that within the prevailing cost structure farmers can increase output with less labour and make profits, it is most inefficient in *energy* terms. Increases in output have been obtained historically by stepping up use of the fossil fuels. The energy efficiency (energy out to energy in ratio) of a battery egg is a mere 0.19, of greenhouse winter lettuce 0.0023, and of a white sliced loaf 0.525; in contrast, a well cared for British allotment can multiply the energy invested in it by 1.30 while corn grown in Mexico without the help of machinery has an energy efficiency factor of 30.60.

If, as we envisage, there is to be a reduction in the use of agricultural chemicals (both as a result of rising costs and of declining efficacy) and of agricultural and agriculture-related machinery (because of rising fuel prices), and in the import of grain, protein concentrates, and foodstuffs generally, the energy needed to replace the reduced inputs of inanimate energy, and to step up production, can only come from an increased input of muscle power. One recent calculation suggests that in a fully self-sufficient Britain there would have to be a net transfer of some eight million people to the rural areas (3). Labour-intensive mixed farming would probably flourish best on the basis of small holdings and small farms, rather than in the context of today's giant agri-businesses and factory farms. There is, however, as I suggest below, room for flexibility and experimentation in actual implementation.

At the moment, there is no organised political demand for such a transformation. There is, though, evidence of diffuse sympathy for movement 'back to the land' and of social forces pushing in that direction. As examples of the first, we may cite the number of individuals, families and groups who have actually given up urban life and taken up farming in the last few years, and the appearance of organisations and periodicals concerned with studying and encouraging the trend; and of the second, the steeply rising demand for allotments, stoked by rising food prices, and the slight increase in rural employment in Britain since the onset of massive industrial unemployment in the 1970's.

The present, or any subsequent, government could, of course, take steps to encourage the movement. The wages of farm workers, at present at the bottom of the pay league (65% below the national average in 1976), could be brought into line and made competitive with industrial wages. Unemployed urban workers could be given training in farming skills in preparation for re-employment on the land. The route mileage and frequency of rural bus and train services could be greatly increased. Housing, education and health provision in country areas could be given priority. By operating upon food prices, subsidies and taxation big agri-business farmers could be induced to redirect their efforts along such lines as replanting hedgerows, re-introducing sound rotations, increasing vegetable production at the expense of livestock rearing (at present Britain quite unnecessarily imports 25% of the vegetables eaten), employing more men and horses and fewer machines, and the like.

## Forces for Transition

Simply to recommend these and other measures would leave us in the realm of exhortatory politics, of disembodied advice offered in a vacuum. What are the social forces ranged on each side? That is the key question. Can we detect the development of social forces potentially strong enough to find reflection in effective political and economic action? There is little need to emphasise the strength of the forces behind the continuation of the present economic course, far less the sheer inertia of traditional ways of doing things. Big landlords, big farmers, exporters, multinationals with EEC links, the giants of the food 'industry' (Unilever, Nestles, etc) and all their political, administrative, judicial, media, and enforcement allies, constitute an impressive coalition. What we have to look for and speculate upon are sources of support for radical change.

Among the middle-classes, deterioration of conditions of life in urban areas is already impelling a steady drift to the country and helping to shape a consciousness of the need for drastic change. For the most poorly paid, the unemployed, and those with least access to land generally, rising food prices must promote receptivity to radical new ideas holding out the promise of jobs and cheap food. If, for the moment, organised labour seems firmly wedded to more traditional approaches, pressures from the membership and grassroots may shift its stance in time. Since British withdrawal from the Common Market (with its Common Agricultural Policy) is an essential prerequisite for implementation of the kind of new policies we have been arguing for here, it is significant that broad sections of the labour movement are now engaged in mounting a campaign for precisely that objective. It is interesting, too, that massive industrial unemployment in Italy has led to large-scale movement back to the land. In 1976, 100,000 workers returned to farming, often in organized groups.

Some of these 'communes' plan to market directly to the public, eliminating middlemen profits and keeping prices down. A member of one such commune of the formerly unemployed was reported as saying that they wanted to show that farming could enjoy a boom by absorbing the jobless.

What the surface shifts mirror is the growing contradiction between the existing relations and mode of production and the further development of the forces of production. Contrary to the conventional wisdom of the mechanical or palaeo-Marxists, the way forward is not through more and more hectic industrialisation and high-technological innovation under centralised 'socialist' planning of the kind favoured by the Webbs, Stalin and the Morrisonian vintage Labour Party. Instead it is to be sought in a reconciliation of British needs and capabilities to changing international realities. True, those presiding over the present dispensation cannot provide the answers; nevertheless the analysis of the present book leads to conclusions about the future very different from those clung to by the palaeo-Marxists.

This is not the place to indulge in fruitless prophecy. The specifics of the transition and the specifics of the society subsequently built cannot be neatly detailed. But I think we may safely speculate that however land is socialised, as it must be, it will *not* be subjected to monolithic bureaucratic nationalisation, that there will be scope for a variety of forms in accordance with particular local social and agricultural circumstances. A partial dismantling of big concentrated bureaucracies should permit the flourishing of more responsive de-centralised authorities, exercising such functions as may be entrusted to them. Scotland and Wales will win their full independence, and there may be substantial regional devolution in England itself. Conventional modern high-technology 'defence' will probably give way to universal militia training for all-out people's war against any aggressor.

It is tempting to speculate further, but we have probably peered as far into the future as is profitable. The outcome in detail may be indeed quite different, but of one thing I am absolutely sure: Karl Marx was typically prescient in his analysis of the post-capitalist Western society of the future when he stipulated that it would have to display, among others, the following features:

'. . . the bringing into cultivation of wastelands, and the improvement of the soil generally in accordance with a common plan . . . Establishment of industrial armies, especially for agriculture . . . Combination of agriculture with manufacturing industry; gradual abolition of the distinction between town and country, by a more equitable distribution of the population over the country . . .' (4)

The oldest overdeveloped country is, if our own analysis is correct, moving in just that direction.

## A NOTE ON POPULATION

Those who wish to cover up the imperfections and injustices of present international economic arrangements frequently resort to the argument that poverty in the Third World is a function of too rapid population growth there. Accordingly, a quite disproportionate share of 'development' funds and thought has been devoted to the demographic aspects of poverty. Though the arguments, such as they are, lurking behind this particular approach have by now often been ridiculed and invalidated, I want to end by alluding briefly to the population dimension. After all, eventual achievement of population stabilisation *is* integral to achievement of general eco-economic-energy homeostasis (allowing for entropy).

We should first abandon the hackneyed but often invoked 'spaceship earth' analogy; whatever merits it may have are greatly outweighed by its disadvantages in obscuring the distinct components of the problem. I suggest it is useful to think instead of a four category model, where the rather distinct segments consist of: first, the rich industrial countries of the capitalist West and Japan (roughly equivalent to the OECD — Organisation for Economic Cooperation and Development — group of countries, consisting of Austria, Belgium, Denmark, France, West Germany, Greece, Iceland, Eire, Italy, Luxembourg, the Netherlands, Norway, Portugal, Spain, Sweden, Switzerland, Turkey, the UK, Canada, the USA, and Japan, but not conterminous: demographically and in terms of per capita GNP Turkey, for instance, is out of place in this company, while Australia and New Zealand should be included); second, the USSR and the East European bloc; third, China; and, fourth, the unliberated countries of the Third World. I am quite conscious of anomalies, overlaps, and omissions, but the scheme enables us to highlight a number of relevant and instructive points.

It is worth pointing out that in the hypothetical event of the four groups of countries being isolated from one another, all but the first could cope fairly readily with the eventuality. Russia and China both possess enormous untapped resources. The poor countries of the Third World could at a pinch backtrack to subsistence production (as several of them indeed had to do during the second World War). But the economies of the rich capitalist countries would collapse, plunged into social chaos by economic paralysis brought on by termination of the complex international exchanges which alone sustain them.

In the first group of countries we observe a very remarkable post-war shift to patterns of behaviour unfavourable to continued population growth, the shift becoming particularly noticeable with the affluence and permissiveness of the 'sixties, but paradoxically being reinforced by the austerity of the succeeding 'seventies. We have already remarked upon the current stagnation in British numbers. This is no isolated phenomenon. In West Germany, Austria, and Switzerland the population is now declining, and Sweden and Belgium are expected to join them shortly. If West Germany's birth rate remains at its present level (at 10 per 1,000 the lowest in the world), its 1976 population of 61.9 million would decline to 44 million by 2020, to 37 million by 2040, and to nil by 2076, other things remaining equal throughout (which of course they won't). Australia faces zero population growth by the end of the century or before if birth rates and the numbers of immigrants continue to fall. In the USA the birth rate has been declining since the beginning of the 1970's, portending a sag in numbers in the foreseeable future.

Anti-natal phenomena range from the obvious, such as the increasing acceptance of homosexuality, the pill and other more widely available and widely used contraceptive devices, liberalised abortion laws, and greater resort to divorce and to promiscuity, to the more subtle and indirect, such as the general attitude of younger people to 'the troubles, worries, sorrows and sacrifices' (as one West German couple put it) occasioned by allowing a child to interfere with their pleasure and 'self-fulfilment' (self-indulgence). Material affluence and the widening variety of possible life styles alternative to the traditional no doubt constitute a factor. I feel, in addition, that there is a correlation, albeit a complex one, between the onset of Western population decline and the beginning of the end of the Western imperial mission, but of that I shall risk no more here.

Turning to the second group, there has long been concern on the part of the Communist governments of Europe at the stubborn determination of their married couples not to have children. The cynical might quip that if you live in societies as unpleasant as those nothing is going to induce you to bring children into them. Housing shortages were for decades a headache more or less dictating childlessness or very small families to young couples. Official concern at the looming spectre of declining population has spurred the various governments to discuss and devise pro-natal measures, ranging from penalties for the parents of one child families to the awarding of material rewards to those having large families. Curiously, East Germany has the second lowest birth rate in the world. Increasing affluence in the European communist bloc, after the grim austerities and consumer good famines of the past, may paradoxically be having the same general effects as the reversed order of events in the West.

Of China, all that needs to be added to what was said above is that there seems to be general agreement among qualified visitors to the country that its leaders are well on their way to accomplishing the goal of a growth rate of under 1% per annum by the end of the century. Many of the major cities already boast growth rates of under — in some cases well under — 1% per annum (notably Shanghai). The birth rate nationally fell from 4.5% in 1949 to well under 2% in 1973 in response to the family planning programme, including its political and ethical aspects. Such a consciously fashioned transition to stability contrasts strongly with the experiences of the first two groups, the governments of which are faced with population phenomena independent of their own actions and profoundly puzzling to them. Professor Carl Djerassi, Professor of Chemistry at Stanford University, was quoted as having said after a visit to China that '(t)he Chinese success in the past ten years is unsurpassed in terms of magnitude, intensity and total self-sufficiency anywhere in the world'. (5)

It is when we come to the fourth group — the poor countries of Asia, Africa and Latin America — that we confront the population problem as it is generally understood. But even here, there are indications of change, two of them admittedly highly negative and intrinsically unwelcome, but the third highly positive and destined eventually to supersede the others. One of the negative checks is the rise in death rates in some of the poorest countries of the world as a result of continuing mismanagement, the series of bad harvests coinciding with the development of the oil crisis, and the general deterioration of life circumstances for the poverty-stricken bulk of the population. The other is the commitment of some of the most ruthless reactionary regimes in the world, such as Chile and Iran, to co-operate with the USA in 'advanced fertility management', a scheme designed to sterilise 100,000,000 women in the Third World in order to reduce revolutionary pressures resulting from hungry and unemployed millions of young people and thus to maintain 'the normal operation of US commercial interests around the world', to quote Dr. A.T. Ravenholt, Director of the US Office of Population, the agency of the State Department in charge of the programme.

The positive factor is the hastening prospect of liberation for more and more countries in Asia, Africa and Latin Ameria; only revolutionary regimes enjoying the confidence of the people and capable of satisfying their aspirations can hope to emulate the Chinese pattern and thus expand the sphere of conscious, planned demographic homeostasis.

Taking the world as a whole, there is therefore a marked deceleration evident in population growth, which appears to have reached an all-time peak in the late 1960's/early 1970's period. In 1970, the number of people in the world grew by an estimated 1.9% (69 million added on to a world population of 3.59 billion). The most recent(1976) data show a marked decline: 1.64% growth in 1975 (64 million added on to 3.92 billion). It seems that, one way or another, with, without, or in spite of, government actions world population numbers are levelling off; it is hard not to conclude that Man, the animal, and his natural environment are at last shaking down into some kind of (entropy-constrained) equilibrium . . .

## REFERENCES: Part I

1. *Peoples Daily*, 7/9/71.
2. *International Herald Tribune*, 29/1/75.
3. B. Wilmot, 'Waste not, Want not in China', *Resurgence*, (September-October, 1974).
4. N. Maxwell, *Sunday Times*, 8/12/74.
5. *International Herald Tribune*, 1/11/76.
6. *Ta Kung Pao*, 5/9/74.
7. *International Herald Tribune*, 11/12/76.
8. W. Burchett, *Again Korea*, International Publishers, (New York, 1968).
9. B. Wideman, 'The Plight of the South Korean Peasant', in F. Baldwin (ed), *Without Parallel*, Pantheon, (New York, 1974), p.276.


## REFERENCES: Part II

1. F. Soddy, *Cartesian Economics*, Henderson, (London, 1922), p.13.
2. R. Bacon and W. Eltis, 'Too Few Producers: The Drift Healey Must Stop', *Sunday Times*, 14/11/76.
3. M. Allaby, 'Must Britain Feed Itself?' in H. Giradet (ed), *Land For The People*, Crescent Press, (London, 1976), p.60.
4. K. Marx, *Communist Manifesto*, various eds.
5. *Ta Kung Pao*, 22/5/77.


## BIBLIOGRAPHY: Part I

1. M. Elvin, *The Pattern of the Chinese Past*, Eyre Methuen, (London, 1973).
2. K. Buchanan, *The Transformation of the Chinese Earth*, G. Bell & Sons, Ltd., (London, 1970).
3. J. Needham, *Science and Civilisation in China*, CUP, (Cambridge, 1954-), (on-going).
4. H. McAleavy, *The Modern History of China*, Weidenfeld & Nicolson, (London, 1967).
5. B. Brugger, *Contemporary China*, Croom Helm, (London, 1977). (Some diverse views and perspectives drawn from a bibliography which is expanding exponentially!)
6. Peter Worsley, *Inside China*, Allen Lane, (London, 1975).
7. K.S. Karol, *The Second Chinese Revolution*, Jonathan Cape, (London, 1975). (Two of the best of the recent crop of books by visitors).

8.   J. Chen, *Inside the Cultural Revolution*, Sheldon Press, (London, 1976).

9.   L. Maitan, *Party, Army and Masses in China*, NLB, (London, 1976). (Two very different interpretations of the Cultural Revolution — the first by a participant, the second by a Trotskyist scholar from his study in Rome; see also Chen's review of the Maitan book in *Journal of Contemporary Asia*, Vol. VII, no. 3, 1977).

10.   K.W. Kapp, *Environmental Policies and Development Planning in Contemporary China*, (The Hague, 1974).

11.   M. Ocksenberg (ed.), *China's Developmental Experience*, Praeger, (New York, 1973).

12.   M. Caldwell & N. Jeffrey (eds.), *Urbanisation and Planning in China*, Pergamon Press, (Oxford, 1977). (Three looks at broad environmental/planning policies in China).

13.   J.G. Gurley, *China's Economy and the Maoist Strategy*, Monthly Review Press, (New York, 1976).

14.   E. Wheelwright & B. McFarlane, *The Chinese Road to Socialism*, Penguin, (London, 1971).

15.   C. Bettelheim, *Cultural Revolution and Industrial Organisation in China*, Monthly Review Press, (New York, 1974).

16.   B.M. Richman, *Industrial Society in China*, Vintage Books, (New York, 1969). (Since it would be inappropriate to omit Jack Gray from this list, I refer the reader to the bibliography of his works in *Journal of Contemporary Asia*, Vol. IV, no.3, 1974, pp.293-4).

17.   M. Selden, *The Yenan Way*, Harvard University Press, (Cambridge, Mass., 1971).

18.   S. Fitzgerald, *China and the Overseas Chinese*, CUP, (Cambridge, 1972).

19.   J. Gittings, *The World and China, 1922-72*, Eyre Methuen, (London, 1974). (Three important contributions by an American, an Australian, and an Englishman).

20.   J. Gittings & G. McCormack (eds.), *Crisis in Korea*, Spokesman Books, (Nottingham, 1977). (A fresh and stimulating look at a long standing crisis area, including analyses of the economies of the North and the South).

21.   Pham Cuong & Nguyen Van Ba, *Revolution in the Village — Nam Hong 1945-75*, Foreign Languages Publishing House,(Hanoi, 1976).

22.   G. Chaliand, *The Peasants of North Vietnam*, Penguin, (London,1969). (There are, as of 1977, no book-length studies of post-1975 developments in Indochina suitable for citation here).

## BIBLIOGRAPHY: Part II

23.  HMSO, *Food from Our Own Resources*, Cmnd.6020, (London, 1974).

24.  K. Mellanby, *Can Britain Feed Itself?* Merlin Press, (London, 1975).

25.  H. Girardet, (ed.), *Land For The People*, Crescent Press, (London, 1976).

26.  T. Beresford, *We Plough the Fields*, Penguin, (London, 1975).

27.  J.G.S. & Frances Donaldson, *Farming in Britain Today*, Penguin, (London, 1972).

28.  M. Allaby, C. Blythe, C. Hines & C. Wardle, *Losing Ground*, Earth Resources Research, (London, 1975).

29.  C. Wardle, *Britain and the World Food Crisis*, Earth Resources Research, (London, 1974).
(A variety of views on the present state, likely prospects, and desirable targets of British agriculture).

30.  P. Kropotkin, *Fields, Factories and Workshops Tomorrow*, Harper Torchbooks, (London, 1974).

31.  P. Kropotkin, *The Conquest of Bread*, Allen Lane, (London, 1972).

32.  P. Kropotkin, *Mutual Aid*, Allen Lane, (London, 1972).
(The latest of numerous re-printings of three of the highly influential and relevant works of one of the greatest 19th century thinkers — b.1842, d. 1921.)

33.  E.F. Schumacher, *Small is Beautiful*, Abacus, (London, 1975).

34.  L. Kohr, *The Breakdown of Nations*, C. Davies, (Swansea, 1974).
(Two 'heretical' views that are becoming less and less so).

35.  F. Soddy, *Cartesian Economics*, Henderson, (London, 1922).

36.  F. Soddy, *Wealth, Virtual Wealth and Debt*, Allen & Unwin, (London, 1926).
(These two contributions show that the basic ideas underlining the argument of this book have a long parentage).

37.  H.T. & E.C. Odum, *Energy Basis for Man and Nature*, McGraw Hill, (New York, 1976).

38.  G. Foley, *The Energy Question*, Penguin, (London, 1976).
(Two up to date discussions).

39.  A. Sauvy, *Zero Growth?* Basil Blackwell, (Oxford, 1975).

40.  Susan George, *How the Other Half Dies*, Penguin, (London, 1976).
(Two recent works on food-resource-population problems — both critical and sceptical of much establishment thinking, but from perspectives different from those I have adopted in this volume).

41.  H.G. Wells, *The World Set Free*, Collins, (London, 1914), Corgi, (London, 1976).

42.  D. Wallis, *Only Lovers Left Alive*, Blond, (London, 1964).
(And, finally, two novels with plenty of food for thought for economists prepared to think through the fictional particulars and allegories to the underlying morals.

## APPENDIX A

The complete history of the production of any fossil fuel must display the following characteristics:

'The curve of the rate of production, plotted against time on an arithmetic scale, must begin at zero, rise until it passes over one or more maxima, and finally decline gradually to zero.

If Q be a quantity of a given fuel, and t the time, then: $P = dQ/dt$ will be the production rate, where d signifies the amount of change. Then, if the production rate P be plotted on an arithmetic scale as a function of time . . . the element of area under the curve with a base of dt and an altitude P, will be: $dA = Pdt = (dQ/dt) dt = dQ$

Hence, on such a graph, the cumulative production Q up to any given time t will be proportional to the area between the curve of production rate and the time-axis from the beginning of production until the time t.

For the entire cycle of production, where the production rate begins at zero, and eventually returns to zero, the total area under the curve is a measure of the ultimate amount, $Q_\infty$ , of the given fuel produced during the cycle, as is illustrated in the figure below. This fact provides a powerful means of keeping within reasonable limits in our estimations of the future course of the production of a given fuel. If an estimate can be made from geological data of the amount $Q_i$ of the given resource which was initially present in the geographical area considered, then any extrapolation of the production curve for that area must be such that the ultimate area under the curve satisfies the condition: $Q_\infty \lesseqgtr Q_i$

Mathematically, such a curve may assume an indefinite number of shapes, but the technology of production essentially requires that the early phase be one of positive exponential rate of increase, and the declining phase an exponential rate of decrease, so that between these two requirements, and that of the limitation of the area circumscribed, the amount of latitude in such a curve is greatly reduced.'

(Source: National Academy of Sciences-National Research Council, *Resources and Man*, W.H. Freeman & Co., (San Francisco, 1969), pp.167-168.)

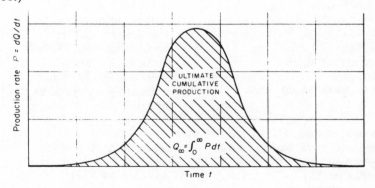

Using this technique with the information on reserves and rates of consumption available in the early 1960's, peak production of oil was forecast for 1990 to 2000, and of coal for 140 to 170-200 years from the 1960's (see *ibid* pp.195 and 203-4); more recent data suggest that these projections may have given what would now be regarded as optimistic horizons.